QUILTS & WOMEN
OF THE
MORMON MIGRATIONS

Daughters of Utah Pioneers

We, the International Society Daughters of Utah Pioneers, are pleased to have the opportunity to assist Mary Bywater Cross in her Mormon Migration Quilt Project. Recognizing the high quality in her previous work on 19th century quilts associated with the Oregon Trail migration, our Board of Directors concluded her project would enhance our mission of perpetuating and perfecting the record of Utah Pioneers.

The thoroughness of Ms. Cross' research has contributed greatly to the documentation information about our quilt collection. The connections she has made between the quilts and the women who made or brought them to the West as presented for the first time in this important publication are significant.

Recognizing the limitations of a volunteer-managed and staffed organization, Ms. Cross' respect of our capabilities has been of the highest. In return, we greatly value her personal contributions of time and energy.

The International Society Daughters of Utah pioneers are pleased to have this major accomplishment dedicated in our honor in celebration of our mothers' and grandmothers' contribution to Mormon settlement in the West.

Sincerely,

Louise C. Green
Louise C. Green - Pres.

Edith Menna
Edith Menna - Museum Director

300 North Main, Salt Lake City, Utah 84103-1699 / (801) 538-1050

QUILTS & WOMEN

OF THE

MORMON MIGRATIONS

TREASURES OF TRANSITION

Mary Bywater Cross

RUTLEDGE HILL PRESS

NASHVILLE, TENNESSEE

In honor of the dedicated work
and commitment to history of
The International Society of
Daughters of Utah Pioneers

Copyright © 1996 by Mary Bywater Cross

Published in Nashville, Tennessee, by Rutledge Hill Press, Inc.,
211 Seventh Avenue North, Nashville, Tennessee 37219.
Distributed in Canada by H. B. Fenn & Company, Ltd.,
34 Nixon Road, Bolton, Ontario L7E 1W2.
Distributed in Australia by Millenium Books,
33 Maddox Street, Alexandria NSW 2015.
Distributed in New Zealand by Tandem Press,
2 Rugby Road, Birkenhead, Auckland 10.
Distributed in the United Kingdom by Verulam Publishing, Ltd.,
152a Park Street Lane, Park Street, St. Albans, Hertfordshire AL2 2AU.

Cover and text design by Harriette Bateman
Book concept by Mary Bywater Cross and Robert A. Burco
Layout by Mary Bywater Cross
Typography by E. T. Lowe, Nashville, Tennessee

Library of Congress Cataloging-in-Publication Data

Cross, Mary Bywater, 1942–
    Quilts & women of the Mormon migrations : treasures in transition /
Mary Bywater Cross.
        p.   cm.
    Includes bibliographical references and index.
    ISBN 1-55853-399-0 (hardcover). — ISBN 1-55853-409-1 (pbk.)
    1. Morman women—United States—Biography.   2. Church of Jesus
Christ of Latter-Day Saints—History—19th century.   3. Quilts—
United States—History—19th century.   I. Title.
BX8693.C76   1997   96-31708
289.3'082—dc20   CIP

Printed in HONG KONG
1 2 3 4 5 6 7 8 9 — 02 01 00 99 98 97

CONTENTS

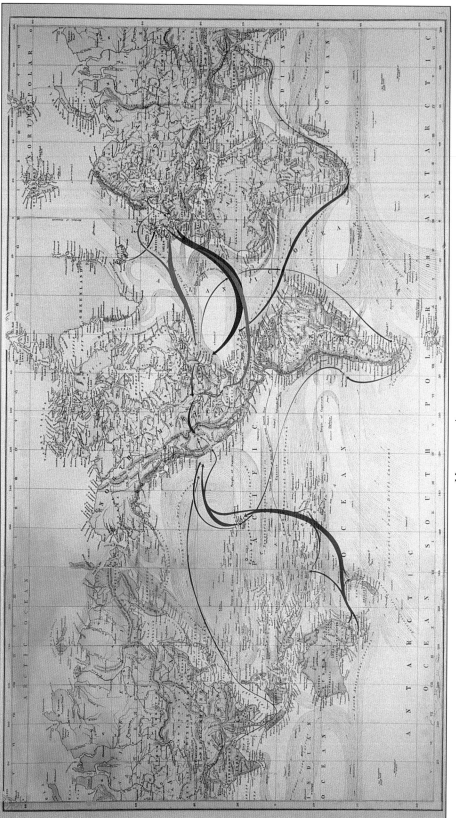

Mormon emigrant sea routes

PREFACE

"I shall try to present them in their terms and judge them in mine. That I do not accept the faith that possessed them does not mean I doubt their frequent devotion and heroism in its service. Especially their women. Their women were incredible."—Wallace Stegner, *The Gathering of Zion: The Story of the Mormon Trail*, 1964[1]

THESE WERE THE WORDS I READ IN WALLACE Stegner's well-respected book as I began the research for the Mormon Migration Quilt Project. With his book, he joined the ranks of many earlier popular writers and artists who had witnessed or studied the Mormon migrations including Charles Dickens, Mark Twain, William Henry Jackson, and C. C. A. Christensen. The group indicates the on-going fascination people had with the Church of Jesus Christ of Latter-day Saints (LDS). Although Stegner's was one of the first written specifically on the migration experience for a general audience. It marked the beginning of new scholarship on the subject to be followed by Mormons and non-Mormons alike including Stanley B. Kimball, James Allen, Glenn Leonard, John D. Unruh, Jr., and Merrill Mattes.

Stegner's text presents the traditional orientation of a narrative study through a balanced study of other mostly male, professionals' work, and the personal journals, reminiscences and letters available at that time. His reference to women as incredible was haunting, but not surprising; perhaps indicating an unknown or unanswered question. Because for him, womens' records were unavailable and/or inaccessible; or perhaps not even sought out.

Now more than thirty years after Stegner's publication, I have had the opportunity to search out these women and research their roles through a set of newly-discovered resource materials, their quilts. This project has been aided not only by previous publications, but also by the significant new scholarship available because of the growing interest in quilt history and womens' history. Valuable contributions of both quilts and expertise have been made by quilt historians such as Jean Christensen, Sandi Fox, and Joyce B. Peaden; recent publications by womens' historians such as Carol Madsen, Susan Arrington Madsen, and Lyndia Carter; and interpretations of pioneer womens' personal narrations by Edith Menna, Director of the International Society of Daughters of Utah Pioneers' Pioneer Memorial Museum, and Maureen Ursenbach Beecher, Professor of English and Research Historian at BYU's Joseph Smith Institute for Church History.

This study is part of a continuing interest in the quilts and women of migrating populations as I pursue the focused goal to educate the general public about quilts as material culture artifacts and how they represent the lives of the people who made and used them.

Several unique opportunities have broadened my perspective and sharpened my skills in preparation for this study of nineteenth century migrating women. Most significant academically was the 1994 Larom Summer Institute of the Cody, Wyoming's Buffalo Bill Historical Center with Glenda Riley, Professor of History at Ball State University. Her history course was framed around the question of womens' experience, "Was the West a Place to Grow?"

Another experience that particularly gave me empathy for the handcart pioneers and other self-reliant Mormon women was a Pacific Crest Outward Bound Backpack and Canoe Trip in 1994. During those eight days, I developed a trust in the leaders, a self-reliance, and a concern for others not unlike that described by the Mormon pioneers. Just as they repeatedly experienced, we were eight total strangers who came together as a unified group under the guidance of trained personnel. Supportive leaders who confronted us with unfamiliar challenges, yet offered encouragement to succeed. Other similarities were the daily tasks of unloading and reloading the group gear to carefully balance the weight; and preparing and eating meals, often after dark, after walking our day's planned distance. Sleeping on the ground under a low tarp and doctoring sore feet were other common experiences.

For my work, I define the parameters of the project and seek the quilts meeting stated requirements for valid documents of history. The result is a book of quilts found during a western regional search with defined qualifications but not preconceived notions to what artifacts to seek. In this manner, it is unlike other recent publications where authors could choose examples from a collection to illustrate their points. The quilts, preserved for whatever reason, became the basic objects around which the project was shaped. Most of these artifacts appear here for the first time, in full view and in professional photographs of selected details.

To be considered a valid artifact of material culture or document of history, a piece had to conform to requirements derived from textile historian Rachel Maines's work. A quilt must have a continuous and traceable history from time of construction until the present. It must reflect the experience of the mainstream culture for the time in which it was made; as migration does. It must be honest in representing the free expression of the maker.[2]

For this project, a quilt had to be traceable to one of several categories of women: a woman who was part of the Mormon Church and participated in its early efforts to seek and migrate to a gathering place; a woman who, once in the Salt Lake Valley, moved out from there to colonize the State of Deseret, or the Intermountain West between Canada and Mexico; or, a woman who later served a requested "mission" assignment as the Church's focus changed from bringing converts to the West to serving them in their home areas. Using these broad criteria allowed the project to go beyond quilts of Utah's pioneer women alone. The Utah pioneers are identified by the International Society Daughters of Utah Pioneers (ISDUP) as those who arrived in the Salt Lake Valley prior to May 10, 1869, the date of the transcontinental railroad completion.

Quilt historians are able to read visual clues from the stitched works and interpret their significance and meaning. From experience, particularly with the support of diaries, interviews, and other sources, I am able to place quilts into a broader historical context of discoveries and associations.

What I discovered was the microcosm of quilts representing the broad expanse of quilt history, the diversity of the women's prior experiences; the diversity of their cultural origins; the various modalities of travel; and their significant participation in the development of the Intermountain West.

The quilts are organized by the woman's date of arrival in the Salt Lake Valley and by her traveling company. The arrival date signifies the major achievement of having survived the journey across the Great Plains and, in many cases, the Atlantic Ocean. The arrival dates are divided into four time periods: 1830–1848; 1849–1855; 1856–1869; and 1870–1900. These time periods are defined by the goals of the Church to seek the place, to gather in Zion, to welcome the faithful, and to settle the Intermountain West. Each section begins with C. C. A. Christensen painting of the Mormon history, and an overview of the migration and settlement, the women, and the quilts.

The traveling company provides the identification of the mode of transportation, the length of the journey, and the opportunities offered the women to participate in the westering tasks, to share their experiences, and to stitch their treasures.

Information about each quilt includes the technical data of size, method of construction, and unique features; and often it also may include a statement about the quilt's visual impact from a design consideration in order to enhance appreciation by quilters and nonquilters alike. Specific information about block and border size and construction methods may benefit quiltmakers who like to recreate historic designs. For nonquilters, I have provided a point of information or unique feature as what to look for in a quilt.

The heirlooms represent the wide diversity of cultures sought by the Church during their effort to gather the converts together in an isolated geographic area. Once the converts had gathered, the Church leadership imposed policies of economic and social self-sufficiency. These policies had major ramifications on women's lifestyles and their choices related to quiltmaking.

Because of this unique situation, I made the important decision not to date these quilts using the traditionally accepted timeline of decades or quarter centuries. Instead, I used broad time periods that fall within the framework of Mormon migration history. Each quilt is then focused more specifically to the dates within the maker's life when the quilt would have been made. The exact date is given if valid information was available.

The periods are labeled Early (1800–1850); Mid (1860–1890); and Late (1890–1935). The period before 1850 represents for many women their early life prior to and during their major overland migration . The decade between 1850 and 1860 saw a major interruption in general migration and settlement patterns. The period of 1860 to 1890 was a time of imposed self-sufficiency and isolation from outside resources. The period after 1890, marked by the Manifesto that changed Church policy, began a time of normalization with access to the broader world of textiles and resources for quiltmaking.

For a unit of study, I have devised a system of identifying the quilts, assigning each quilt a Roman numeral and an Arabic numeral within a section. A chart is included referencing the maker's name, the quilt name, quilt number and page number. I have used the word "fragment" to reference a preserved part of a consumed quilt; and the word "segment" to refer to a unit of unfinished piecework. By examining patterns, fabrics, quilting motifs, and styles, I have sought to identify common themes related to migration and settlement.

Summarizing the findings as artifacts of textile history, I have placed selected examples on charts in the appendix.

For each quiltmaker or owner, I have included her full name, including all married names; the dates of her life; the year of migration across the Plains and/or the year of emigration across the ocean; the company which she traveled with; her family relationship to her immediate traveling party; the date of arrival in the Salt Lake Valley; and the counties in which she resided. All counties are in Utah unless otherwise specified. This information is readily available through the rich resources of the Mormon Genealogical Library and its Family History Center network including the European Emigration Index and the Crossing the Plains Index. A word of caution about the Ancestral File resource, however, the material contained is not checked so double entries and inaccurate information does exist. Further checking can usually identify the correct data. The International Genealogical Index (IGI) is considered accurate. I have used the spelling for the cities and towns as well as their county locations for the time of the person's life because as population has grown, boundaries have changed. According to Accredited Genealogist Ann Leppich, this information is vitally important is tracing documentation for family history.[3]

I have also used the three words "migration," "emigration," and "immigration" to define three distinct situations. "Migration" refers to movement within the North American continent. "Emigration" refers to movement away from a foreign location. "Immigration" refers to movement by those from abroad to or within North America.

The ship lists, handcart lists, and wagon train lists are included in an appendix. These lists give an indication of the extensive recordkeeping done by the Saints and the general scope of the migration.

For clarification, within the Church structure, a "stake" is the basic unit of regional Church administration and the "ward" is the local congregation.

Then, in the description of each woman's life, I have included her parents' names, her birth location, her husband(s)' names, and her life experiences within the historical context of events and circumstances occurring around her. The general context is described in the introduction text to each section and in the Chronology of Mormon history appendix. Much of the information on the women came from personal histories written by granddaughters or from published family records generously made available to me by the owners or by the institutions in which the quilts are located. Drawing on these rich available

"She was a true pioneer, taking each new situation in its stride, holding on to the lovely things of life and making them a part of her home, whether it be an apartment in Southampton, a wagon box, a dugout or an adobe home."

Ruby Shepherd Karpowitz, granddaughter of Eliazbeth Jane Rogers Shepherd[4] (Quilt III-15)

resources of their written and spoken words, I have included quotes to give the quilts a personal dimension. At times, I found conflicting data about the basic facts or I found information giving a truer sense of the individual. For example, when I found reference to a marriage that ended in a divorce which may or may not have been mentioned in her history, I included that name in parenthesis. In cases of conflict, I followed a mentor's advice to be "to be true to the woman."

To complete the study, I have made some generalizations about quiltmakers' lives as nineteenth century women in the West. Nearly all these women came west as part of a social and religious movement that strongly expected a woman to be a wife, a mother, and a support to those who needed her. Yet I discovered details of their lives and their involvement that went beyond these basic responsibilities that I found deserving of recognition.

Pursuing the question of was the West a place to grow, I have attempted to describe social and economic conditions that affected the lives of these Anglo women. I have tried to include specific examples both of how their "transitioned mindset" or changed attitudes enabled them to take care of themselves and their children; and of how they faced the new challenges, conflicts, contests, contacts that confronted them as they sought to achieve their personal conquests of survival and adaptation to their new environment of living in the American West.

To paraphrase Wallace Stegner, I will present these stitched "treasures in transition" in their terms and analyze them in mine.

INTRODUCTION

And so it was. Thousands of anglo women gathered together from North America and Europe, following their faith, to find and build a Zion for the Church of Jesus Christ of Latter-day Saints in the American West.

Zion was the name given to a permanent place where these Saints could live, work, and practice their religion within a style and custom they had chosen or was chosen for them by their parents. It would be a safe place, free of wars, persecution, and plagues, for converts to gather where they could live in anticipation of Jesus Christ's second coming, the Millennium. This unifying goal as led by Joseph Smith and Brigham Young between 1830 and 1877 was met with steadfast belief that God and their faith would see them through, no matter what the odds. They brought with them their native heritages, their needlework traditions, and their strong desire to achieve a peaceful life.

Presented here are the women's previously unheard stories communicated through their visual records stitched in cloth quilts; their words written in records of their family's journeys and settlement; and their reminiscences of detailed individual responses to their vision of Mormon pioneer settlement.

THE WOMEN

These women would begin their migration to the anticipated Zion with their individual life experiences that varied according to age, stage in personal relationships, educational level, societal background, and economic wherewithal. Yet, unlike other nineteenth-century western migrations across America, these Anglo women shared that common goal of gathering together

". . . After weeks of hard work, Father had the cows broken so that he could drive them, and on the ninth day of May, 1849—my brother Riley's sixteenth birthday—we said good-bye to our friends and relatives, got into our wagon, and started on our long, eventful journey. Oh, how Mother's countenance beamed with joy! What did she care for hardships, if she could only reach the goal?"
Margaret Gay Judd Clawson[1]

whether they joined in the East in the 1830s or later in Europe in the 1870s. The early American and Canadian women were often from established New England and Southern families whose desire was for better land and personal freedoms. For those coming from Europe, their migration was taking place anywhere from twenty to fifty years ahead of the major wave of European ethnic groups who came around the turn of the twentieth century. For all, their life experiences during these years of 1830 through 1900 were being played out in self-sufficient isolation against a background of advancing technology in production and communication, and improved transportation systems for migration to Zion.

Initially, their lives were shaped by their informal training in domestic skills within their homes by mothers and grandmothers, and formal education from books, classes, and religious experiences by teachers and ministers. While exposure to formal education varied with each, all were trained in the domestic skills necessary to create and maintain a home and family. They brought their expectations of being a wife and mother with them as they traveled westward and established their own homes within the unifying world of the Church. Most all would live out this role in an isolated, self-sufficient society defined by the male-dominated church structure. They produced numerous babies with hopes that some would survive against the ever present threat of death. They helped one another whether it was gleaning fields, producing food and textiles at home, birthing babies, or preparing the dead. They took active roles of teaching, training, and leading as members of the Female Relief Society within the structured church.

In addition, unlike other nineteenth-century women, many of these feminine Saints often were solely responsible for earning their livings for their homes and children as the men of the larger community tended to be away living with their other families, conducting business, sometimes fleeing to avoid prosecution by federal authorities, or serving on missions, defined as an assignment requested by the Church.[2]

"Working like a man, yoking up, outspanning, walking fifteen or twenty miles a day through brush and sande beside the slow churn of the wheels, hunting up strayed oxen on mornings when the sun stretched enerrying incredibly long up the Platte's long valley . . . [she] began to feel that it was 'a pleasure to take hold and do something.' She was one type, a rather common type, of Mormon woman, capable, indefatigable, unquestioning, She gives the myth of the Pioneer Wife footing in reality."

Wallace Stegner[3]

THE VISION

From the founding of the Church by Prophet Joseph Smith in 1830 in New York state, the Saints believed they were chosen as a covenant people to establish a Zion. They placed emphasis on education with an ethic of integrity, industry, and thrift. They had a common desire to live according to the teachings and ordinances of early Christianity. They believed in a second coming of Christ for which they would prepare by being organized along the lines of the early church with a prophet, apostles, and a governing body of seventy men.

This uniqueness was in part the cause of both their success and abrasion.

Almost immediately upon the founding, the Saints initially migrated west seeking the free or inexpensive land to establish their homes and families and nurture the tenets of their faith. In this regard, they were not unlike many others, especially religious groups like the Methodists, the Congregationalists, and the Amana Colony Inspirationalists coming together in the "Burned-Over District" of New York.

In this area, after the American Revolutionary War and concurrent with this wave of westward migration in the first half of the nineteenth century came the period known as the "Second Great Awakening." Reaching a peak in 1825–1827 were new grass-roots religious movements with such methods as revivals and new leaders such as evangelists and circuit-riding preachers. This followed an earlier "Great Awakening" in the 1740s that had given rise to new levels of social acceptability including participation by laymen in religious organizations and new interest in previously unchurched populations. As a result, there were significant amounts of religious-based activities outside the traditional framework of the established churches, offered by non-college educated men through local grass-root efforts. The concept of free association with others by individual choice of interest, needs, or goals became important.

Another significant concept was the recognition of the common man's abilities to accomplish important challenges and achievements. This led to the acceptance of them as leaders. Andrew Jackson's election as president of the United States in 1828 was recognized as the "uncommon common man" brought to Washington.[4]

In western New York, with its large numbers of transplanted populations from the agriculturally depleted areas of New England, many new forms of identification and association were developed. Once formed, they moved on westward to enable or maintain their individual identities and practices among their followers. This area became known as the "Burned-over District" because it proved a fertile ground for birth of new affiliations through revivals and other forms of evangelism. Leaders had only to reap their harvest and move on.[5]

For the Mormons, every convert considered herself or himself a missionary desirous of spreading the message that

"We were called rebels and some of the members, including my father, were carried to prison. All these things were conducted against us by our old neighbors. What a change this doctrine had made in our friends. They were almost ready to take my life simply because I had started to serve the 'God of my Fathers.'"

William Burton, brother of Rebecca Burton Jones (Quilt II-2)[6]

European harbor

salvation came only through becoming a Saint and following the Prophet to the designated gathering place of Zion. This important mission took them immediately to other areas of America to proselytize. It was along the corridor served by the waterways of the Erie Canal, the Great Lakes, the Ohio, Missouri, and Mississippi Rivers that the work advanced most rapidly between the years 1830 to 1840. By 1837, over sixteen thousand persons were baptized from every state in the Union, much of Upper Canada, and Great Britain.

For the women, to accomplish this vision required sharing a common bond reaching beyond all levels of previous friendship and kinship. They shared not only their duties, their lives, their dreams and expectations, but also often their most private spaces, their homes, their families, and sometimes their husbands.

THE MIGRATION AND SETTLEMENT

As in much of nineteenth-century society, migration for social and economic reasons was the accepted expectation for both sexes. A person was born, raised and trained in the basic tasks, and moved on or "took leave" to establish their own farm and family. The desire to explore and settle the nation was a virtue to be celebrated in the days of building the country and strengthening the economy. Migration was a profession with financial opportunity as well as cultural exercise. Men migrated to seek their fortunes in gold, free land, or employment. Single women migrated to serve the rural communities' growing need for teachers, laundresses, missionaries, and prostitutes. Many migrated to find locations where they could live out their lives according to their personal choices, decisions and opportunities.

Migration for religious purposes was not unique to just the followers of Joseph Smith but to many of the various sects or groups. They were conducting revivals, publishing their idealogy, and reaching out to serve the needs of potential new members, both male and female, single or married. Many would have a similar focus to gather together in a common place to practice their faith. Several major differences did exist. These groups would establish working relationships with others within their chosen areas. Or, if they had chosen to follow a charismatic leader, after his death, the group would often dissolve.

To accomplish their vision, the Mormon men were

Council Bluffs Ferry and Cottonwood
Trees *by Frederic Piercy*

unique among these nineteenth century populations. They were skilled in their ability to design and execute plans to bring in new members, to get them to Zion, to settle their part of the American West and to accommodate their lifestyle and enterprise to the changing pressures of a developing nation. They sought people with talents and abilities to build their communities and sustain their vision from artisans to accountants and teachers to printers. As with many American immigrants, most were also farmers who could conquer the land.

Through their religious vision, the early Saints joined together in a pattern of precise structure, supervision and community cooperation. Then, in later years, the foreign emigrants, often unknown to each other, were rapidly shaped into a cooperative community, especially after having traveled together in a crowded ship's hold with little privacy, quiet, and calmness.

Over the years, the plans and programs for migration and settlement evolved as the Church confronted the challenges offered by demographical complexities of the converts, technological advances in transportation, and political and social challenges at home. Added to these were the factors of rising costs, public health and safety, and economic opportunities within Utah. Like all projects, some efforts were successful, others were not. By 1849, the Mormons claimed a territory, the State of Deseret, that spread from the Rocky Mountains to the Pacific Ocean. By 1900 they had colonized settlements from Canada to Mexico in the Intermountain West between the Rockies and the Sierra Nevadas.

Wagon outfit

THE TRANSITIONS

Women's abilities to transition to frontier living were shaped by many factors. Uppermost would be their mental attitudes formed by previous background and exposure to outdoor living. Many came from long established self-sufficient early American or Scandinavian farms where life activities and domestic tasks took place on a seasonal calendar based on weather. They knew the circumstances of outdoor living and how to adapt. While those from the British Isles had less developed outdoor skills and abilities. Their urban city experiences were based on established class levels and defined commercial jobs.

For all, the challenge was adapting to the new environments of the American West and the arduous travel and community building—sometimes again and again. The land journey

"It was quite a task for me to drive the team and care for the six children, but I got along very well. We had a snowstorm while traveling along the Sevier River, but we had a good tent which we pitched every night, and we were comfortable. We did not travel very far during the day. We had a cow which gave us milk. The road was very bad in places, but I drove all the way, except over one hill just after we had crossed the Big Colorado. We had no serious trouble on the journey."

Sarah Dall Weech[7]

"My Emigrant ship [Amazon] lives broadside on to the wharf. Two great gangways made of spars and planks connect her with the wharf; and up and down these gangways, perpetually crowding to and fro and in and out, like ants, are the Emigrants who are going to sail in my Emigrant Ship. Some with cabbages, some with loaves of bread, some with cheese and butter, some with milk and beer, some with boxes, beds, and bundles, some with babies—nearly all with children— nearly all with brand-new tin cans for their daily allowance of water, uncomfortably suggestive of a tin flavor in the drink. To and fro, up and down, aboard and ashore, swarming here and there and everywhere, my Emigrants. . . . Now I have seen emigrant ships before . . . and these people are so strikingly different from all other people in like circumstances. . . . The weather-browned captain of the 'Amazon' is at my shoulder, and he says, 'What indeed! The most of these came aboard yesterday evening. They came from various parts of England in small parties that had never seen one another before. Yet they had not been a couple of hours on board, when they established their own police, made their own regulations, and set their own watches at all the hatchways. Before nine o'clock, the ship was as orderly and quiet as a man-of-war.'"
Charles Dickens[8]

was covered slowly on foot, by wagon, and later, by railroad car. Plus, for most Saints, the journey over water was by ocean-going sailing vessel, or steamboat. During both, the exposure to vast environmental desolation, constant movement, and cramped living quarters was ongoing for a long time. The broad expanses of the horizon, the wind, the rain, and the dust were not what they had been previously accustomed to. This would have a pervasive impact on every aspect of a woman's life, whether physical, social, emotional, or mental.

Church leaders were unique in helping people to cope with these impressive changes and their overall ability to transition. They organized them into traveling companies of small groups for supervision and contact with each other. They arranged for agents to handle the transfer between water and land transportation. They commissioned artists to record the images in oil paintings and printed engravings to project the migration as something able to be successfully accomplished.

They used other artists, musicians, and choral leaders to write and perform songs and dances to encourage, inspire, and celebrate their accomplishments. They encouraged writers and poets to record and publish their thoughts and responses to their journeys. Often, these painted and written observations were by non-Mormon artists as well.

For those who succeeded in getting to Zion, and most did, the patterns of their lives were often repeated, with requirements to pioneer new areas while living in tents and wagon boxes, and then, eking out subsistent livings from the arid land. At times, those who had come from a more settled Europe, were thrown into confusion or despair by the primitive quality of the living conditions.

Here again, church leadership would help by organizing companies of families and friends from selected areas to band together with skills, abilities, social networks, and common objectives to be successful in many varied tasks, locations, and troublesome times. Often, the male leaders would turn to women, wives or friends, for support and leadership. Women "clubbed" together for economic buying power in rural areas. Women supported the efforts of Utah Silk Association in sericulture. Utah women were given the right to vote on February 12, 1870.

THE QUILTS

These quilts, defined as layered textile sandwiches, are a particularly unique body of stitched works made by diverse cultures of Anglo women committed to a common religious goal. They serve as artistic textile responses to their life experiences made at a time when many women were unable to read or write.

Because these visual records were saved, all were and are valued heirlooms to their descendants as symbolic of the ability to adapt and persevere. Those they brought with them often triggered the visual memories of those family members and homes far away and long ago. Those made later often celebrated the maturing stories of personal accomplishment and satisfaction.

Now, with celebration of the Utah Statehood Centennial and the Mormon Trail Sesquicentennial, these treasures are presented as part of these pioneers' contributions.

The initial survey was for quilts made by individual women who migrated as members of the Church. From the response of about five hundred, not counting the large reviewed inventories of state quilt projects, the final group of period quilts and well-documented women's histories were chosen.

They are unique as a study.

The discoveries represent a broader span of time and place of origin because of the changing focus of migrations from North America to Europe. Fabrics and techniques range from the early American hand-wovens to the European exported factory prints. They include the various textiles produced within their isolated territory of forty years.

Each quilt, no matter the condition, the purpose it served, or the technical skill mastered, led to rich and compelling discoveries of these previously unknown women's life experiences.

PART ONE

1830–1848 SEEKING THE PLACE

"In the fall of 1837 a mob organized and came with a force which the saints were unable to resist, thrust our Prophet and Patriarch and others in prison, which are all matters of history. Here too Sister Margaret Smoot's courage and heroism was put to the test and was equal to the occasion. She cut patches, run bullets, cooked meals for the men, dressed their wounds, made their beds, gave the fevered ones drink, shared her few comforts with those in need, cheered the spirit of those who were ready to sink." —*History of Margaret T. McMeans Smoot, Pioneer of 1847*[1]

detail from Defense of Nauvoo in September 1846 *by C. C. A. Christensen*

EARLY GATHERING OF SAINTS TO OHIO AND MISSOURI

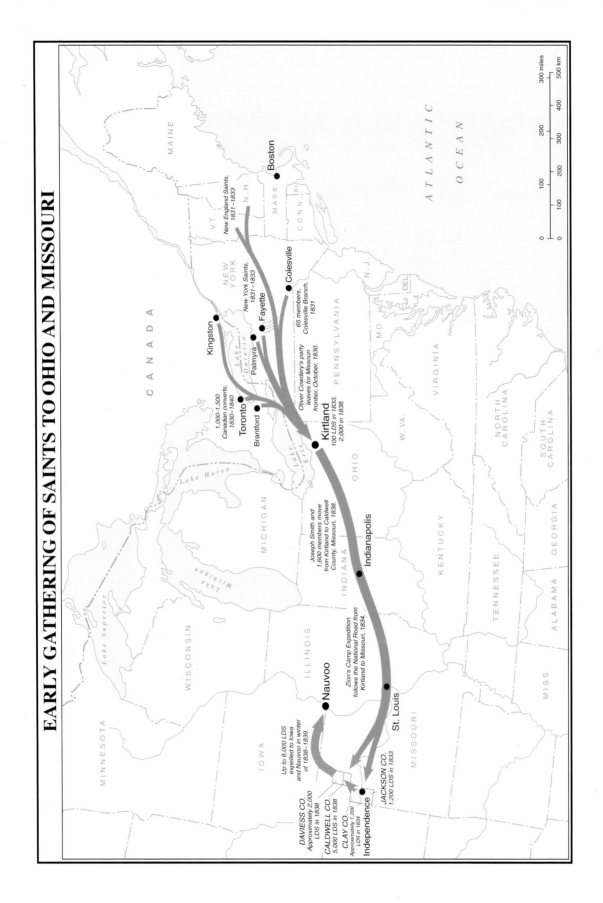

New England Saints,
1831–1833

New York Saints,
1831–1833

65 members,
Colesville Branch,
1831

Oliver Cowdery's party
leaves for Missouri
frontier, October, 1830.

1,000–1,500
Canadian converts,
1830–1840

100 LDS in 1833,
2,000 in 1838

Joseph Smith and
1,600 members move
from Kirtland to Caldwell
County, Missouri, 1838.

Zion's Camp Expedition
follows the National Road from
Kirtland to Missouri, 1834.

Up to 8,000 LDS
expelled to Iowa
and Nauvoo in winter
of 1838–1839.

DAVIESS CO.
Approximately 2,000
LDS in 1838

CALDWELL CO.
5,000 LDS in 1838

CLAY CO.
Approximately 1,200
LDS in 1834

JACKSON CO.
1,200 LDS in 1833

Boston

Colesville

Fayette

Palmyra

Kingston

Toronto

Brantford

Kirtland

Indianapolis

Nauvoo

St. Louis

Independence

MAINE

N.H.

VT.

MASS.

CONN.

R.I.

N.J.

DEL

MD

NEW YORK

PENNSYLVANIA

VIRGINIA

W. VA.

NORTH CAROLINA

SOUTH CAROLINA

OHIO

KENTUCKY

TENNESSEE

GEORGIA

ALABAMA

MISS.

MISSOURI

INDIANA

ILLINOIS

IOWA

WISCONSIN

MICHIGAN

MINNESOTA

CANADA

Lake Superior

Lake Michigan

Lake Huron

Lake Erie

Lake Ontario

ATLANTIC OCEAN

0   100   200   300 miles

0   100   200   300   400   500 km

THE MIGRATION

IN THE EARLY YEARS OF MIGRATION (1830–39), the Saints focused on finding an appropriate location for building their Zion on what was then the western edge of Anglo-American settlement. This goal, as published and circulated by the Mormons themselves, often caused suspicion and fear among their neighbors. Non-Mormons worried about their own prosperity if Mormons were to move in, establish their own commerce, create their own markets, and control the local political and legal decisions. Often the Saints' activities were met with fear, resentment, and violence.

In response to these threats, Thomas Butterfield, husband of Mary Jane Butterfield (Quilt II-4), was asked to assemble the outfits and oversee the animals needed to transport the many Saints in Kirtland, Ohio, who were eager to join the Prophet on the western edge of previously settled areas. This wagon journey, referred to as "Zion's Camp," was to serve as the basic organizational pattern for all migrations, whether across the Plains or across the ocean. This group of 515 people with their 27 tents, 59 wagons, 97 horses, 22 oxen, 69 cows, and one bull was divided into companies of tens, with a captain overseeing each. Ten groups of ten were organized into a group of 100 and so forth.[2]

Having tried without success to relocate in previously unsettled land within the political boundaries of Missouri, they looked to neighboring states. The governors of Iowa, Robert Lucas, and of Illinois, Thomas Carlin, both issued invitations to settle there. These invitations served as important indications of possible governmental support and protection, which would give the families a sense of safety.

Many women had lost loved ones, and all were worried about the lives of Church leaders with whom they were personally acquainted. The two states were in the initial stages of settlement, and additional citizens would stimulate economic

"We sold our beautiful home in Kirtland and traveled all summer to Missouri—our teams poor and with hardly enough to keep body and soul together. We journeyed about six months as we were forced to stop at times and work for food and clothes. We were often threatened . . . and sometimes traveled at night and laid over during the day to avoid mobs. Several times we were warned of mobs waiting ahead for us and we would then leave the road and journey over unbroken prairies and through the woods. . . ."
Amanda Barnes Smith
(Quilt II-6)[3]

development. Furthermore, because the leading political parties, the Whigs and the Democrats, were about equally divided in numbers, politicians were eager to gain new supporters.

After much consideration the Mormon leaders selected the two areas of Hancock County, Illinois, and Lee County, Iowa, on opposite banks of the Mississippi River. One factor contributing to their decision was the availability of temporary housing for families in the Fort Des Moines army barracks near Montrose in Lee County. However, Mormon settlement was not limited to these two counties alone, as indicated by the number of families of quiltmakers and owners who settled along both sides of the river and inland toward central Illinois.

Soon, the townsite of Commerce on the Mississippi River in Hancock County became the focus for establishing their next Zion, called "Nauvoo" from the Hebrew word meaning "beautiful resting place." This provided a brief seven-year (1839–46) period of stability during which the majority of Saints could pursue their dream in one location. They lived their lives in relative peace and joy and went about building their homes, farms, families, and community. Here they began construction on their Temple, the ceremonial building in which they could practice the full dimension of their faith. Here the women formalized their work of supporting each other socially and economically by creating the initial Relief Society in 1842.

The following words by Joseph Smith addressing the sixth meeting of the Relief Society on April 28, 1842, formed the basis of how the organization would operate. It was through the Relief Society that the Church would have a major influence on the lives of the women.

This is a charitable Society, and according to your natures; it is natural for females to have feelings of charity and benevolence. You are now placed in a situation in which you can act according to those sympathies which God has planted in your bosoms.

If you live up to these principles, how great and glorious will be your reward in the celestial kingdom! If you live up to your privileges, the angels cannot be restrained from being your associates.

Let this Society teach women how to behave towards their husbands, to treat them with mildness and affection. When a man is borne down with trouble, when he is perplexed with care and difficulty, if he can meet a smile instead of an argument or a murmur—if he can meet with mildness, it will calm down his soul and soothe his feelings; when the mind is going to despair, it needs a solace of affection and kindness.

You will receive instructions through the order of the Priesthood which God has established, through the medium of those appointed to lead, guide and direct the affairs of the Church in this last dispensation; and I now turn the key in your behalf in the name of the Lord, and this Society shall rejoice, and knowledge and intelligence shall flow down from this time henceforth; this is the beginning of better days to the poor and needy, who shall be made to rejoice and pour forth blessings on your heads.[4]

Unfortunately for the Saints and their neighbors, the same issues of local political and economic control began to resurface. In an effort to resolve the conflict and work within the framework of the court system of the state of Illinois, Joseph Smith and other leaders agreed to submit to a trial by jury in Carthage, Illinois. A writ, which was imposed without a proper hearing, charged Smith with treason for declaring martial law in Nauvoo. The culmination of the conflict came on June 27, 1844. A mob rushed the Carthage, Illinois, jail and murdered Joseph Smith and his brother Hyrum Smith and injured John Taylor. Willard Richards escaped harm.

After the martyrdom, the question immediately arose as to who would lead the Saints, while the broader concerns dealt with the Church's overall organization. Renewed life and commitment resulted from this challenge to survive the death of their Prophet. Brigham Young was chosen President, and with the support of the Council of Twelve Apostles, he continued the policies previously outlined by Joseph Smith. These included putting the missionary work in order, developing a plan for an expansion of gathering places, and promoting the industrial development and building construction in Nauvoo, particularly the last stages of their Temple.[5]

As political and social conditions evolved, however, it became obvious that the Saints had to move on to a more remote area in order to be able to live in peace. Over the next eighteen months, Brigham Young negotiated with state and local authorities of Illinois and Iowa in preparation for leaving Nauvoo. A November 23, 1845, inventory showed 3,285 families organized into groups of tens, fifties, and hundreds. There were also 1,508 wagons ready and another 1,892 wagons under construction.[6] It became almost a race against time to complete the Temple before leaving the area. The Temple was completed in late 1845 and immediately members began flocking there as the only place where their special ceremonies would be performed.

In early February 1846, the tension and pressure had risen to such a level that the Saints were driven out of Nauvoo—at great sacrifice and personal loss—by angry mobs of neighbors, who felt threatened by their presence. While many were able to withstand the rigors of the journey in the depth of winter, many others were not prepared or able to travel. The Saints realized that they were committed to transporting people of a wide range of ages, degrees

"[As near as we could estimate] about fifteen thousand Saints, three thousand wagons, and thirty thousand head of cattle . . . a great number of horses and mules . . . [and] an immense number of sheep."
John Taylor, 1846 Exodus from Nauvoo[7]

An announcement that appeared in the Nauvoo Neighbor, *October 29, 1845*

BILL OF PARTICULARS

For the emigrants leaving this government next spring.
Each family consisting of five persons, to be provided with—

1 good strong wagon well covered with a light box.
2 or 3 good yoke of oxen between the age of 4 and 10 years.
2 or more milch cows.
1 or more good beefs.
3 sheep if they can be obtained.
1000 lbs. of flour or other bread, or bread stuffs in good sacks.

1 good musket or rifle to each male over the age of twelve years.
1 lb. powder.
4 lbs. lead.
1 do. Tea.
5 do. coffee.
100 do. sugar.
1 do. cayenne pepper.
2 do. black do.

½ lb. mustard.
10 do. rice for each family.
1 do. cinnamon.
½ do. cloves.
1 doz. nutmegs.
25 lbs. salt.
5 lbs. saleratus.
10 do. dried apples.
1 bush. of beans.
A few lbs. of dried beef or bacon.
5 lbs. dried peaches.
20 do. do. pumpkin.
25 do. seed grain.
1 gal. alcohol.
20 lbs. of soap each family.
4 or 5 fish hooks and lines.
15 lbs. iron and steel.
A few lbs. of wrought nails.
One or more sets of saw or grist mill irons to company of 100 families.

1 good seine and hook for each company.
2 sets of pulley blocks and ropes to each company for crossing rivers.
From 25 to 100 lbs. of farming and mechanical tools.
Cooking utensils to consist of bake kettle, frying pan, coffee pot, and tea kettle.
Tin cups, plates, knives, forks, spoons, and pans as few as will do.
A good tent and furniture to each 2 families.
Clothing and bedding to each family, not to exceed 500 pounds.
Ten extra teams for each company of 100 families.

N. B.—In addition to the above list, horse and mule teams can be used as well as oxen. Many items of comfort and convenience will suggest themselves to a wise and provident people, and can be laid in in season; but none should start without filling the original bill.[8]

of physical condition, and abilities to adapt to the outdoor living. There were also a large number of animals.

As a result, between the years 1846 and 1848, the Saints altered and expanded their migration plans in an attempt to find a new permanent gathering place. They also looked for temporary safe places in which families could rest and recover. Temporary sites were built across Iowa at Mt. Pisgah and Garden Grove.

Mt. Pisgah was the place for recruitment and celebration of the Mormon Battalion. On June 26, 1846, a request was made for volunteers to serve in a military unit known as the "Army of the West" led by Colonel Stephen W. Kearny. This was a volunteer group of 541 men who participated in a contract with the federal government in the declared war against Mexico. Accompanying them were about one hundred others—including some officers' wives and children and twenty Battalion wives serving as laundresses—who would spend a year traveling to the Pacific Coast through the Southwest. They would gather and earn supplies, money, and valuable information on the western migration experience, while not having to participate in combat.

The initial reaction was similar to that voiced by Sarah Pea Rich (Quilt I-2), who regarded it "as 'a cruel demand made upon us' from a government that had rendered the Mormons no aid in their own time of need."[10] But ever-practical Brigham Young saw the opportunity differently. They could move men and supplies west at government expense. In addition, they could acquire capital for the rest of the Saints to make the migration by drawing in advance on the federal government $42 clothing allowance. The women and children, however, would be delayed in the bleak cold wilderness of the Midwest for at least a year.

"Large turnips, hollowed out to hold candles and hung from the ceiling or walls, 'imparted a very peaceable, quiet, Quakerlike influence, and the light reflected through these turnip rinds imparted a very picturesque appearance.' The celebration included a simple meal of corn and pea kernels presented with 'short speeches full of life and sentiment, spiced with enthusiasm, appropriate songs, recitations, toasts, conundrums, exhortations, etc.' She noted the evening ended when 'all withdrew, feeling as happy as though they were not homeless.' "
Eliza R. Snow quoted on a Mt. Pisgah evening in 1846[9]

"Mary says the scene [at Mt. Pisgah] that followed, she will never forget. Widow mothers parting with sometimes their only son. Sweethearts, husbands and wives being parted. A scene which only the ones who have witnessed it can realize the sadness thereof. The Battalion bravely underwent the terrible hardships as did their loved ones whom they left."
Annie Caroline Carlston Bills, granddaughter of Mary Young Wilcox (Quilt I-6)[11]

B. Y. Calling Volunteers for the Mormon Battalion *by C. C. A. Christensen*

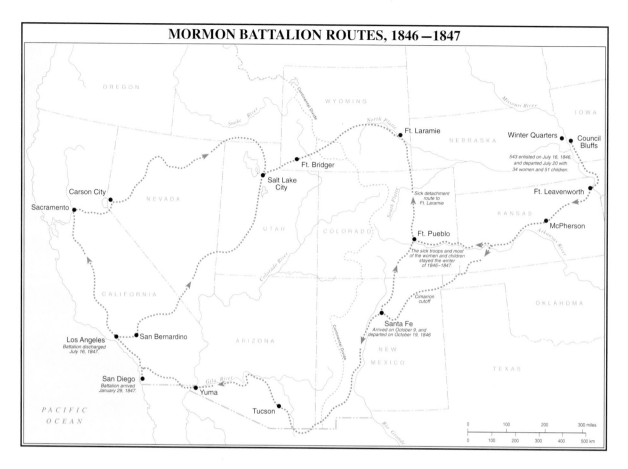

MORMON BATTALION ROUTES, 1846—1847

Winter Quarters was established on Indian land on the west bank of the Missouri River opposite Kanesville, which later became Council Bluffs. This place became the launching point for the Mormon Battalion. Many also waited here for family and loved ones journeying from the East or the West to rejoin them. Again, using their organizational ability, they set up ecclesiastical and municipal councils with a ward structure for the 2,980 women and children and 502 men.[12] Each especially needy family was assigned to several others who could assist them.

The Saints hoped that Winter Quarters would become a recovery place for many who needed to restore their strength before they could continue the migration. Instead, exposure and malnutrition, especially from the lack of fruits and vegetables, led to starvation and diseases such as scurvy (called black canker), consumption, and malaria. The sexton recorded 365 for whom the burial fee of $2.50 was paid, but many more deaths may have gone unrecorded. Many people could not afford the fee, and deaths were occurring frequently. As many as six hundred people may have died in Winter Quarters and the surrounding area.[14]

EMIGRATION CROSSING THE PLAINS FROM 1847 TO 1869					
(Andrew Jenson's Compilation)					
1847	About	2,000	1858	About	179
1848	About	4,000	1859	About	809
1849	About	3,000	1860	About	1,409
1850	About	5,000	1861	About	1,959
1851	About	5,000	1862	About	3,599
1852	About	10,000	1863	About	3,646
1853	About	2,603	1864	About	2,697
	(foreign)		1865	About	1,301
1854	About	3,167	1866	About	3,333
1855	About	4,684	1867	About	660
1856	About	3,756	1868	About	3,232
1857	About	1,994		Total	68,028
Source: "Church Emigration Book," Mormon Church Archives					

The experiences of the 1846 migration across Iowa to Winter Quarters on the Missouri River and westward in 1847 to the Great Salt Lake Valley under the leadership of President Brigham Young would serve to define and refine their major migration patterns. Returning to Winter Quarters in 1848, Brigham Young led nearly twenty-five hundred Saints west in about one thousand wagons.

They used all types of wagons and carriages. The most common was a five-by-ten-foot farm wagon, outfitted with a canvas cover and reinforced for the journey with caulking or waterproof canvas for crossing rivers. They were uncomfortable for passengers, but excellent for hauling freight, and they offered the needed protection from the weather. The five-foot width had two advantages: a bed could be set up in one permanently and the wagon wheels would fit existing trail ruts.

The Saints used oxen, mules, horses, and even cows to pull the wagons. They preferred oxen for their strength and patience; oxen also were easy to care for. They also cooperated more readily in crossing mud and quicksand. The equipment required for oxen was the easiest to acquire and maintain: a simple yoke rather than complicated harnesses. Furthermore, because oxen were gentle, women and children could handle them easily by walking beside them and guiding them. Using reins was not necessary, as it was with horses or mules.

Mules were the second animal of choice, followed by horses. Both of these were subject to being stolen; therefore, they had to be watched more closely. They also tended to be more independent.

Cows were used only in situations in which no other choice existed. If another animal died or was injured, a cow might be the only replacement.

Mormon Panorama Twenty-one/Winter Quarters *by C.C.A. Christensen*

Under normal conditions, an organized Mormon company could travel by wagon at an average speed of about two miles per hour.

THE WOMEN

In this group of early quilt owners are women who joined the Church as daughters and wives early in its history. They participated in many of the early migrations "seeking the place." This common bond of shared experience and knowledge helped them to survive. Most personally knew or were married to Church leaders. Many had witnessed death, personal loss, destruction, and verbal attacks from non-Mormon neighbors or "gentiles."

An important consideration for most of these women was their stage of pregnancy at the time of the February exodus from Nauvoo. Women close to delivery were encouraged to remain behind after the initial exodus. Women with very young babies often suffered the worst, because they left Nauvoo in weakened condition from just recently having given birth. They subjected themselves and their babies to the extremes of winter weather with very little possibility of decent food and shelter. Many had tents, either finished or unfinished, to sleep in, while others camped in wagons, but some had no shelter at all.

"With drawn sword and pistols pointing at me and telling me if I did not tell where my husband was they would blow my brains out and when they would see that I was not frightened they would give vent to the most wicked oaths and vulgar language that their tongues could utter and then leave with wicked threats what they would do if I did not tell [where] my husband was. For three months I lived under these cruel threats . . ."

Sarah DeArmon Pea Rich
(Quilt I-2)[15]

In 1847, several quiltmakers and quilt owners were among the first Mormon women to cross the Plains. They were in the best physical condition to travel after leaving Nauvoo and spending the months at Winter Quarters awaiting better traveling conditions in the spring. Their husbands were among the Church leaders heading up small companies of fewer than two hundred people, following the vanguard group that had gone with Brigham Young. These were the women who took a physically active part in the migration, since the organization was not as refined and disciplined as it became in later years. Their experiences gave rise to the generalized image of the Mormon Pioneer woman who drove her wagon while holding her baby on her lap.

Following in 1848 was a company of more than two thousand people with five thousand animals, traveling in five different companies of about five hundred people each, under the controlled leadership of Brigham Young. From the challenges faced by so large a group, the men and women learned the procedures and skills necessary to orchestrate a major migration over time and space. The men developed a cadre of trained professionals and well-cared-for oxen who would make between five and forty journeys between Salt Lake and the Missouri River over the next twenty years. The women perfected their pioneering skills of surviving in a bleak environment of unknown conditions and resources with the added burden of continuous movement.

THE QUILTS

The first group of quilts and their makers and owners represent the migration period between 1830 and 1848. The quilts range from family heirlooms made with fabrics from the earliest textile industries in America and Europe, to the later unfinished projects of these pioneer women. Because these women were traveling by wagon, they had space in which to pack a finished quilt. They knew it could serve multiple purposes: keeping them warm, protecting them from the weather, and serving as a visual record of family members left behind. Other quilts in this section are those that women made late in their lives after years of residing in the West. They represent these women's abilities to succeed and survive the challenges of pioneering. That some tops remained unfinished indicates that these women were involved in other activities. Often they made important economic and social contributions to their families, as directed by the Church or allowed by the family social structure. The first quilt, Whig's Defeat, and the last, Mormon Mothers, are especially symbolic of "seeking the place."

Family Portrait: Mary Burton White, Robert T. Burton, Rebecca Burton Jones, Melissa Burton Coray Kimball (about 1855)

Quilt: WHIG'S DEFEAT (I-1)

Category: Pieced
Size: 91¾" x 93"
Date: circa 1850–1870
Maker: Elizabeth Ann Whitmer
    Cowdery (22 January
    1815–January 1892)
Migration: Seneca County, New York,
    to Missouri
Place Joined the Church: New York
Year Crossed the Ocean: ————
Ship: ————
Year Crossed the Plains: ————
Company: ————
Arrived: ————
Came: ————
County Where Settled: Jackson,
    Missouri; Cuyahoga, Ohio;
    Caldwell, Missouri; Wisconsin;
    McDonald, Missouri

Elizabeth Ann Whitmer Cowdery

Because the quilt is mounted in a plexiglass display case, it is difficult to access for study and photography. It appears to be either a summer quilt, a top finished without a batting and backing, or handwork mounted on a cotton foundation for preservation. The pieced pattern sections are stitched in place with what appears to be machine-stitching. The pattern sections appear to be older than the surrounding fabric. How-

Detail of piecing

ever, since a quilt must be dated by the most recent fabric or technique used, and since the sewing machine was in general production by 1856, the quilt may be dated between 1850 and 1870.

The pattern name Whig's Defeat is often attributed to the 1844 election victory of Democrat James K. Polk over Whig Henry Clay.[16] For Mormons, who were actively involved in the expansion and settlement of the West, this defeat reflects the decline of a political party whose philosophy and ideals they opposed. For Elizabeth Ann Cowdery personally, this pattern may have symbolized her husband's political victory over a Whig opponent in Kirtland, Ohio, where he ran for elective office in the mid-1830s. His victory and those of other Mormons constituted a first step in creating Mormon control over local government.[17]

During this time in Ohio, Elizabeth faced personal tragedy. Between 1835 and 1846, their six children were born, and the five youngest died before the age of six.

To trace the history of the quilt is a challenge. The accession records indicate it was transferred to the

Latter-day Saints Museum of Church History by the Relief Society, who had received it as a gift from a Mary A. Stephens. Property records at the Reorganized Church of Latter-day Saints Archives in Independence, Missouri, indicate a Stevens family owned land in the same township as the Cowderys in Caldwell County. The quilt could have been a gift from the Cowderys to someone who was active with the Relief Society, or perhaps it was taken from the home after they were forced to leave the area.[18]

Elizabeth Ann Whitmer Cowdery was born the daughter of Peter and Mary Musselman Whitmer in Fayette, Seneca County, New York. The Whitmer log home was the site of much of the Church's early history. In 1829 the "revealed narrative" was dictated by Joseph Smith to recorder Oliver Cowdery. On April 6, 1830, the Church was formally organized when thirty of the believers gathered here to officially accept Smith and Cowdery as teachers. The house was also the site of Joseph Smith's allowing eight men to see the golden plates, in order to validate their existence. Among these men were Elizabeth's four brothers and a brother-in-law.

In October 1830, Oliver Cowdery, Elizabeth's brother Peter, and two others left for the Missouri frontier. She and her family migrated to Jackson County, Missouri, where she married Oliver on December 18, 1832. He served as the first recorder and editor of the Church's printing office in Independence. Two years later, they moved to Kirtland, Ohio, where in 1838 he was excommunicated from the Church for disagreeing with the Church's administrative procedures in Missouri. Ten years later, however, while he was practicing law in Wisconsin, a leader called on him. Having decided to return to the Church, he appeared at an October 24, 1848, convention in

Full view of Whig's Defeat Quilt

Kanesville, Iowa, reaffirming his faith and sharing his early experiences. The family began to plan to migrate to Salt Lake. However, Oliver died on March 3, 1850, in Richmond, Missouri. Elizabeth and their only child, fifteen-year-old daughter Maria Louise, remained in Richmond with Whitmer family members. In 1856, when Maria Louise married Dr. Charles Johnson, Elizabeth joined them in settling in Southwest City, Missouri. Here both women lived out their lives together, dying within four days of each other in January 1892.

Quilt: STAR TOP (I-2)

Category: Pieced
Size: 37" x 62"
Date: Mid (1880–1890)
Maker: Sarah DeArmon Pea Rich
    (23 September 1814–12
    September 1893)
Migration: Illinois to Utah
Place Joined the Church: Missouri
Year Crossed the Ocean: ———
Ship: ———
Year Crossed the Plains: 1847
Company: Capt. Charles C. Rich's
    Guard
Arrived: October 2, 1847
Came: With her husband, his other
    wives, and family
County Where Settled: Salt Lake; Bear
    Lake, Idaho; Salt Lake

The size of the sixty 6" assembled blocks indicates the piece was "a work in process." The blocks are hand-pieced and machine-stitched together. The documentation submitted with the quilt says "Made by Sarah D. Rich when 82 years old."[19]

The significance of this quilt top is that it leads to the discovery of an important Mormon pioneer whose life experiences span much of the migration story. Referred to as "Sarah D." within the family and "Sarah Pea" in other publications, this woman, like other early Church members, has served as a role model for many Mormon women. Her responses to the demands placed upon her life as a member of the young Church demonstrated her leadership ability. She earned a position of respect among other women, and her husband sought her counsel. Early Church leaders recognized her position of leadership by placing her portrait alongside her husband's in the Nauvoo Temple.

Sarah DeArmon Pea Rich

———

Sarah DeArmon Pea Rich was born the youngest daughter of John and Elizabeth Knighton Pea in St. Clair County, Illinois. She and Charles Coulson Rich had been recommended to each other by friends. He proposed to her by letter, and she accepted before she had actually met him. They were married in Far West, Missouri, on February 11, 1838.

When the mobs began their raids on the Saints in Caldwell County, Missouri, Charles was recognized as a Mormon leader and forced to flee.

Sarah remained behind in her parents' home with seven other refugee families. She and Samantha Stout, the wife of exile Hosea Stout, vowed to stay together through the ordeal until they could make their way to safety in Quincy, Illinois.

Once they were reunited, the Riches settled in Nauvoo. Charles was then called to go on a mission to Michigan and Canada. To finance the mission, the Riches sold their home and Sarah Pea rented a room in her parents' home. Called back to Nauvoo after Joseph Smith was murdered in 1844, forty-year-old Rich was elected to the Quorum of Twelve Apostles, the leadership group.

Charles Rich consulted Sarah Pea about what their position should be in the practice of polygamy, or plural marriage. She accepted the concept and urged him to marry before leaving Nauvoo, since marriage ceremonies could be performed in its Temple. He, in turn, requested she choose the women. She selected, taught, and converted four women: Eliza Ann Graves, Sarah Jane Peck, Mary Ann Phelps, and Emeline Grover. Throughout their lives these women shared roles of leadership and cooperated with

Salt Lake City home of Sarah DeArmon Pea Rich

one another in mutual respect and admiration.[20]

When they traveled west in 1847, their extended family included five wives ranging in age from fourteen to thirty-six, and six children under six, including four babies. At least three wives drove ox teams across the Plains. Sarah Pea and Emeline were often irritated that the men seemed more eager to hunt than to cover distance.

In 1851, when Charles was called to help settle the San Bernardino, California, area, the couple decided Sarah Pea would remain in Salt Lake City to recover from childbirth and to assist the other pregnant wife, Sarah Jane, with her expected delivery. During this time, she received a love letter from Charles expressing his appreciation for her wisdom and understanding and his increasing affection for her. She recorded this letter in her diary with the accompanying words: "for future generations of my family to read so that they will fully understand and never criticize Charles for leaving us at this time."[21] This was, no doubt, a difficult time for her as Charles divided his time as a husband, father, and Church leader between San Bernardino; Centerville, Utah; and Salt Lake.

In order to be with her husband when Charles was asked in 1864 to colonize the Bear Lake area in northern Utah/southern Idaho, Sarah Pea, now age fifty, accepted the challenge of pioneering again. However, the difficulties faced during the long cold winters forced her to return to Salt Lake. Her home in Salt Lake served as a refuge for all family members. She maintained lovely gardens, from which she produced fruits and flowers. She had brought a rose cutting from Nauvoo, which she grafted to a wild rose. Brigham Young awarded her a certificate for growing the first cultivated rose in the Salt Lake Valley.

Full view of Star Quilt top

Quilt: FLYING GEESE (I-3)

Category: Pieced
Size: 70½" x 71¾"
Date: Mid (1870–1890)
Maker: Sarah Jane Peck Rich (25 September 1825–29 November 1893)
Migration: Chenango County, New York, to Utah
Place Joined the Church: New York
Year Crossed the Ocean: ————
Ship: ————
Year Crossed the Plains: 1847
Company: Capt. Charles C. Rich's Guard
Arrived: October 2, 1847
Came: With her husband, his other wives, and family
County Where Settled: Salt Lake; Davis; Bear Lake, Idaho

Sarah Jane Rich

"[She] went cheerfully to work to prepare for the long cold winters ahead . . . She also made quilts and added to their beauty by gathering sagebrush and wild herbs, which she used as dyes for the different materials."

Ethel May Rich Morgan, her granddaughter [22]

This popular old pattern traditionally has several different names. Here, the pieced triangles or "flying geese" express the theme of nature and the outdoors. While Flying Geese is the pattern name used by the maker's family members, another commonly used one is Fox and Geese, the "fox" being the larger triangle. Both names evoke a spirit of action, important elements of migration and pioneer life.

The forty-two 7¾" pieced blocks are set "on point." In an "on point" arrangement, the blocks are set on the diagonal rather than being set square. The quilting lines are a grid set 1¼" by 1¾". The batting is wool. The quilt's puffiness indicates shrinkage as a result of improper laundering prior to its acquisition.

One significant feature is the use of sagebrush blossoms as the dyestuff for the cloth backing. This is an example of the pioneer women seeking and using the local resources available. Since the plant does not grow in the East or Midwest, the quilter would not have known of this dye source prior to her migration. Formerly for a yellow dye, she would have used plants such as sumac, sassafras, goldenrod, hickory, oak, or ash. Western women could create a dye liquid by soaking the blossoms, bark, roots, and stems of the one plant readily available in their desert climate, sagebrush. [23]

———

Sarah Jane Peck was born the youngest of five children of Benjamin and Phoebe Crosby Peck in Bainbridge, Chenango County, New York. Soon after Benjamin's death, his widow became a member of the first branch of the Church at Colesville. Her marriage to Joseph Knight, Sr. brought her daughter Sarah Jane directly into one of the early Church families that had a close friendship to Joseph Smith. Over the years, the Knight family followed the Church and its leaders, at great sacri-

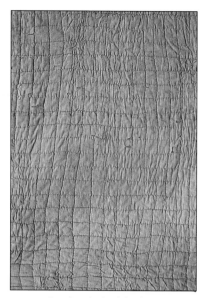

Sagebrush-dyed backing

fice, to Ohio, Missouri, Illinois, and Utah. [24]

At the age of twenty-one, Sarah Jane Peck, accepting the principle of plural marriage and with the encouragement of Sarah DeArmon Pea Rich, became the fourth wife of Charles Coulson Rich on January 9, 1845. After leaving Nauvoo in the winter of 1846, she bore her first child in Mt. Pisgah, Union County, Iowa. There the family lived temporarily in log houses, using their wagon boxes as sleeping areas.

They spent their first year in the West in Salt Lake County. In 1849, Rich obtained land in Centerville and moved two of his wives, Sarah Jane and Eliza, there. They were pleased to be near other relatives, including Sarah Jane's sister Henrietta, wife of Charles Rich's cousin Thomas Rich, and Charles's father.

In 1851, when the Church asked Charles Rich to move to San Bernardino, California, these two wives with their children chose to remain in Centerville. With the help of a hired man, they raised crops and livestock for themselves and for Sarah D. Rich in Salt Lake City.

Full view of Flying Geese Quilt

In 1864, Rich was called to help colonize the Bear Lake area. He planned to move the entire family of all six wives and their children, to Paris, Idaho, despite the challenges of relocating and re-establishing a productive farm. His two wives in Centerville were reluctant, yet accepted the plan to sell their farm and leave their friends. Identical three-room log cabins with chimneys and fireplaces were built for each wife.

After Charles Rich died on November 21, 1883, three wives continued to reside in Idaho. Sarah Jane received a $25 allowance from the Church and income from her property. Having already buried six children, she was especially grieved when two adult sons died within five days of each other in January 1893. She died eleven months later at the age of sixty-eight.

Quilt: FRIENDSHIP (I-4)

Category: Appliquéd
Size: 75½" x 90"
Date: Mid (1870)
Maker: Members of the Twentieth Ward Relief Society
Owner: Margaret McMeans Thompson Smoot (16 April 1809–2 September 1884)
Migration: South Carolina to Utah
Place Joined the Church: Tennessee
Year Crossed the Ocean: ————
Ship: ————
Year Crossed the Plains: 1847
Company: Capt. Abraham O. Smoot
Arrived: September 25, 1847
Came: With husband, other wives, and family
County Where Settled: Salt Lake, then Utah

This silk Friendship quilt was presented to Margaret M. T. Smoot by the sisters of the Twentieth Ward Relief Society when she resigned as president to move to Provo in 1872. Thus, it serves as a tribute to this woman for her dedication to their social organization. As with many group quilts, each woman who contributed a block drew upon one of her basic domestic talents, the ability to sew, in order to create a symbol of respect and celebra-

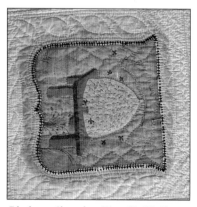

Block attributed to Zina D. H. Young

Detail of center with key blocks: one identifying that the quilt was made for Margaret Smoot and one attributed to Eliza R. Snow.

tion. It is included here because many of its images and texts reflect themes of migration. Each contributed one of the fifty-six 11¼" silk quilt blocks featuring symbols of their native culture such as the American Stars and Stripes flag (1795–1818), the British Navy ensign, and the Irish shamrock.[25]

Many blocks contain phrases proclaiming the values of Mormonism, including "Let Sisterly Love Continue," "Consider the Lilies," "United We Stand," "Faith, Hope, and Charity," "Humanity and Affection," and "Man is the lofty rugged pine—Woman the slender clasping vine." Others have political references such as "Our Mountain Home and Celestial Marriage," and "Woman's Rights in Utah."[26]

Many contributors were early residents and important leaders in Utah. Eliza R. Snow, the second general president of the Relief Society from 1866 to 1887, contributed the block with the lion and lamb and the inscription from Isaiah: "And there shall be nothing to hurt or destroy in all my holy mountains, saith the

Lord." Zina D. H. Young contributed the block with the beehive with the inscription "Holiness to the Lord" and her name and the date "Sept. 9, 1870."

Margaret McMeans Thompson Smoot was born the daughter of Anthony and Esther Hunter McMeans in Chester County, South Carolina. In 1818, her father died and her mother moved west to Roane County, Tennessee. Nine years later, Margaret entered into a difficult marriage. In order to prevent her husband from taking her young son, she was forced to leave her family and friends. In 1834, she joined the Church and migrated to Far West, Missouri. There, she married Captain A. O. Smoot on November 11, 1837. Forced to leave in 1839, they moved to Nauvoo where they prospered and entered into plural marriage, a decision she supported.

The Smoots left Nauvoo on May 14, 1846, and wintered over in Pottawattamie County, Iowa, before leading one of the first companies to Utah. There, they lived in Salt Lake City for twenty-one years during which Captain Smoot served as the mayor part of the time. In 1868,

Margaret McMeans Thompson Smoot

Full view of Friendship Quilt

they moved to Provo City when Brigham Young asked him to supervise the woolen mill there. He again served as mayor as well as on the board of directors of several livestock and woolen cloth manufacturing companies.

Respected among her peers, Margaret Smoot also served as president of the Provo Relief Society and president of the Utah County Silk Association. In 1870, she was one of the twelve women to sign the letter of gratitude to Territorial

Governor Mann for signing the women's right-to-vote bill. Her husband, A. O. Smoot, had directed the bill through the legislature. Joining her were Amanda Barnes Smith (Quilt II-5) and Zina D. H. Young (Quilt I-13).[27]

Quilt: LOG CABIN (I-5)

Category: Pieced
Size: 59" x 67"
Date: Late (1890–1910)
Maker: Sophronia Ellen Turnbow
   Carter (23 February 1841–
   5 February 1925)
Migration: Perry County, Alabama,
   to Utah
Place Joined the Church: Alabama
Year Crossed the Ocean: ———
Ship: ———
Year Crossed the Plains: 1847
Company: Capt. Abraham O. Smoot
Arrived: September 25, 1847
Came: With her parents and family
County Where Settled: Salt Lake;
   Washington

This silk-and-velvet Log Cabin quilt is composed of seven narrow (¼" to ⅜") strips (logs) built around very small (¼" to ½") centers. Each block consists half of light fabrics and half of dark. Careful placement of the squares creates the larger 8" alternating color blocks known as the Light and Dark variation. The blocks are hand-stitched. The detail of the black silk with a white stripe gives an unusual effect to the quilt's overall appearance.

Since Sophronia Carter was known to be very successful in the business of raising silkworms, it is very likely that the quilt contains some Utah-produced silk fabric. "There being at one time over one thousand silkworms in her business. She gathered the silk from the worms, spun it into skeins and later wove it into cloth from which she made her own dresses."[28]

Sophronia Ellen Turnbow Carter was born the seventh child of Samuel and Sylvira Hart Turnbow in Perry County, Alabama. Her family joined the Church and moved to Nauvoo in 1845. They spent the winter of 1846 in Winter Quarters before starting west in 1847.

Ten years later in 1857, at the age of sixteen, she married into polygamy as the third wife of William Carter. As an early scout, William was one of the first men to enter the Salt Lake Valley on July 22, 1847. He plowed the first furrow in the Salt Lake Valley, and later he did the same in southern Utah's Dixie area in 1861.[29]

As a member of one of the families called to settle the Dixie area, Sophronia reportedly drove a three-ox team while holding her baby on her lap. It was in the Carters' large tent that the entire company celebrated a rainy Christmas Day.

Settling in Dixie permanently, she made significant contributions to pioneering the area. She helped to

Sophronia Ellen Turnbow Carter

make the adobe bricks used for their home. During the first year, she prepared the soil and planted fourteen rows of cotton. At harvest time, she gathered four hundred pounds of cotton, which she picked, carded, and wove into cloth for her family. She reportedly wove over four hundred yards of unbleached muslin, commonly called "factory."[30]

She did her share of caring for the sick and needy, often also preparing the dead for burial. She was known to go out at all hours of the day and night. She was also active in Church-related affairs, including helping to clean the St. George Temple every Monday morning for ten years.[31]

Block showing use of stripes and print fabrics

William Carter Home in St. George

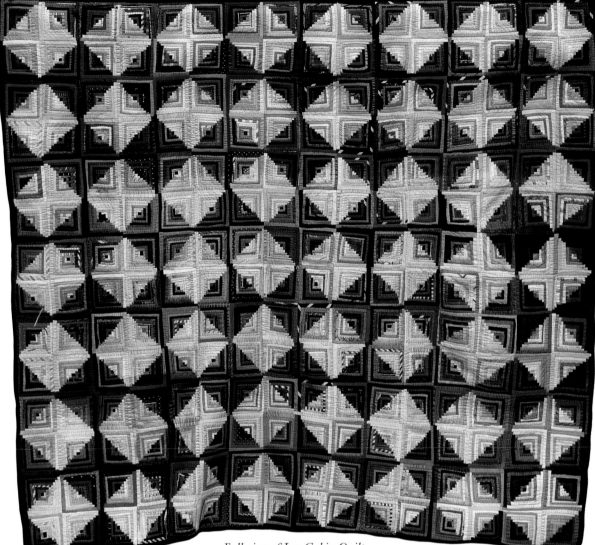

Full view of Log Cabin Quilt

Quilt: DOUBLE IRISH CHAIN
   (I-6)

Category: Pieced
Size: 72½" x 86"
Date: Late (1890–1910)
Maker: Mary Young Wilcox (6 June
   1831–16 May 1929)
Migration: Ontario, Canada, to Utah
Place Joined the Church: Canada
Year Crossed the Ocean: ————
Ship: ————
Year Crossed the Plains: 1847
Company: John Taylor (also known
   as Joseph Horne, Captain 1st
   Fifty)
Arrived: September 29, 1847
Came: With her parents and family
County Where Settled: Salt Lake;
   Sanpete; Salt Lake; Weber; Utah;
   Salt Lake

This mint-condition quilt still has
the pencil lines used to mark the
quilting lines, indicating it has never
been washed. It has always been
treasured as a special family heirloom.

The finished blocks are 11¾" by
12¼" consisting of 2¾" machine-
stitched squares of blue-and-white
print. The diagonal chain of color
creates the sense of movement across
the quilt's surface. The simple
quilted lines across the pieced
squares enhance this movement.

In all the solid blocks but one, the
quilting pattern is a wreath of leaves
with a center cluster of five leaves.
The one different block is located on
the corner edge. Here the design is a
4" open gridwork inside the wreath
of leaves.

The ⅜" binding is worked continu-
ously around the edge. One unique
treatment is the way the quiltmaker
finished the two ends. One end is
carefully folded over the top of the
other end making a seam line invisi-

ble. This shows a careful attention
to detail.

———

Mary Young Wilcox was born the
first daughter and second child of
James and Elizabeth Seeley Young
in Whitney Township, Ontario,
Canada. Her family was converted to
Mormonism by Parley P. Pratt during his 1836 mission to Canada. The
family traveled by steamer and river-
boat to Missouri in 1838. Forced to
flee almost upon their arrival, they
settled in Burlington, Iowa, across
the Mississippi River from Nauvoo.

In 1846, the Youngs joined the
trek west to Winter Quarters, where
they lived in a small, windowless log
cabin. The family headed west in the
John Taylor Company. John Taylor
was another Canadian whose conver-
sion from Methodism to Mormonism
was significant in the development of
Church doctrine and policy. Seventeen-year-old Mary walked three
yoke of oxen pulling a heavy wagon
across the Plains. Part of her responsibility was yoking and unyoking
them, a difficult task for anyone.

Arriving in the Salt Lake Valley as
a healthy young woman committed
to her faith and her family, Mary remembered her eager response to Captain Taylor's blessing: "Mary, there
doesn't stand within the lids of any
history, a record of a girl your age

Mary Young Wilcox

who has taken such an important part
as you have in such an endeavor. You
will become the mother of a great
nation. You will live as long as life is
desirable." To which she responded:
"I shall live forever."[32]

On March 14, 1848, Mary and
John Henry Wilcox had the distinc-
tion of being the first white couple
married in the Salt Lake Valley.
Brigham Young presented them with
a wedding gift of ten acres of land.
To prepare their farm, Mary worked
beside her husband. While he
grubbed the brush, she piled and
burned it.

The young couple, with their
growing family of eventually eleven
children, answered the call to help
settle and build new colonies in the
territory six different times between
1848 and 1860. While John worked
to develop the land, Mary provided
food, clothing, and bedding for her
family by using the natural resources
available to her.

She lived to be ninety-eight and
had 625 descendants. The state of
Utah presented her with a plaque
recognizing her contributions to
building the territory and establishing her family.

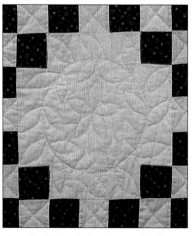

Quilting design in one block

Full view of Double Irish Chain Quilt

Quilt: FEATHERED STAR (I-7)

Category: Pieced
Size: 77½" x 99"
Date: Late (1860–1875)
Maker: Elizabeth Whitaker Cain
  (4 August 1828–26 March 1880)
Migration: Worcester, England, to
  Utah
Place Joined the Church: England
Year Crossed the Ocean: 1846
Ship: Unavailable
Year Crossed the Plains: 1847
Company: John Taylor
Arrived: September 28, 1847
Came: With her husband
County Where Settled: Salt Lake

This quilt's unusual appearance comes from the color choice for the background fabric in the pattern blocks and in the sashing strips. Here the quiltmaker has done the reverse of what usually happens in quilt construction. Usually the stars of the twelve 14½" blocks are set against the light fabric and the 5¾" sashings would be the print. The effect is that the stars become more static and less dramatic when set within the print. For visual comparison, see the quilt made by Eleanor Young (III-4). The outer border of continuous pieced

large triangles creates a sense of movement around the quilt. Note how the quilter has adjusted the triangle size to fit the length of the quilt on each side, yet maintained a consistent corner design.

The quilting stitches in the pattern blocks create wheels in the star's center and in each corner square. In the pink-print and large green-print triangles, the quilting lines follow the piecing patterns. A trefoil is centered in each of the large green triangles. The chevron pattern, quilted in the sashings, continues the sense of movement.

Elizabeth Whitaker Cain was born the daughter of Thomas and Sophia Turner Whitaker in Blakedown, Worcester, England. She married Joseph Cain on February 1, 1847, after meeting him on board the ship bringing them to America. They were married between the two phases of their migration. They migrated to Utah in that same year, settling permanently in Salt Lake City on what proved to be valuable real estate at First South and Main Streets. They were able to use this lot to their economic advantage. After Joseph Cain's death in 1863, Elizabeth leased the property to a retail clothing store. She was the first customer and annually received a birthday gift from the owners. The

construction materials from the old home were used to build a new home on West Temple between Second and Third Streets South.

Elizabeth was recognized in her home as "the presiding genius who kept both action and order in perfect harmony."[33] She instilled in her only daughter, Elizabeth Turner Cain Crismon, a sense of commitment to the women's social organizations. Elizabeth Crismon provided assistance to these organizations from the time she was a small child until she served on the Relief Society General Board. She was also a charter member of the International Society of Daughters of Utah Pioneers. She donated this quilt to their Pioneer Memorial Museum.[34]

Detail of quilt block

Salt Lake City, c. 1870

Full view of Feathered Star Quilt

Quilt: FRAMED CENTER
    MEDALLION (I-8)

Category: Pieced
Size: 72½" x 81"
Date: Early (1835–1850)
Maker: Unknown
Owner: Susan Mandeville Fairbanks
    (23 September 1819–2 March
    1899)
Migration: Morris County, New
    Jersey, to Utah
Place Joined the Church: New Jersey
Year Crossed the Ocean: ———
Ship: ———
Year Crossed the Plains: 1847
Company: John Taylor
Arrived: September 29, 1847
Came: With husband and family
County Where Settled: Salt Lake; Utah

Quilt documentation

This treasured heirloom quilt contains a center section (46" by 56") of fabric known to have been part of the bed curtains and valance made for the marriage of the owner's mother, Jane Jones, to Brig. Gen. Cornelius William Mandeville in Pompton Plains, New Jersey, in 1810. This was and continues to be an acceptable way of preserving special fabrics as family treasures. Here it is presented so that the print design can be fully appreciated. The vertical match of the two finished 23" sections is almost perfect. Comparable pieces of the same wax-resist printed fabric are in the Winterthur Museum Collection and the Cooper-Hewitt Museum of Design, Smithsonian Institution. The comparable fabrics have shades of indigo blue on white while this one has only the single shade. Because this difference would indicate a less-complicated

production process, the piece may be American-made. According to the Roster of American Calico Printers and Print Works, 1776–1900, there was a print works (name unknown) in Pompton, New Jersey, starting in 1796.[35]

Surrounding the quilt on three sides are 6" by 6⅜" blocks of an early quilt pattern called Orange Peel. Oval curved slices are cut from and then exchanged between two squares of cloth.

The quilting patterns are straight lines spaced one inch apart across the center section. The pattern in the three framing sections are repeats of the piecing pattern spaced ½" to ⅝" apart. There are nine stitches per inch.

Susan Mandeville Fairbanks was the youngest of the couple's five children. Her mother, Jane, died in 1821 when Susan was two years old and her older sisters were five and seven. Her father was a leader in the New Jersey State Militia and a northern slaveholder.

Susan's education was not typical of that of most young women of the period. Since help was available to do most of the domestic tasks, her education was more intellectual. She at-

tended the academy owned and directed by her father. As his favorite, she would accompany him on business trips and handle his correspondence.

Susan Mandeville married David Fairbanks on November 26, 1838, in Pompton Plains. They lived with his family, and his mother taught her homemaking skills. The extended family joined the Church in 1842 and migrated to Nauvoo in 1844. The couple's first three children were born in New Jersey and their fourth in Nauvoo in 1846.

In Winter Quarters in 1846, David Fairbanks became a ward bishop overseeing the construction of log cabins for those families, widows, and orphans left there during the travels of the Mormon Battalion. Susan was very ill with the major disease of the time, scurvy. Yet, she agreed to leave in the spring of 1847, when the family was one of the six hundred chosen to migrate west.

Two more children were born in Salt Lake City. The next daughter was born in Pond Town, a settlement they helped to found. Their last six children were born in Payson, Utah County. Susan also raised a grandson. Respected by friends and neighbors, David was one of the first elected Justices of the Peace in Utah. Susan was active in the Utah County Silk Association.

Susan Mandeville Fairbanks died on March 2, 1899, after falling on the ice and breaking her hip.

"I have travelled from the Atlantic almost to the Pacific in a wagon. I do not think I shall undertake it again very soon."

Susan Mandeville Fairbanks,
April 2, 1854[36]

Full view of Framed Center Medallion Quilt

Quilt: LOG CABIN (I-9)

Category: Pieced
Size: 78" x 86"
Date: Late (1890–1900)
Maker: Nancy Garr Badger
    Stringham (17 October 1822–
    1 April 1900)
Migration: Indiana to Utah
Place Joined the Church: Illinois
Crossed the Ocean: ————
Ship: ————
Year Crossed the Plains: 1847
Company: Captain Jedediah Grant's
    Hundred
Recorded: October 2, 1847
Came: With father and family
County Where Settled: Salt Lake;
    Millard

Nancy Garr Badger Stringham

This woolen quilt has alternating blocks of one dark and one light fabric in "logs" in the Light and Dark variation. The blocks are constructed of solids, paisleys, and plaids around a center of the same color as the light fabric of the block. This is unique and creative because usually the center piece is either yellow or red and the logs are of various fabrics. The sixteen full blocks are each 9½" finished with ½" strips or logs.

Nancy Garr Badger Stringham was born the second daughter of Field-ing and Pauline Turner Garr in Richmond, Wayne County, Indiana. In 1840 her mother became the first family member to join the Church. The family moved west to near Nauvoo, where Nancy's mother died in 1844. When she was on her deathbed, her husband promised to keep the family together and to remain with the Church. Nancy married Rodney Badger, a young Vermont native, in La Harpe, Illinois, in 1845. He was ordained an elder and was asked to help move families west from Nauvoo. Leaving his wife and child with her father, Rodney left to help build the road and bridges for others to follow. After the family reunited at the Sweetwater River, they continued on to Salt Lake Valley.

Later, Rodney served as a lieutenant of the Territorial Militia and sheriff of Salt Lake County. He drowned on April 29, 1853, while rescuing a migrating mother and her four children in the Weber River.

This tragedy left Nancy a widow with four young children. She went to live with her father on Antelope Island in the Great Salt Lake, where he and her brothers cared for the Church cattle. She cooked and kept house for the cowboys living and working there. When she remarried Briant Stringham in 1858, her family continued to live and work on the Antelope Island Church farm. She became a widow again in 1871 when Briant died of typhoid fever. She then lived with her sons and daughters in Holden until she died in 1900.[37]

Woolen fabrics used in quilt block

Full view of Log Cabin Quilt

Quilt: CRAZY QUILT (I-10)

Category: Pieced
Size: 78" x 84"
Date: Late (1915)
Maker: Lydia Rebecca Baker Price
    Johnson (9 June 1841–1 April
    1934)
Migration: Iowa to Utah
Place Joined the Church: Iowa
Year Crossed the Ocean: ————
Ship: ————
Year Crossed the Plains: 1847
Company: Capt. Jedediah M. Grant's
    Hundred
Arrived: October 2, 1847
Came: With her father, stepmother,
    and family
County Where Settled: Salt Lake;
    Rich; Sweetwater, Wyoming;
    Uinta, Wyoming

This quilt was made while Lydia Rebecca was visiting her youngest son, Claud. Her daughter-in-law, Annie B. Johnson, had started the project and was unable to finish because of other responsibilities. Lydia had wanted to

*First-prize ribbon from
Bridger Valley Fair, 1918*

make something special for Claud so she offered to complete it.

It began as a name quilt so that she could record her family's names. But when her son objected to that idea, she changed her plan. This explains why names and initials appear in the top right corner blocks, while flowers and other symbols are in the rest. Her son was very pleased and proud of her workmanship. In the center of the quilt is a ribbon with "1841 Mother 1915," her birthdate, and the year she completed the quilt. The corner designs were stamped by Annie.

A significant image is the Old Dutch Cleanser trademark. This striding Dutch woman with her wooden shoes was a popular figure at the time the quilt was made. Its inclusion here symbolizes the ongoing effort to keep a home clean in the windy, dusty, arid region of Wyoming's high plateau area. It also acknowledges the success of the manufacturer's marketing campaign. Originally the woman was conceived as an image of Dutch cleanliness for Cudahy Packing Company of Omaha, Nebraska. The design was taken directly from a framed decoration in the home of E. A. Strauss. He was trying to create an image American housekeepers could strive for in cleaning their homes. Actually, the figure became so popular and recognized that it was featured in cartoons satirizing Teddy Roosevelt's trust-busting crusades. The image was also used on World War I bond posters to represent the effort needed to clean up the war-torn areas of Europe.[38]

Wanting something to back the quilt, Lydia Rebecca selected a burgundy sateen and reproduced a portrait of Abraham Lincoln. Her son Claud greatly admired Lincoln. The reproduction was done by perforating the picture and stamping it onto the back for stitching.[39]

*Block with Dutch cleanser and initials
J. A. J. and M. P.*

Lydia Rebecca Baker Price Johnson was born the seventh child of Simon and Mercy Young Baker in Montrose, Lee County, Iowa, on June 9, 1841. Her mother died in March 1845, leaving her husband with eight children. A month later, he married Charlotte Leavitt.

The family moved west, arriving in Salt Lake in 1847. As a child and young woman, she worked to help

Detail of backing

Full view of Crazy Quilt

the family by sewing, cooking, building furniture, and doing other household chores. She was married to William Price in 1857 at the age of sixteen. After that marriage ended, Lydia Rebecca was married in polygamy to Snellen Marion Johnson as his second wife in 1862. His first wife, Sarah Hunt Greer, was one of her good friends. The family lived in harmony together and helped to pioneer Mormon settlements in Utah, Idaho, and Wyoming. Aunt Becky, as she was known, had nine children.

She died at age ninety-three while living with her daughter Cora in Robertson, Wyoming.

Quilt: WHOLE CLOTH (I-11)

Category: Pieced
Size: 76½" x 83"
Date: Early (1820–1840)
Maker: Samantha Crismon Chase
(27 March 1840–9 July 1899)
Migration: Kane County, Illinois,
to Utah
Place Joined the Church: Illinois
Year Crossed the Ocean: ————
Ship: ————
Year Crossed the Plains: 1847
Company: Capt. Jedediah M. Grant's
Hundred
Arrived: September 29, 1847
Came: With her parents and family
County Where Settled: Salt Lake; San
Bernardino, California; Salt Lake;
Weber; Utah

This quilt, defined as a whole cloth
for its overall visual appearance, is
actually three 25" panels of early
roller-printed fabric. The repeat of
the printed design is 11¾". This
measurement allows one to determine if a roller plate or flat copper-
plate was used in the printing
process. This size repeat indicates the
fabric was roller printed because the
circumference of most rollers was
twelve inches. The red-and-blue floral images were applied by wood-
blocks in the second stage of
printing.

The original colors would have
been red, blue, and black or purple
printed on a white ground. The
change to pink, buff, and brown is

due to factors of aging, soil, and oxidation.[40] The overall quilting pattern
is the elbow with eleven to twelve
sweeps about ⅜" apart. The backing
is an indigo-blue-dyed fabric. The
binding is an early red resist-dyed
fabric.

According to the accession file,
the quilt was part of Samantha
Crismon's hope chest when she married Dudley Chase in 1857. Both of
her parents' families lived along the
eastern seaboard and, for a time
around 1800, in the Pendleton district of western South Carolina.
They would have had access to imported fabrics through the markets
in such seaports as Charleston, South
Carolina. The fabric is similar in
color and style to examples of
printed Indian cottons exported
through Marseilles, France, to
America.[41]

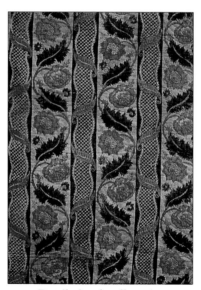
Detail of early roller print

Samantha Crismon Chase was
born the daughter of Charles and
Mary Hill Crismon in Geneva, Kane
County, Illinois, on March 27, 1840.
Her uncle was Thomas Carlin, the
Illinois governor who invited the
Mormons to settle there in 1839.
Her mother had joined the Church.
Samantha's family moved to Han-
cock County before migrating to
Winter Quarters. After arriving in
Salt Lake in 1847, the family went to
the California goldfields in 1849.
This was not unusual for Mormon
men at the time.

Unhappy with the living conditions, the Crismons moved on to
San Bernardino County, California,
to join the growing Mormon colony
there. Samantha married Dudley
Chase on July 19, 1857. Responding
to Brigham Young's call to return to
Utah in anticipation of the arrival of
federal troops known as Johnston's
Army, or the Utah War, the young
couple returned with Dudley's family
members. The Chases settled briefly
in Salt Lake before moving to Harris-
ville in Weber County. There they
built and expanded their log cabin to
a six-room home and raised their
family of ten children. Spending
much of her time caring for her large
family and the hired men, Samantha
also provided medical assistance to
those in need. She died of pneumonia in 1899.[42]

*"Many textiles which today appear to
have been printed in brown originally
may have been black or purple . . .
apparently due to staining or
oxidation."*
Florence Montgomery[43]

Full view of Whole Cloth Quilt

Quilt: STAR TOP (I-12)

Category: Pieced
Size: 70" x 88"
Date: Late (1890–1910)
Maker: Elizabeth Rebecca Ashby
Snow (17 May 1831–12 June
1915)
Migration: Essex County,
Massachusetts, to Utah
Place Joined the Church: Illinois
Year Crossed the Ocean: ————
Ship: ————
Year Crossed the Plains: 1848
Company: Capt. Brigham Young
First Company
Arrived: September 20, 1848
Came: With husband and family
County Where Settled: Salt Lake;
Washington; Mexico; Washington;
Salt Lake

Erastus and Elizabeth Snow family

The eleven whole and four split 22" blocks are basted on a white muslin backing. The raw edges are folded under, ready for stitching. The vivid contrasting red-and-green diamonds create a sparkle of action. The center red stars are accentuated by the paired green arrows. The quiltmaker's family was known to appreciate her design and decorating abilities.

The quilt most likely remains un-finished because the maker (Libby, as she was known) had an important role in her extended family's contributions to settling the Dixie area of southern Utah. In the "Big House" in St. George, they hosted paying guests and important visitors. Gentiles Thomas L. and Elizabeth Kane spent the winter of 1872–73 in the house planning the colonization in Mexico and writing about visits to Mormon homes. Libby was the wife in charge, serving as hostess and managing the affairs of providing beds and substantial meals.

Elizabeth Rebecca Ashby Snow was born the daughter of Nathanial

and Susan Hammond Ashby in Salem, Massachusetts. The relatively wealthy Ashbys had built the first shoe factory in America. "When persecution became too great, Nathanial sold some of the property and sent the money to his friend Erastus [Snow] in Nauvoo and asked him to have a home built for his family as well as the Snow family."[44] The Ashbys migrated to Nauvoo in 1842 where Libby was baptized by the man she would later marry. As her family moved across Iowa toward Winter Quarters, her father died, leaving her mother with eleven children. They spent the winter of 1847–48 in Winter Quar-

Ashby/Snow home in Nauvoo, c. 1845

Snow's "Big House," St. George, Utah

Full view of Star Quilt top

ters, where Elizabeth became the fifth of Erastus Snow's sixteen wives. Their wedding on December 19, 1847, was the largest social event that winter and was attended by Presidents Young and Kimball and other leaders.[45]

Crossing the Plains in 1848, the family had to use cows to pull their two wagons. They carried with them eight hundred pounds each of flour and corn meal, fifty pounds of sugar, some molasses, and honey.

Once in Salt Lake, they spent the winter in the Old Fort as was the pattern of pioneering Saints during the first year or so in a new location.

In October 1849, Erastus was called to go on a mission to Scandinavia, leaving Libby and the other wives to adapt to supporting themselves by doing sewing and other tasks. During the next eight years, he served on mission assignments, keeping in contact through detailed cor-

respondence and visits. He returned permanently to Utah in 1857.

Four years later in 1861, he was called with his cousin George Albert Smith to head the Dixie Mission. In 1884, Erastus Snow went "underground" to Mexico. Libby was one of the wives to accompany him. After his death in 1888, she returned to the home in St. George where she lived a number of years before moving to Salt Lake City's Eighteenth Ward. She died in 1915.[46]

Sugar Creek by C. C. A. Christensen

Quilt: WOOLEN WHOLE CLOTH
(I-13)

Category: Pieced
Size: 93" x 97"
Date: Early (1820–1835)
Maker: Eliza Baker Lathrom (30
   August 1800– ?)
Owner: Zina Diantha Huntington
   Jacobs Smith Young (31 January
   1821–27 August 1901)
Migration: Jefferson County, New
   York, to Utah
Place Joined the Church: New York
Year Crossed the Ocean: ———
Ship: ———
Year Crossed the Plains: 1848
Company: Capt. Brigham Young
   First Company
Arrived: September 21, 1848
Came: With husband and his
   extended family of wives and
   children
County Where Settled: Salt Lake

This quilt illustrates some of this
study's unusual findings. Containing
features not usually found in the West,
it represents the time and place from
which a woman began her migration.

It is a whole cloth composed of

Detail of backing

three separate pieces of homespun,
home-dyed, and handwoven fabric
made by the New Hampshire quiltmaker.

The overall quilting patterns of
sweeping feather plumes, leaves, and
flowers are balanced symmetrically on
the quilt's surface. The large plumes
are 25" from end to end while the
center circular design is 13½" wide.
The ground or background is filled
with parallel lines and gridwork. There
are six stitches per inch.

Surprisingly, no initials, name,
or date are quilted on the surface.
Often a quilted masterpiece like this
contains such a reference.

According to the quilt's documentation, it was made by Eliza Baker
Lathrom for her sister Zina Baker
Huntington, mother of Zina Diantha
Huntington Jacobs Smith Young, a
plural wife of Brigham Young. The
Ancestral File and the New Hampshire Census of 1820 and 1830 list
only an Elizabeth Baker Durkee born
August 30, 1800, in Sullivan County
as Zina's sister and wife of Bela Durkee. No additional biographical material could be located about the maker.
After Zina Baker Huntington's death
in Nauvoo in 1839, the quilt was
brought west by her daughter.

Zina D. H. Young was born the
daughter of William and Zina Baker
Huntington in Jefferson County, New
York. Her parents were descendants of

early prominent New England colo-
nial families from Great Britain. Following the pattern of other New
Englanders, they moved from Sullivan
County, New Hampshire, to Water-
town, New York, near the eastern
shore of Lake Ontario. Having joined
the Church there in 1835, the family
then moved west to Kirtland, Ohio.
As they continued west, her father
served a major role in the emergency
migration from Caldwell County, Missouri, to Nauvoo, where her mother
died of fatigue and privation on July
8, 1839.[47]

Zina D. married Henry Jacobs and
had two sons before they separated.
She then accepted the principle of

*Zina D. H. Young and daughter
Zina Young Card*

Full view of Woolen Whole Cloth Quilt

plural marriage and married Joseph Smith as one of his thirty-one wives. After his martyrdom June 27, 1844, she married Brigham Young on February 2, 1846. This was just seven days prior to the Saints' being forced to leave Nauvoo on February 9. She and her sons crossed the frozen Mississippi River and Sugar Creek to join her father and family in Mt. Pisgah, a site about 172 miles west of Nauvoo in Iowa. A year later in March 1847, she and her sons continued on to Winter Quarters where she rejoined Young's family in the company of Charles C. Rich and his five wives. In May 1848, she started crossing the Plains, actively participating in all trail activities, including driving the teams.

Zina's contributions to the development of the Church and its society were significant. The formal education and the foundation of religious beliefs provided by her parents prepared her well for the personal challenges and leadership roles she undertook. As a plural wife, she was freed from domestic responsibilities and therefore could take on greater involvement in the political and economic development of their community.[48] In 1870, Brigham Young assigned her the mission of establishing the silk culture to produce the desired silk cloth within the territory. She successfully sought to overcome her personal dislike of the silkworms, learn sericulture, and teach other

women how to raise the worms. In 1875, she became the head of the Deseret Silk Association, which was organized to dispense information on sericulture, from nurturing the worms to weaving the cloth. Under her leadership, the Relief Society sponsored silk projects in nearly 150 communities.

Active in the Relief Society, Zina served as first counselor to President Eliza Rozey Snow, and as the third general president. This position she held from 1888 until her death in 1901. As a result of her national perspective and leadership abilities, the society became incorporated and affiliated with the National Council of Women.[49]

Quilt: STENCILED QUILTS
(I-14 and I-14a)

Category: Pieced
Size: 54" x 84"
Date: Early (1830–1840)
Maker: Elizabeth Terry Kirby
    Heward (17 November 1814–
    9 March 1878)
Migration: Wayne County, New
    York, to Utah
Place Joined the Church: Ontario,
    Canada
Year Crossed the Ocean: ————
Ship: ————
Year Crossed the Plains: 1848
Company: Brigham Young First
    Division[50]
Arrived: September 25, 1848
Came: With her second husband,
    brother, niece, and baby
County Where Settled: Salt Lake

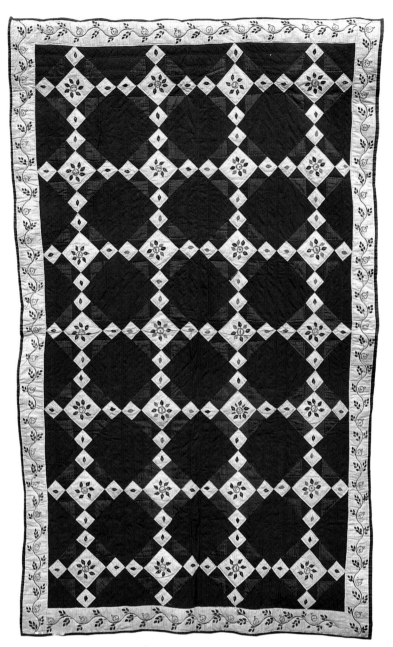

Full view of Stenciled Quilt

These two stenciled quilts have a place of origin similar to others that are known to exist in America. Stenciling was done extensively in the first decades of the 1800s in New England. Walls and floors, in addition to textiles, were decorated with patterns of birds, flowers, and cornucopias.[51] During this time textiles were not yet being produced in America. The presence of individual stencils, as opposed to a complete design unit, in each block illustrates this production process. The quiltmaker's design flexibility is evident by the varying numbers of leaves around each flower in the white 4" center pieces.

The 8" blocks are set on point, creating a secondary lattice pattern in the chain of small white squares. The contrasting rich, dark-brown dye is made from black walnut or butternut bark or from nut husks. This dye stuff helps to date the quilt to pre-Utah days because these nut-producing trees do not naturally grow in the

Utah area.[52] Another possible dye source for brown would be the mineral manganese, which was available.[53]

The quilt shows the practical quiltmaker's frugality. Three colors of thread—brown, green, and white—are used but in no particular pattern. Although it is often possible to have

thread take on the color of the fabric through which it is stitched, that is not the case here. Instead, it appears the quiltmaker simply used the thread on her needle until it was consumed. There are several places on the quilt where she has left a line unfinished after quilting only a part of it.

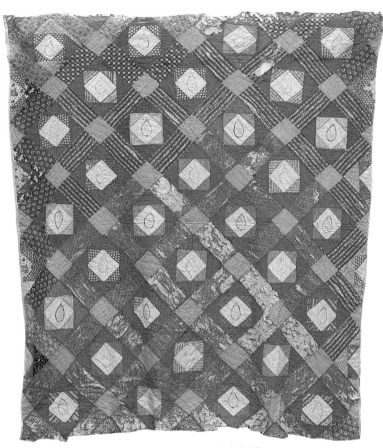

Second quilt: Stenciled Quilt

fort in 1848, they made their first home in a tent of willows until the cold temperatures became intolerable. This pioneer resourcefulness served the family well for years. Elizabeth made a dress from a wagon cover for her daughter Sarah. Using the cotton cloth wrapper from the rolls of woolen fabric produced at the mill, she painted a red bud and two green leaves in an all-over pattern. A cousin then made the fabric into a beautiful dress.[54]

Early on, Elizabeth saw the need for proper education for children and approached Brigham Young with the idea of starting a school. Seating the children on low, hand-hewn log benches in her home, she taught personal health habits and morals, especially respect for their elders. She called these sessions "children's meetings" and once a month would encourage them to share their testimonies. She filed a report of her school activities at each Church conference. She continued to teach as her family moved about the territory.

The Hewards' last home was in Draper. Elizabeth died in 1878.[55]

The second quilt shows a more simplified design of a single leaf motif in the center square of the 9" blocks. This pattern is a variation of the square within a square. The use of perhaps early Turkey-red prints and a simplified green print with yellow dots suggests the fabrics were imported to southern Canada where Elizabeth lived.

Elizabeth Terry Kirby Heward was born in Palmyra, New York, to cousins Parshall and Hannah Terry and moved with her family to Ontario, Canada. Her life journey is well documented in her own reminiscence, taken from her diary. The bulk of the diary unfortunately ends about 1860, and the reminiscence was written around 1875. The richness of the document reveals the strength, determination, and commitment of this early Mormon pioneer woman to face the contests, conflicts, and confrontations in her daily life. She overcame an unfortunate marriage in Canada and the death of her first baby in the cold of Nauvoo. She adapted to her life as a mother, teacher, and wife in the earliest days of the Mormon settlement in Utah.

Her struggle to survive during the Nauvoo years of 1844–46 is included in Carol Madsen's *In Their Own Words: Women and the Story of Nauvoo*. Here in 1844, she married John Heward, an Englishman who had worked as a hired man for her first husband in Canada and knew the difficulty of her earlier marriage.

Arriving at the Salt Lake Valley

Elizabeth Terry Kirby Heward

Quilt: ALBUM BLOCK (I-15)

Category: Pieced
Size: 81⅕" x 90"
Date: Early (1835–1845)
Maker: Matilda Caroline Fuller
   McArthur (1 May 1820–7 January
   1914)
Migration: Saratoga County, New
   York, to Utah
Place Joined the Church: New York
Year Crossed the Ocean: ———
Ship: ———
Year Crossed the Plains: 1848
Company: Capt. Brigham Young's
   First Company
Arrived: September 21, 1848
Came: With her husband and
   stepson
County Where Settled: Salt Lake;
   Utah; Washington

The quilt's three colors and pieced
sashings connecting the blocks give
it a sense of liveliness. There is a
great deal of movement and tension
with the diagonal lines and the 9½"
blocks set on point. The colors,
the fabrics, and the absence of
white were all common among
mid-nineteenth-century quilts made
in the Mid-Atlantic states. Here
women had access to the rich
fabric resources imported and produced along the East Coast in the
second quarter of the nineteenth
century. According to family history, the quilt was brought across
the Plains.

This quilt provides an opportunity
to clarify the pattern's name. Often,
the name Album Block is chosen for
a quilt that has names written on a
single centered strip of light fabric.
However, when there is not a single
strip of cloth, no indication of
names, and instead, clear evidence
of a cross in the yellow fabric pieces,
the more appropriate pattern name is
Christian Cross, a popular early pat-

Matilda Caroline Fuller McArthur

tern name in Ohio and New England.[56] For comparison, notice the
block construction in the Butler
Album Quilt (Quilt IV-4).

Matilda Caroline Fuller McArthur
was the third of ten children born to
Edward Meeks and Hannah Elizabeth Eldridge Fuller in Providence,
Saratoga County, New York. Her
family moved west to Nauvoo where
she married Church leader Daniel
Duncan McArthur after the death
of his first wife.

Her extended family's experience
in crossing the Plains through Win-

ter Quarters is one of this study's
best documented. Matilda Caroline's
parents, brothers Thomas Eldridge
and Mix, and sister Hannah all died
and were buried there in 1847.
Many people died from chills and
fever during that particular summer.
Her sister Sarah Ann Fuller married
Samuel Gully in the winter of 1847;
she gave birth to and buried a son,
Edward Meeks Gully, in the spring
of 1848. Matilda Caroline was with
them after having spent the winter
of 1846 at Punea, about 150 miles
south on the Missouri River where
her husband and others went to obtain work.

After leaving Winter Quarters
in the summer of 1848, Matilda
Caroline gave birth to her first child.

*"On the 18th day of August my Wife
Bore me a Son, weight eight pounds
and three quaters, we were then fifteen
Miles west of the Devills Gate on the
Sweet Water, We cauld his name
Daniel D. McArthur Junior. on the
19th we resumed our journey and
Caroline done first rate Bro Heber C
Kimball Daughter hade a Daughter
the same night we continued our
journey all doing firstrate and the
Camp landed in the Salt Lake Valley
on the 26th of September 1848."*
       Daniel D. McArthur[58]

*"On the 14th Day of December 1845
I married me a nother Wife by the
name of Matilda Caroline Fuller who
was Born in the town of Providence
Saratoga Co State of New York on the
first day of May 1820 Daughter of
Edwin M. and Hanna Fuller we were
maried by the Patriarch John Smith
uncle to the Prophet Joseph Smith
Father Fuller maid a good Supper for
the invited on the occation we hads a
fine Dance after the Supper was over
all felt well."*
       Daniel D. McArthur[57]

*Daniel D. McArthur
home in St. George*

Full view of Album Quilt

Three additional children were born in Salt Lake. A fifth child, Edward Meeks, was born in Pleasant Grove in 1860, and the sixth, Mahala, was born in St. George in 1862. Five of the six children died before age ten, with two dying in August 1860 and two in February 1863. Daniel, her first born, died before his tenth birthday in August 1858.

Matilda Caroline Fuller McArthur maintained her home and family while her husband guided other Saints' migrations. He served a mission to Scotland from 1852 until 1856, when he returned and led one of the first handcart companies from Iowa City, Iowa.

The McArthur family settled in St. George where Matilda, as the first wife, was the leader in her home and community. In 1875, she established and took responsibility for much of the operation of the Ladies Co-op. By organizing the group more efficiently, she helped them to save costs.

"There was perfect harmony among the (three) wives and children, but they seldom mentioned the wife Caroline Fuller, but always spoke of Mary Frances and Elizabeth Bullock. Wilford says some people thought it would be awful to be raised in a polygamist home, but he thought it was wonderful, because he had two mothers instead of one. All children were equally obedient to either mother who asked them to do anything. They never dared to disobey."

Lola H. McArthur, a granddaughter[59]

Quilt: FOUR PATCH (I-16)

Category: Pieced
Size: 73" x 83"
Date: Late (1926)
Maker: Matilda Ann Duncan
  (Stoddard) Winters (25 April
  1836–19 June 1932)
Migration: St. Clair County, Illinois,
  to Utah
Place Joined the Church: Illinois
Year Crossed the Ocean: ————
Ship: ————
Year Crossed the Plains: 1848
Company: Heber C. Kimball's
  Company
Arrived: September 24, 1848
Came: With her parents and family
County Where Settled: Salt Lake;
  Davis; Rich County, Nevada;
  Oregon; Davis

Mormon Panorama Thirteen/Joseph Mustering the Nauvoo Legion
by C. C. A. Christensen

This quilt was made late in the maker's life. Its high degree of precision indicates a knowledge of quilt-making and a desire to maintain the maker's level of skill. The diagonal arrangement of the 8" blocks adds visual interest for the viewer. The eye is carried across the surface from left to right by the placement of the dark fabrics and the repeat of matching light prints and plaids. Then, at places along the right edge, the viewer's eye is halted and turned back by the block's rotation so that the dark fabrics turn back into the quilt. The blocks are hand-pieced and set together with machine-stitched sashing.

The blue sashing strips are 5¼" wide. This width provides enough space for the double-wedding-ring quilting pattern to nicely fill the space and hold the batt in place. Intersecting diagonal lines are quilted individually through each square of the block. The backing is a period print of the 1920s. The quilting thread is light blue.

Matilda Ann Duncan (Stoddard) Winters was born the daughter of James and Hulda Jones Duncan in Belleville, Illinois. Her family moved to Hancock County, about six miles from Nauvoo. Her father was a personal friend of Joseph Smith and provided him with the horse known

Quilt front and back

in Church history as the "Joe Duncan Horse," which Smith used when he commanded the Nauvoo Legion.

The Duncan family moved to Winter Quarters in 1846. They crossed the Plains in 1848 when Matilda was twelve years old. Her father was assigned the responsibility of hunting for fresh meat during their journey, so Matilda was the one who drove the family wagon's two yoke of oxen. She drove from the Sweetwater River to Salt Lake without a mishap.

In 1858, she married Charles Henry Stoddard as his second wife and they became the parents of three children. After the marriage ended in divorce, Matilda taught school at Randolph before marrying William Winters in 1876. They settled first in Nevada and then Oregon where he drowned in the Snake River in 1892.

Moving back to Bountiful after his death, Matilda became very active in the Latter-day Saints and civic work. She was celebrated as being the oldest resident in Davis County when she died in 1932 at the age of ninety-six.[60]

Full view of Four Patch Quilt

"*Her House was always one of order. Cleanliness was her hoby [hobby]. She was methodical in every thing she did. An example of this is seen in the blocks of this quilt, each block cut almost to a thread, each corner when sewed meeting almost to pin point. These blocks were put together when she was ninety years of age, all sewing done by hand.*"

Matilda Burningham, her granddaughter[61]

Detail of early fabrics

Quilt: NOONDAY or SUNBURST (I-17)

Category: Pieced
Size: 68" x 89"
Date: Early (1835–1845)
Maker: Susan Crosby Harris (15 July 1815–29 May 1897)
Owner: Nancy Crosby Bankhead (1825–1916)
Migration: Monroe County, Mississippi, to Utah
Place Joined the Church: Tennessee
Year Crossed the Ocean: ————
Ship: ————
Year Crossed the Plains: 1848
Company: Heber C. Kimball's Company
Arrived: September 23, 1848
Came: With husband, family, and slaves
County Where Settled: Salt Lake; Box Elder; Cache

This quilt validates the life story of the maker and her family. The high-quality fabrics, the mathematically complicated pattern, and the labor-intensive effort required to create it all indicate a level of wealth and success for this Southern family.

The old popular pattern names reflect the importance of daylight and sunshine in Southern plantation agricultural production. The extended family owned slaves, bringing some of them with them to Utah.

The forty pieces of diamonds and triangles in each of the 12" sun blocks separated by narrow sashing strips, and the four borders of varying widths, offered a challenge to this quiltmaker. She made it as an unmarried woman probably living at home with flexible time in her schedule of responsibilities.

The center circle and ten of the diamonds in eighteen blocks are made from an early imported print of purple, now turned brown by oxidation. The red print and two indigo-blue-and-white pieces are examples of fabrics made from improved dyes that began to be more readily available in the mid-nineteenth century. The red print fabric may have been an imported textile available to the quilter through southern seaports such as New Orleans. The strength and intensity of the blue is a clear illustration of why the indigo plant became so popular as a dyestuff. It was the first real colorfast dye that was available.

The overall quilting pattern is a latticework of four parallel lines creating a grid of diamonds. Within each diamond, there are as many as twenty-one stitched lines—a further example of the quiltmaker's attention to detail and precision.

The quilt was donated by the maker's grandniece. The maker did not have children of her own. The quilt probably came west with the family of the donor's grandmother, Nancy Crosby Bankhead, who was the maker's sister for whom the quilt was made.

The quiltmaker, Susan Crosby Harris, was born the fifth child of John and Elizabeth Glenn Coleman Crosby in Monroe County, Mississippi. Her sister Nancy was ten years younger. Their parents had migrated south from Indiana a couple of years before her birth. The father died on August 19, 1840, leaving a widow with adult children, most of whom were married except for Susan. It was not until October 25, 1860 that she, at the age of 45, married Wyley Harris. She was baptized into the Church in September 1890.[62]

Susan and Nancy's older brother William organized the Mississippi Saints, a party of forty-three Mormons from Monroe County, Mississippi, long celebrated for their eagerness to gather with Brigham Young. This small group started west on April 8, 1846, wintering over with members of the Mormon Battalion in Colorado. The records are clear that neither Susan Crosby Harris nor Nancy Coleman Crosby Bankhead was part of the party. At the time, Nancy Crosby Bankhead and her family were living in Tennessee, where they joined the Church and then decided to migrate to Utah in 1848.

On the journey, when Nancy thought she was dying, company leader Heber C. Kimball offered her a ride in one of his carriages. Her husband assisted by providing a pair of his best mules, a black man to

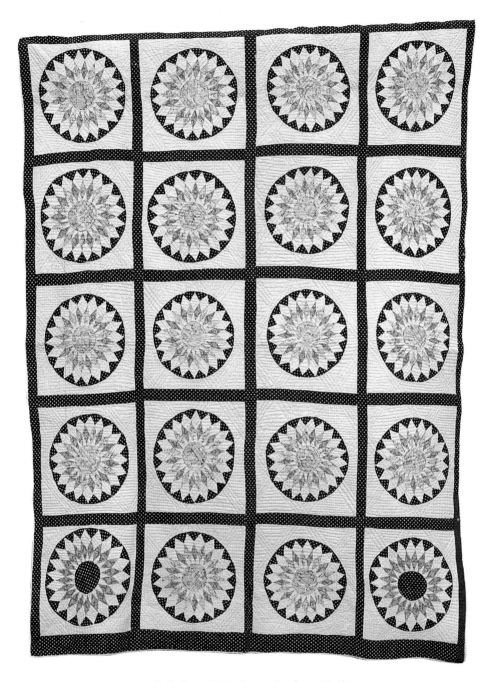

Full view of Noonday or Starburst Quilt

drive the carriage, and a woman to attend her. The man was one of their slaves who was taken west with the family. In Utah they were freed and lived in small houses built by John Bankhead. The slaves began to use the name Bankhead.[63]

Freeing the slaves caused a significant change in Nancy's lifestyle. She adjusted to the additional workload and joined with other women in their cooperative work and in sharing their provisions. The family lived in Maughn's Fort in the Cache Valley before settling the Wellsville area.

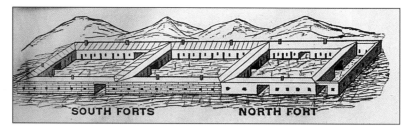

Fort, Great Salt Lake City, 1848

Quilt: STAR WITH NINE PATCH
(I-18)

Category: Pieced
Size: 69¼" x 74½"
Date: Mid (1875–1885)
Maker: Hannah Johnson Huffman
Wheaton Staley (31 July 1806–27
October 1888)
Migration: Albany County, New
York, to Utah
Place Joined the Church: Canada
Year Crossed the Ocean: ————
Ship: ————
Year Crossed the Plains: 1848
Company: Heber C. Kimball's
Company
Arrived: September 23, 1848
Came: Unavailable
County Where Settled: Salt Lake;
Summit

This intricately designed quilt is
the masterpiece of a woman known
to be a perfectionist, expert seam-
stress, and meticulous housekeeper.
The mathematics are complicated
for figuring the necessary template
sizes. The piecework is technically
advanced.

The 5¼" center Nine Patch is incorporated in a larger Nine Patch of
squares and triangles, creating a finished block size of 16½". Each block
is expanded by a border of pieced 1½"
triangles. All the blocks are pieced ex-
actly the same except for the center
one. Here the green and pink triangles are cut and placed in a different
arrangement. This gives an element of
surprise in the quilt's central focal
point. The skilled quiltmaker most
likely placed it there intentionally.

The blocks are sashed horizontally
and vertically with various sizes of
strips. Three borders of various sizes
surround the quilt. The binding is a
red-and-white print attached from
the front to the back.

The quilting is the elbow pattern
with nine sweeps ½" apart. Note in
the detail of the center block the
point where the quilting lines inter-
sect from each side.

The backing is from fabric for her
last dress, a gift from her son John.

Hannah Johnson Huffman
Wheaton Staley was born the daughter of Abraham and Hannah Wheeler
Johnson in their Albany, New York,
home along the Erie Canal. Her life
followed the traditional pattern for
young girls born and raised in the
early nineteenth century. She was
trained at home to be a wife,
mother, and provider for her home
and family. While living in Canada
and the eastern United States, she
had five children and was widowed
several times. She then married Con-
rad Staley, a widower with three children. They had two additional
children, giving them a family of ten.

According to her history, she
worked long hours to supply her
family's needs. She was proud of saying that the sun never found her in
bed. To stay in good health, her rit-
ual was to never let her bare feet
touch the floor.

She died at age eighty-two after
falling and breaking her hip.[64]

*"In that day there was little could be
bought from the stores, so the housewife
made nearly everything she used, and
almost all clothing. They wove their
sheets, made quilts, cleaned feathers
for pillows, made candles, soap and
most utility items."*
*Sarah Ann Huffman Pitkin,
her daughter*[65]

Detail of center quilt block

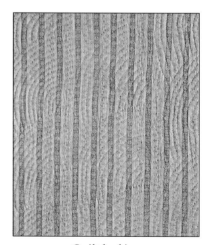

Quilt backing

Full view of Star with Nine Patch Quilt

Quilt: TRIPLE IRISH CHAIN
   (I-19)

Category: Pieced
Size: 69" x 82"
Date: Late (1890–1895)
Maker: Ellen Fielding Burton
   (9 February 1841–8 March 1906)
Migration: Lancashire, England,
   to Utah
Place Joined the Church: England
Year Crossed the Ocean: 1841
Ship: Tyrian
Year Crossed the Plains: 1848
Company: Heber C. Kimball's
   Company
Arrived: September 24, 1848
Came: With parents and family
County Where Settled: Salt Lake;
   Weber; Lincoln County,
   Wyoming; Weber

William Walton Burton family

The machine-pieced 1⅜" pieces of red and white are set in 13½" blocks. The diagonal hand-quilted lines reinforce the sense of movement created by the piecing pattern. They are placed 2¼" apart and have five stitches per inch. In the white solid blocks, an original floral design, perhaps a coxcomb, is repeated four times. This is one of the few pieced quilts in this survey to contain a floral pattern. It reflects Ellen Burton's creative ability to seek a design from her outdoor environment to beautify her indoor living space. This quiltmaker's ability to draw on her knowledge both of pieced quilt patterns and of representational designs for her quilting further shows her skill.

Ellen Fielding Burton was born in Preston, Lancashire, England, the second daughter of seven children born to Joseph and Hannah Greenwood Fielding. Her father had joined the Church in Canada and was one of the first seven missionaries sent to Liverpool, England, in 1837. The Fielding family of four sailed from England in 1841 with her father in charge of a company of more than two hundred Church members. They arrived in Nauvoo in November 1841.

Ellen's reminiscences of the 1848 wagon train experience as a seven-year-old included walking barefoot and tending her little brothers in the wagon as the adults drove the cattle.

Growing up in the Salt Lake Valley, Ellen married William Walton Burton on November 2, 1862. He also married two of her sisters: Rachel on March 28, 1856, and Sarah Ann on May 23, 1870. The three sisters were the only children of their family to grow to adulthood. William also married a fourth wife, Eliza Hooper. The families were settled in Weber County, Utah, and Lincoln County, Wyoming.

While living in Afton, Wyoming, in 1886, Ellen helped to manage the Burton store. They conducted business first from a covered wagon, then a tent, and later, one end of their log home.[66]

Back in Ogden in 1896, she was noted as hosting some of the Young Ladies Mutual Improvement Association (YLMIA) members in her home. Ellen's daughter Mercy R. Stevens taught them how to reel silk from cocoons. The course was a daily class taught for two weeks using a reeling machine purchased by the Weber Stake Board of the YLMIA. The machine is now part of the collection of the Daughters of Utah Pioneers.[67]

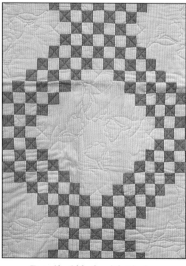

*Detail of block with piecing
and quilting designs*

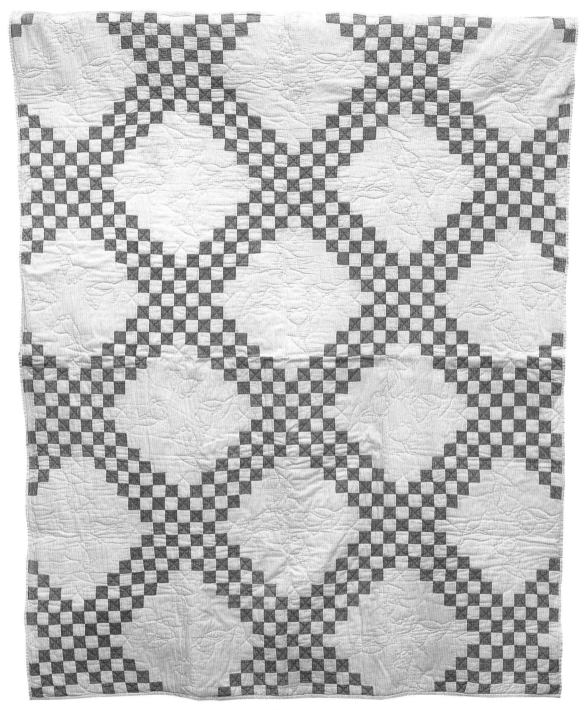

Full view of Triple Irish Chain Quilt

Quilt: ROCKY MOUNTAIN
variation (I-20)

Category: Pieced
Size: 79½" x 79½"
Date: Early (1840–1846)
Maker: Mormon Mothers
Migration: Unknown
Place Joined the Church: Unknown
Year Crossed the Ocean: ————
Ship: ————
Year Crossed the Plains: ————
Company: ————
Arrived: ————
Recorded: ————
Came: ————
County Where Settled: ————

This fragile pieced and stuffed-work quilt has served its owners well and is a significant document in a study of the quilts of the Mormon migration. If only the threads could talk! Its history remains a mystery but it is deserving of being included.

The documentation on the fairly recent acquisition from Eva P. Stevens reads "Made by Mormon mothers enroute from Zion, Illinois to Springfield, MO." The name "Green B. Franklin" is divided between two blocks. It was supposedly quilted in Winter Quarters.[68]

The quilt does reference times and places consistent with the Saints' ac-tivity in the area. "Zion, Illinois" would refer to Nauvoo. But the reference to "Springfield" most likely means the state capitol of Illinois, not the town in Missouri. Between 1839 and 1845, there was much travel and communication between the two locations as Mormons worked to develop and protect their Zion. The Mormon women were keenly aware of and actively involved in the situation. For example, during their first summer of Relief Society work in 1842, President Emma Smith, accompanied by Eliza R. Snow and Amanda Barnes Smith (Quilt II-5), traveled to Quincy to present their signed petition to Governor Carlin requesting protection from illegal suits against the Prophet Joseph Smith.[69] These women could have worked on the quilt during this journey.

The documentation saying that this quilt was quilted in Winter Quarters is most likely true, though difficult to validate. This was a winter characterized by isolation, illness, and inactivity. Women gathered together for support and assistance. Sometimes they lived together in their windowless cabins. Sewing was a mainstay of their social lives, yet because they had very few materials, it was not a time of major textile and clothing production. Quilting was a popular social activity among these women, especially during the inactivity of the long cold winters.

No viable leads to a Green B. Franklin were found in any of the many Church history resources.[70]

The generic, or more common, name for this quilt pattern is New York Beauty. Another name variation, Sunrise in the Pines, appears later in this study's quilts (III-1b and III-2).

The blocks are the four white 22" center squares with the stuffed work. When assembled with the 6¾" pieced green sashing strips, they create a circular image of the red pieced seg-ments. The red block at the intersections of the sashings is 6¾". In order to complete the pieced design and to create the desired width, the quilt-makers have added rectangles and squares.

The stuffed-work pattern of flowers in a basket rests upon a ground of quilted parallel lines. The floral design would have been outlined in quilting stitches and then stuffed from the back with pieces of cording and bits of cotton. Fifteen parallel lines are quilted in the sashing strips and across the red squares. A series of double lines are quilted in the pieced red corner sections.

"Saturday 27th the weather warm made a little apron for Clara Sunday 28th a pleasant day took a walk with Rebecca [Rebecca Burton Jones] RM & EA to the river about ½ mile. We talked much about Samuel and Nathanial and wished often that they were with us. after we returned home Reb and Myself went and sat down in the wagon were [where] we had a long talk and enjoyed ourselfs much, talking about our dear companions, who now were far from us, and sympathizing with each other &C [cried] &C [cried]."
Mary Haskin Parker Richards[71]

Detail of quilt: Green B.

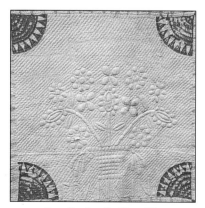

Detail of quilt: Franklin

Full view of Rocky Mountain Variation Quilt

PART TWO

1849–1855 GATHERING IN ZION

"Sun. 17th [May 1846] The meeting held at Taylor's camp which has not mov'd—Yesterday I enjoy'd the novel scenery of a quilting out-of-doors, after which with much conviviality and agreeable sociability the party took tea with sister Dalton, the mistress of the quilting. present Sis. Markham, Yearley, Gleason, Harriet, and Catherine. Our treat was serv'd in the tent, around a table of bark, spread on bars, supported by four crotches drove into the ground; and consisted of light biscuits and butter, dutch cheese, peach sauce, custard & tea." —Eliza R. Snow[1]

detail from Pioneers Crossing the Plains of Nebraska *by C. C. A. Christensen*

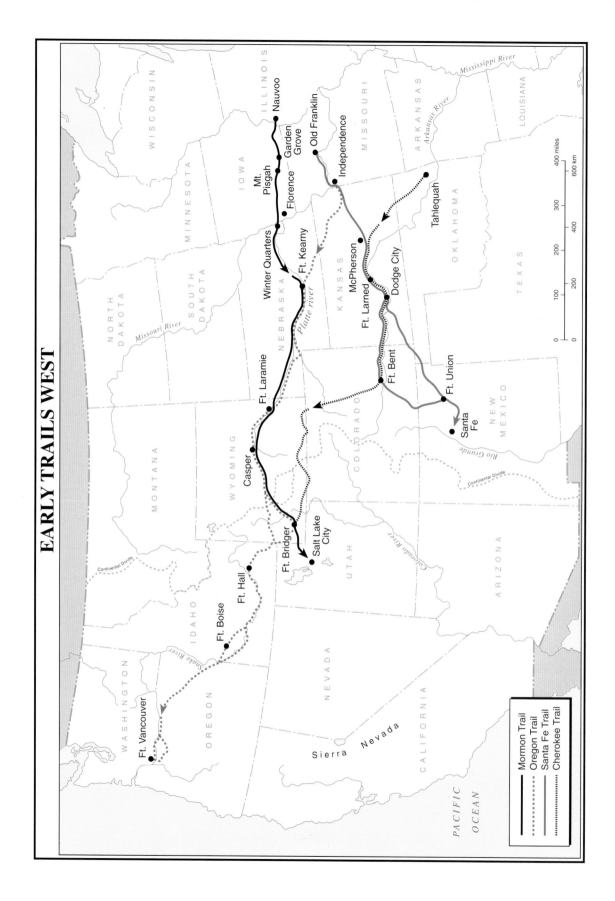

EARLY TRAILS WEST

Mormon Trail
Oregon Trail
Santa Fe Trail
Cherokee Trail

1849–1855 GATHERING IN ZION

THE MIGRATION

AT THIS TIME, THE MORMONS GENERALLY DID not want to go westward but were driven beyond the current settlement frontier by hostile neighbors. In planning and executing an extensive migration, they were as concerned with developing the trail to make the journey easier, more predictable, and more economical for the succeeding waves of migrants, as they were with getting themselves settled.[2] The years from 1849 to 1855 were those of "gathering in Zion," not only for the original Saints but for many new European converts as well.

Brigham Young's 1847 letter to the other migrating company leaders on the Plains that summer, shown on the next page, foreshadows the plans for the future. Its stated intent to return to Winter Quarters before late fall indicates that they planned to use the trail for going back and forth. It asks for a list of the available resources so that they can begin organizing the most

Pioneer Camp *by Frederic Piercy*

"We camped in Council Bluffs, Iowa, for one month waiting for companies to be made up. Oh the monotony of camp life when not traveling! How delighted we all were when we started on our journey for good. Everything was bright and beautiful. I was young and healthy. All was 'color de rose' for me. The responsibilities, anxieties, and cares rested on my parents."
Margaret Gay Clawson,
sister of Phebe Judd Kimball
(Quilt II-3)[3]

Pioneer Camp, Valley of the Great Salt Lake
August 2, 1847

To General Charles C. Rich and
Presidents and Officers of Emigrating Company.

Beloved brethren:

We have delegated our beloved brother Ezra T. Benson and escort to communicate to you by Express, the cheering intelligence that we have arrived in the most beautiful valley of Great Salt Lake, that every soul who left Winter Quarters with us is alive, and almost everyone enjoying good health. That portion of the Battalion that was at Pueblo is here with us, together with the Mississippi company that accompanied them, and they are generally well. We number about 450 souls, and we know of no one, but what is pleased with our situation. We have commenced the survey of a city this morning. We feel that the time is fast approaching when those teams that are going to Winter Quarters this fall should be on the way. Every individual here would be glad to tarry, if their friends were here—but as many of the Battalion, as well as Pioneers, have not their families here, and do not expect that they are in your camp, we wish to learn by Express from you the situation of your camp as speedily as possible. That we may be prepared to council and act in the whole matter, we want you to send us the name of every individual in your camp, or in other words a copy of your camp roll, including the names, number of wagons, horses, mules, oxen, cows, etc., the health of your camp, your location, prospects, etc., if your teams are worn out, if your camp is sick and not able to take care of themselves, if you are short of teamsters, or any other circumstance impedes your progress, we want to know it immediately, for we have help for you, and if your teams are in good plight and will be able to return to Winter Quarters this season, or any portion of them, we want to know it.

We also want the mail, which will include all letters and papers and packages belonging to our camp, general and particular. Would circumstances permit, we would gladly meet you some distance from this, but our time is much occupied, notwithstanding we think you will see us before you see our valley. Let all the brethren and sisters cheer up their hearts, and know assuredly that God has heard and answered their prayers and ours, and led us to a goodly land, and our souls are satisfied therewith. Brother Benson can give you many particulars that will be gratifying and cheering to you which we have not time to write. And we feel to bless the Saints.

In behalf of the Council

Willard Richards, Clerk   *Brigham Young, President*

Source: *Carter, Mormon Emigration, 1840–1869*, pages 255–256.

practical, cost effective, and safe manner to continue the movement of their community.

The eagerness to return to Winter Quarters demonstrates that the Mormons took a different approach to the overland trail than did other populations migrating westward.

For most groups, who traveled first along the south side of the Platte River, it was a one-way "trail" on their journey of "going to see the Elephant" in hopes of economic prosperity in gold or land. For the Mormons, it was a two-way "road." Many traveled back along the river's north side, including missionaries leaving for new destinations; "go backs," or disenchanted Mormons; and Church wagon trains hauling freight to the Missouri River and returning with new immigrants, those coming from Europe.[4]

THE SETTLEMENT

When migrants arrived, Brigham Young would take one of several approaches. He might assign canyons in the area that had water resources available to Church leaders, who would then oversee their settlement. Or individuals were allowed to select the place they wished to locate and then request Young's permission to settle there. Or families would participate in drawing for available lots in the hope of fairness to all.

As more people gathered, Brigham Young started sending out pioneers to define and protect the territory they claimed for the State of Deseret. Church leaders defined the boundaries according to their perceived needs for future population growth; for access to water, both for agriculture and industry and for a port to ocean transportation; and for protection of their religious culture.

Ever aware of what was happening on the federal level and eager to be a part of it, they set the boundaries with attention to both the physical features of the geography of the Great Basin and the political decisions being made between major governments. The area stretched from the Wind River Mountains and the Continental Divide on the east to the northern border of Mexico along the Gila River and extending westward to the Pacific Ocean. The boundary then continued north to the Sierra Nevada Mountains on the west and then across the high plateau area dividing the waters flowing to the Columbia River or to the Great Basin, back to the Wind River Mountains.

The Church leaders chose these boundaries partly as a result of the Treaty of Guadalupe Hidalgo in February 1848. This Treaty transferred the land of the Southwest to the United States. This was familiar land to the Mormons from

"From that time he often called at our wagon, that is, our wagon yard. So when any of the young folks called, I was as much at home sitting on an ox yoke as if I were sitting in an easy chair in a parlor. Such is life on the plains."
Margaret Gay Judd Clawson, sister of Phebe Judd Kimball (Quilt II-3)[5]

"I can tell you one thing and that is where you have put up one fine building for the last 6 years we have put more than you can count on the plains for we can build as fine a house in Utah as you can in New York."
Susan Mandeville Fairbanks (Quilt I-8), 1854 letter to her sister[6]

Fort Supply, Wyoming

their participation in the recent Mormon Battalion march. The land to the east was familiar from their migrations, and the land to the north and west from those who traveled overland to California and the Northwest. Men knew which natural resources were available: water and soil for farming; timber, rock, and mineral deposits for future buildings; and animals for food and clothing.

In the early 1850s, the Church established a variety of settlements, classified as "outer" or "inner" based on their physical proximity to Salt Lake City. Often, those selected as leaders would turn to friends and family for people to assist them in the settlements. The "outer" settlements were located at Mormon Station in the Carson Valley of the Sierra Nevadas along the California Trail; Fort Limhi on the Salmon River near the Oregon Trail; Fort Supply along the Overland Trail; and San Diego and San Bernardino on the Old Spanish Trail to the Pacific Ocean. These could serve as outposts for protecting the Saints and alerting them to possible invasion or approaching difficulties; as "safe" havens for polygamist families; and as a means of enhancing the Saints' transportation system along the trails and for access to ocean traffic.

The "inner" settlements were along the Wasatch Front on the mountains' western side. These were to be mainly agricultural and would provide the necessary food and raw materials. The early settlements north of Salt Lake included Bountiful, Ogden, and Brigham City. The early settlements south of Salt Lake included Provo, Tooele, and Manti for agriculture, and Parowan and Cedar City for iron ore. Since population growth was moving south toward a milder climate and longer growing season, plans were made to build the territorial statehouse at a site to be

Early Salt Lake City

named Fillmore in the county of Millard. Both were named in honor of Millard Fillmore, the President who officially created the Utah Territory on September 9, 1850.[7] (See map on page 150.)

THE WOMEN

In addition to the wives whose husbands had responsibilities in assisting others, a number of women migrating at this time were young and single. Most were members of families who had started the journey but had become separated because of illness, death, or lack of funds. The young women then were often forced to continue their journey by making their own arrangements, with varying conditions and results. Their experiences reinforced the need to develop a two-stage migration plan with layover support in St. Louis.

Although they lacked the unifying experience shared by the settlers of the early years, this next group reveals an eagerness to follow the plans and practices of Church leaders as they journeyed west and adjusted to eking out their living and practicing their chosen faith.

THE QUILTS

The quilts in this second group continue to represent each woman's individual experience. Although several were brought as treasured family heirlooms by women whose husbands' assignments had detained them in the Midwest, for the most part they were made by women who sought to make the best of the circumstances under which they lived in the rugged intermountain region chosen for them.

The successful achievements of these women are evident in two ways. First, there are whole quilts and fragments of others made from cotton and wool produced in the territory. These fabrics demonstrate the territory's self-sufficient, home- or factory-based textile production, as well as the continual effort and need to produce clothing and bedding. Second, the elegant silk quilts, which were made later, show the women's financial stability and their desire to beautify their homes. These quilts display the satisfaction and enjoyment quiltmaking was known to give these women. Several show a particularly high level of sophistication in design and construction coming either from a natural ability or from years of experience.

> *"...Father if you did not know that the man under whose care you had sent Betsy had ill used her, his wife had cursed her and thrown the coffee pot at her head and the father had threatened to throw Betsy into the river so that she was obliged to leave him and his wagons while on the open desert..."*
>
> *Thomas Bullock, husband of Betsy Prudence Howard Bullock (Quilt II-11)[8]*

Quilt: OCEAN WAVES (II-1)

Category: Pieced
Size: 70½" x 80"
Date: Late (1924)
Maker: Ann Mariah Bowen (Call)
    Loyd (3 January 1834–26 July
    1924)
Migration: Genesee County, New
    York, to Utah
Place Joined the Church: New York
Year Crossed the Ocean: ————
Ship: ————
Year Crossed the Plains: 1849
Company: Samuel Gully Company
Arrived: September 22, 1849
Came: With older sister and brother-
    in-law
County Where Settled: Millard; Box
    Elder; Davis; Salt Lake

The maker's choice and placement of fabric colors make this an unusual Ocean Waves variation. The stronger shades of red, black, green, and blue catch the viewer's eye and carry it across the diagonal lines. Part of the success of the design is the placement of the sections of triangles or waves. Note the light-blue color is next to the center on opposite sides of the square. Then, on the next block, the light blue is next to the other two sides. One interesting result is the creation of a pinwheel of red triangles.

Another unusual technique is the use of embroidery to create a different flower, bird, or fruit in each of the twenty-one solid blocks.

Ann Mariah Bowen (Call) Loyd was born the daughter of Israel and Charlotte Louisa Durham Bowen in Bethany, Genesee County, New York. The family joined the Church in New York and moved to Illinois in the late 1830s. In 1847, when the family began making their preparations to migrate to Utah, the father became ill with pneumonia while gathering needed supplies. He died shortly

Ann Mariah Bowen (Call) Loyd

thereafter, leaving a widow and seven children between the ages of three and twenty-one. The family decided to divide for the journey with the older children traveling in 1849 and the mother and younger children traveling in 1851. Ann Mariah went with her pregnant older sister and brother-in-law, Juliaette and Charles Dalton, driving a team across the Plains from the Missouri River to the Salt Lake Valley. She was fifteen at the time.[9] This experience served to forecast her ability to be a strong, responsible, capable woman who could face the difficult challenges of improving her life situation.

In 1851, Ann Mariah married Anson Call as his second wife. As a wife of this prominent Church colonizer, she was one of the first Anglo women to settle three different areas of the territory. First, they pioneered Fillmore as the territorial capital in Millard County. Then in 1855, they moved north to Box Elder County where they built Call's Fort, a 120-foot-square fort with three-foot-thick walls.

Then in April 1856, the Calls were asked to colonize the Carson Valley in the western edge of the Mormon Corridor. The town of Genoa was being established as a polygamist settlement in the isolated outer reach on the route to California.[10] In October, Anson was called to Salt Lake. He

"You knew when she started out to do a thing, it would be done to the best of her ability. The word 'can't' was never known to her. If she hadn't been a strong fearless young woman, who could handle a gun and five horses as good as any man, she could have never made the trip back home. She often told the grandchildren how she would take her children on her horse's back and round up her stock, then tie the horse to the wagon, put the children in and start on her journey once more."

*Her granddaughters,
Leone George Smith and
Hilda Mann Condie[11]*

left Ann Mariah to live alone with her three small children in an unfinished log wall home with only a wagon canvas for a roof. They survived the winter and joined Anson back in Bountiful in the spring of 1857.

Returning to Bountiful, near Salt Lake City, Ann Mariah remained there while Anson was away colonizing the Colorado River warehouse supply town of Callsville.[12] In 1866, she left Bountiful because of "unpleasant conditions," leaving her three older children in the care of Mary Call, the first wife. Taking her five-month-old baby, Harriet Louisa, she rode on horseback to her

Detail of piecing and quilting

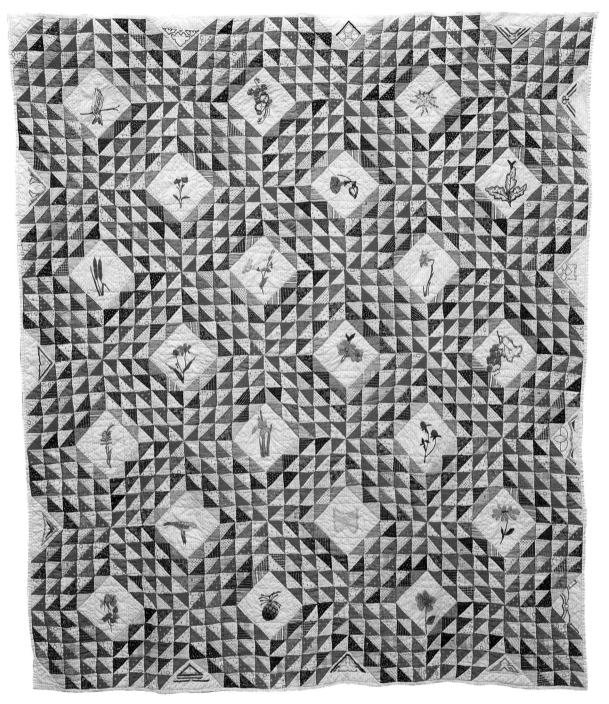

Full view of Ocean Waves Quilt

mother's home in southern Utah. Ann Mariah later divorced Anson Call and supported herself by teaching school. When her daughter was five, Ann Mariah sent her to live with her father in Bountiful.

Ann Mariah later married William Loyd and had two additional children, both of whom died. After her husband's death, she returned to Bountiful to live in a small house next to her oldest son, Israel.

"In the few months that she lived in her ninety-first year, she pieced eight ocean wave quilts, each containing 2381 pieces."

Her granddaughters[13]

Quilt: TULIP (II-2)

Category: Appliquéd
Size: 81" x 85"
Date: Mid (1875–1885)
Maker: Rebecca Maria Burton Jones
  (16 February 1826–19 November
  1888)
Migration: Ontario, Canada, to Utah
Place Joined the Church: Canada
Year Crossed the Ocean: ————
Ship: ————
Year Crossed the Plains: 1849
Company: Howard Egan's
  Independent Company
Arrived: August 7, 1849
Came: With husband Nathaniel Vary
  Jones and child
County Where Settled: Salt Lake

Signature: Rebecca M. Jones

This heirloom quilt with its extensive attention to detail and execution typifies much of the quiltmaker's life. The amount of detail verifies that the quilt was made during a relatively stable time in her life. She lived out her life in Salt Lake City after having arrived in 1849.

The Tulip pattern is one of the few floral patterns in this study. It reflects several themes seen in other quilts included here, such as the beauty of nature, the outdoor experience, and a sense of survival in the arid desert climates, as represented by a flower that has a self-contained food source. In the nineteenth-century lexicon of flowers, a tulip suggested a sense of "renown, fame, spring, dreaminess."[14]

The finished block size is about 15" with each block exhibiting a bit of whimsy and flexibility in its construction. The set of blocks is on point, with the orientation of the base of the blocks toward the sides of the quilt. Both features are seen often in this study.

The quilting pattern in the solid white blocks repeats the appliqué design. Princess feather plumes are quilted in the solid white, triangular blocks. The documentation accompanying the quilt identifies them as beehives. The quiltmaker's signature "Rebecca M. Jones" appears quilted in one of the triangles.

The finished border is 9" wide with a continuous appliquéd vine of sprigs of flowers and buds. Note the green triangular piece as the vine root in each corner. One interpretation of this detail is a desire for connection to one's roots as a pioneer migrating in America.[15] Another is the need for water and soil nutrients in order to sustain growth in the West.

The elbow quilting pattern in the border has series of ten sweeps or rows each ⅜" apart.

Rebecca Maria Burton Jones was born the daughter of Samuel and Hannah Shipley Burton in Mersea, Essex County, Ontario, Canada. As a daughter, wife, and sister of one of the most active extended families in early migrations, her life was influenced greatly by the surrounding circumstances. The family joined the Church in December 1837 and began immediately to notice the controversial anti-Mormon feelings. They migrated west to Missouri in October 1838, unaware of the persecution underway there. Once they discovered it, they fled to the small communities of Hancock County, Illinois, until forced to seek protection in Nauvoo after the 1844

Corner border treatment

Rebecca Burton Jones

Full view of Tulip Quilt

martyrdom of Joseph Smith. In Nauvoo, Rebecca married Nathaniel Vary Jones, a native of New York, on March 14, 1845. He had served as a missionary to Illinois, Michigan, and Ohio with her older brother Robert Taylor Burton in 1843.[16] Their first child was born in Nauvoo in May of 1846. Fleeing west across Iowa to Mt. Pisgah, the Burton family was part of the more than five hundred volunteer members of the Mormon Battalion. Nathaniel Jones served as diarist. Her newly wed sister Melissa Burton Coray was one of the twenty women who, working as laundresses, accompanied the men.[17] Rebecca spent two years at Winter Quarters waiting with others for word of their loved ones.

Reunited with her husband, she and her family migrated west in 1849. They settled in Salt Lake County where she and her children lived. Nathaniel took additional wives and continued his active role as a missionary, military man, and leader in the manufacturing of lead in southern Utah. He died in 1863 and she died in 1888.

Quilt: ONE PATCH (II-3)

Category: Pieced
Size: 68½" x 68½"
Date: Late (1890–1900)
Maker: Phebe Teresa Judd Kimball
    (1 July 1837–23 September 1909)
Migration: Ontario, Canada, to Utah
Place Joined the Church: Canada
Year Crossed the Ocean: ———
Ship: ———
Year Crossed the Plains: 1849
Company: Allen Taylor Company
Arrived: About October 10, 1849
Came: With her parents and family
County Where Settled: Salt Lake

This collection of 1¾" silk patches or squares would have added brightness and warmth to the quiltmaker's family parlor in her turn-of-the-century, Victorian, Salt Lake City home.

The silk of this quilt and of several others of the period shows the level of wealth and success achieved by the Mormon families after their migrations and settlement. Although it is impossible to verify without explicit documentation and fabric samples, these quilts may contain significant information about the silk industry in Utah. Some may contain Utah silk produced by the women in the period between 1875 and 1900. The fabrics may also reflect the

Church's effort to normalize their relations with industries and suppliers outside of Utah after 1890 by allowing commercial activities. This Kimball quilt with its wool batt and elbow quilting may represent the continuous connection to outside resources that those families in the freighting business were able to maintain throughout the period of isolation.

Phebe Teresa Judd Kimball was born the daughter of Thomas Alfred and Teresa Hastings Judd in Westport, Leeds County, Ontario, Canada. The family, having joined the Church in 1836, migrated to Illinois in 1841. When they arrived and were confronted with the scarcity of housing and food, the family settled in nearby Springfield. After the Saints left, the Judds redoubled their efforts to be able to go west comfortably by staying in Springfield. The reminiscence of Phebe's older sister Margaret Gay Judd—as published in Susan Madsen's *I Walked to Zion: True Stories of Young Pioneers on the Mormon Trail*—relates their journey as young, healthy, unmarried women enjoying their opportunities.[18]

Phebe Judd settled in Salt Lake City, and in November 1855, she married Heber Parley Kimball, the son of Church leader Heber C. Kimball and his first wife Vilate. They became the parents of ten children born about every two years between 1856–75. The names of two of the children, Brigham Willard and Heber

Section of quilt

Parley, reflect the parents' respect for the Church leaders Brigham Young, Willard Richards, Heber C. Kimball, and Parley P. Pratt.

They resided in Salt Lake City their entire lives. Heber P. Kimball was involved in freighting. During the early years of the Church or the "down-and-back" trains, he was a teamster or "Utah boy," as they were called. He was captain of the fifth Church train, which brought merchandise and ninety emigrants in 1861.[19] Because of his business, he was able to travel. His family acquired a taste for style and culture, as reflected in their beautiful parlor furniture, which is now part of the Pioneer Memorial Museum collection.[20]

Full view of One Patch Quilt

Mormon Panorama/Zion's Camp *by C. C. A. Christensen*

Quilt: LOG CABIN (II-4)

Category: Pieced
Size: 71" x 78"
Date: Late (1890–1900)
Maker: Mary Jane Parker Butterfield
  (27 January 1817–21 July 1901)
Migration: York County, Maine, to
  Utah
Place Joined the Church: Maine
Year Crossed the Ocean: ————
Ship: ————
Year Crossed the Plains: 1849
Company: Capt. Allen Taylor
Arrived: About October 10, 1849
Came: With husband and family
County Where Settled: Salt Lake

The Log Cabin pattern would have had special meaning to Mary Jane since a cabin was her home for nineteen years. This Light and Dark variation of the Log Cabin quilt is composed of 11" blocks made of eight 1¼" logs or strips cut from the same four fabrics.

For a quiltmaker in Utah, this meant acquiring the Utah-produced factory cloth and producing the dyes at home to achieve the desired col-ors. The white ground fabrics in the quilt were commercially produced back East and brought to Utah. These help to date the quilt to after the Manifesto of 1890 when regular commercial trade was established and such fabrics became more readily available to the eager homemaker.

The double quilting rows are in the elbow style with each pair of lines spaced 1¼" apart. The lines were quilted starting from the sides of the quilt, working toward the center. This method indicates how the quilt was placed on the frame.

Mary Jane Parker Butterfield was the first of two daughters born to Samuel and Hannah Edgecomb Parker in Parsonsfield, York County, Maine. Within a year of her birth, her mother died in childbirth. On February 15, 1835, Mary Jane married Thomas Jefferson Butterfield at Farmington, Kennebec County, Maine.

In the late 1830s, after hearing the Prophet Joseph Smith speak, the Butterfields joined the Church. They were baptized by Thomas's uncle, Church leader Josiah Butterfield. The young couple moved west to Kirtland, Ohio, and then to Far West, Missouri. Thomas took a lead role in planning each of these mass migrations, especially from Zion's Camp from Ohio to Missouri.

Mary Jane independently maintained her family and farm through the many trials of migrating and establishing their homes while her husband assisted others. In the spring of 1839, forced to leave Missouri without his help, Mary Jane loaded and drove her wagon to Nauvoo.

Forced to flee again in 1846, they crossed the icy Mississippi River.

*Detail of Utah-produced,
home-dyed fabrics and
commercially produced fabrics*

"She was very artistic. She gathered weeds, flowers, and bark. She seemed to have an inborn knowledge of colors. She would have cans on the stove steeping sage, berries, etc. then she would add just a little of this shade and then something else, until she achieved the color she wanted to dye the wool."

Cornelia Cran Butterfield,
her granddaughter [21]

Mary Jane Parker Butterfield

Full view of Log Cabin Quilt

When they arrived in Kanesville, Thomas was again asked to select the animals and find the wagons and supplies for crossing the Plains.

In 1849, they successfully migrated west themselves. They outfitted their wagon with a Franklin stove, a butter churn, and several hives of bees. Mary Jane and her two youngest children, both under two, rode in the wagon. Their five-year-old son, Almon, drove the sheep while their thirteen-year-old daughter, Mary Jane, drove the cows and extra horses.

Eight years later in 1857, "Mary Jane's greatest trial came when Brigham Young told Thomas to marry a young English girl, Mary Farmer."[22] Life continued to be a challenge as she faced moving her family and livestock by herself during the 1857 threat of Johnston's Army, federal troops sent to Utah by the government (see pages 107, 108). Holding her youngest child, two-month-old Hannah, she drove the wagon south to temporary safety while the second wife moaned through her labor pains. The two women lived in a wagon box with the children for five months until able to return home.

After many years, as a symbol of their ultimate success in Utah, Thomas built each wife a two-story house of rock.

Four Patch center section

Quilt: FRAMED FOUR PATCH CENTER MEDALLION (II-5)

Category: Pieced
Size: 61" x 71"
Date: Mid (1860–1880)
Maker: Amanda Barnes Smith
(22 February 1809–30 June 1886)
Migration: Berkshire County, Massachusetts, to Utah
Place Joined the Church: Ohio
Year Crossed the Ocean: ———
Ship: ———
Year Crossed the Plains: 1850
Company: Warren Smith Own Company [23]
Arrived: September 18, 1850
Came: With second husband Warren Smith and son
County Where Settled: Salt Lake; Cache

This quiltmaker's life experiences evolved around significant events in Mormon migration history. Amanda Barnes Smith was celebrated as a heroine of the 1838 Haun's Mill Massacre in Missouri in *Heroines of "Mormondom": The Second Book of the Noble Women's Lives Series*, published by the Juvenile Instructor Office in 1884. Her experiences led to her being a leader in efforts to seek peace with the Mormons' Nauvoo neighbors.

According to family tradition, the brown fabric came from an overcoat worn by an officer in Johnston's Army during the Utah War from 1857 to 1860. John Mercer, father of Amanda's daughter-in-law Elizabeth Echo Mercer Smith, traded a horse for the coat.[24]

Creating a quilt of recycled garments was a typical pioneer solution to the need for bedcovers. Note the repair patches are placed to main-

tain the quilt design integrity by continuing to show the important fabrics.

The yarn for the backing was spun by quilt donor Mary Mercer McCarthy, another daughter of John Mercer. The plaid fabrics are typical of home-produced textiles. The hand-quilting is in the elbow pattern with a repeat of seven lines.

Amanda Barnes Smith was born in Becket, Berkshire County, Massachusetts, the daughter of Ezekiel and Fanny Johnson Barnes. The family

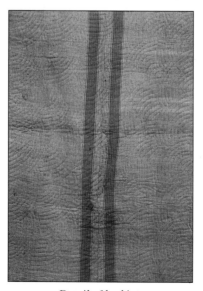

Detail of backing

moved to Amherst, Lorraine County, Ohio, where she married Warren Smith in 1827. Joining the Church, they moved to Kirtland. After the economic recession there, they left for Missouri in early 1838, arriving six months later at Haun's Mill in Caldwell County. (See page 70.)

Barely had the Smiths arrived with their six children and set up their tent next to the blacksmith shop, then the local mob massacred Amanda's husband and their son Sardis. Another son, Alma, was badly wounded by a bullet to his hip joint. Forced by his needed recovery period to remain in the area rather than leave as ordered,

Amanda Barnes Smith

she had to endure public bragging about the massacre.

This time was one of her greatest trials. She fought to help her son recover while living in a tent during one of the coldest winters on record in Missouri.[25] Finally in February 1839, she was able to take her four small children and drive her team and wagon back to Illinois.

She remarried in 1839 to a man who was also named Warren Smith but who was no relation to her first husband. They had three children of their own. In Nauvoo, she was an early member of the Relief Society

Full view of Framed Four Patch Center Medallion Quilt

when it was first organized in 1842. They left Illinois in 1847 but remained in Iowa to replenish their supplies before migrating west in 1850. In Salt Lake, he became disenchanted and left the Church. After the couple divorced, she and her children remained active in the Church.

In 1854 in Salt Lake, she became an officer in a group of women whose goal was to make clothes for the Indians and to do other charitable work.

Respected by all, she was one of the fourteen women leaders to sign a letter of gratitude to Governor Mann for giving women the right of suffrage in February 1870.[26]

Mormon Panorama Eight/Haun's Mill *by C. C. A. Christensen*

"I sat in my tent. Looking up I suddenly saw the mob coming—the same that took away our weapons. Before I could get to the blacksmith's shop to alarm the brethren who were at prayers, the bullets were whistling amongst them. . . . Afterwards this William Mann showed the boots on his own feet in Far West saying: 'Here is a pair of boots that I pulled off before the d__d Mormon was done kicking!' The murderer Glaze also boasted over the country, as a heroic deed, the blowing off the head of my young son."

Amanda Barnes Smith[27]

Quilt: WOOLEN QUILT
 FRAGMENT (II-6)

Category: Pieced
Size: 12" x 10"
Date: Mid (1860–1890)
Maker: Rozilla Whitaker Dalton
 (12 December 1828–June 1898)
Migration: Buncombe County,
 North Carolina, to Utah
Place Joined the Church: Missouri
Year Crossed the Ocean: ———
Ship: ———
Year Crossed the Plains: 1850
Company: Capt. Gardner Snow
Arrived: October 5, 1850
Came: With father, stepmother, and
 family
County Where Settled: Weber

This quilt fragment with the maker's picture attached was donated by her daughter with the following note:

> They raised the sheep, washed the wool, carded it, spun it into yarn, then colored the yarn, had it woven into cloth, sewed the top together, and quilted the quilt.[28]

The hand-dyed colors are probably madder roots or berries for red, and indigo for blue. The quilting pattern appears to have been the elbow style with lines spaced about 1⅛" apart.

Cutting a quilt into fragments is one way of preserving and sharing heirlooms among family members. More appropriate ways of maintaining the integrity of the original are to distribute photographs of the quilt among family members, to schedule a rotation of ownership, or to arrange for preservation in one permanent public location.

Rozilla Whitaker Dalton was born the daughter of James and Milinda Fishel Whitaker in Fairview, North Carolina. In 1833, her family moved west to Missouri where her mother died. Here her father joined the Mormons in 1836 and remarried Nancy Woodland in 1838. Forced to flee after the Haun's Mill massacre, the family moved to Quincy, Illinois, in 1839 and to Nauvoo in 1844.

Leaving Nauvoo in 1846, her family planted crops for the Church's use in Mt. Pisgah, Iowa, before moving on to Kanesville in western Iowa. In 1850, they started for the Salt Lake Valley. Rozilla, as a young single woman, enjoyed the journey's challenges and its fun. She joined in the dances on the dusty brown ground, accompanied by accordion and fiddle music.

Rozilla met her future husband at a similar dance held in her family's new home just prior to their moving in. Matthew Dalton was headed to the gold fields of California when he decided to stop in Ogden. There he was hired to build her father's new home. As a non-Mormon, he was not allowed to join in the dancing but they singled each other out for later introductions. He joined the Church on December 8, 1850, and they were married on the fifteenth.

In 1855, they joined the company of fifty families moving north to settle the area now called Willard in Weber County. Willard was the town nearest the transcontinental railroad line. Since the Daltons had the largest house in town, Brigham Young inquired if they would operate a hotel to serve the coast-to-coast railroad passengers. The alternative of housing travelers with different families was considered improper because it gave "the strangers too many privileges with the young people." Rozilla, with the help of her daughters, did all the cooking while Matthew loved to entertain the guests after dinner.[29]

Woolen Quilt fragment

Quilt: BOW TIE (II-7)

Category: Pieced
Size: 74" x 79"
Date: Late (1890–1900)
Maker: Nancy Casady Bybee
    (22 October 1822–19 January
    1901)
Migration: Alabama to Utah
Place Joined the Church: Iowa?
Year Crossed the Ocean: ————
Ship: ————
Year Crossed the Plains: 1850
Company: Church Record of
    Company Lost
Arrived: ————
Came: With her husband
County Where Settled: San
    Bernardino, California; Weber

Nancy Casady Bybee

This quilt is one of two by the
maker in the collection in the
Ogden, Utah, Daughters of Utah
Pioneers Museum. This one shows
the level of design sophistication the
maker was known to exhibit in her
beautiful quilts and rugs. The second
quilt is a Log Cabin in the Light and
Dark variation.

Note the visually pleasing arrangement of "bow ties" across the design
surface, as created by the 5¼" blocks
of contrasting dark and light silks.
The use of plaids and interesting patterns to complement the solid darks
further enhances the design. A
secondary pattern of circles also
appears.

The fragile silk squares are constructed on foundation blocks of a
stronger fabric to give additional stability. The quilt is assembled with a
backing of brown silk, which is tied
invisibly to the seams of the top. The
construction details indicate a high
level of technical expertise.

Nancy Casady Bybee was born the
daughter of Charles and Elizabeth
Latham Casady in Alabama. Little is
known of her early life except that
both her parents died. By the early
1840s, she and her husband Lee
Bybee were members of the Church
in Iowa. An early experience that left
a lifelong impression was the taking-
over of her home one night by a
group of non-Mormon men while
she and her young baby were alone.
They were forced to flee to a neighbor for the night, and the baby died
of illness brought on by the exposure.

Her ability to recover was challenged several more times as the
family sought to achieve personal
and financial success. The family
was part of the experiences in Nauvoo and Winter Quarters before
moving west. Arriving in Utah
in 1850, they wintered over at
Farr's Fort near present-day
North Ogden.

In the spring of 1851, they
answered the call to colonize an
"outer" settlement in the San
Bernardino area of California. The
purpose of this colony was to establish the outer limits of the Mormon
Corridor and give the Saints an access to the sea for bringing in converts from around the world. This
party of about five hundred was led
by Amasa Lyman and Charles Coulson Rich, husband of two quiltmakers (Quilts I-2 and I-3). After the
party purchased 35,509 acres of an
old Spanish ranch and built irrigation canals, the project became a financial success. Lee Bybee obtained
a good tract of land and water rights
and built a large home and ranch.
However, when the call came in
early 1857 to return to Utah in anticipation of the arrival of Johnston's
Army, the sacrifice for the Bybees
was great. They were able to take
only one heavy wagon, one spring
wagon, and seven horses.

Later, they returned to Ogden
before permanently locating in
1861 on a thickly wooded property
of cottonwood and willows near
Riverdale. Here they again established a successful farm before Lee
Bybee passed away in 1873. Nancy
continued to manage the home
and farm for another twenty-eight
years.[30]

Detail of quilt piecing

Full view of Bow Tie Quilt

"*Because their own sheep did not supply enough wool for their clothing needs, Nancy obtained additional wool to spin on shares. A great deal of this work she did at night by the light of the fireplace. The fuel used for this was small willows, which made it necessary for one of the children to continually feed the fire to make enough light. She corded, spun and wove the wool to make clothing, blankets and yarn for knitting stockings to supply her family of eight children and did all the sewing by hand. She also made beautiful rugs and quilts.*"

Mamie Bybee Stephens, *her granddaughter* [31]

Quilt: BASKET (II-8)

Category: Pieced
Size: 72½" x 87"
Date: Mid (1860–1890)
Maker: Lucy Jane Clark Barkdull
    (8 January 1830–19 January 1914)
Migration: Chautauqua County,
    New York, to Utah
Place Joined the Church: New York
Year Crossed the Ocean: ———
Ship: ———
Year Crossed the Plains: 1851
Company: John G. Smith
Arrived: September 1851
Came: With husband and family
County Where Settled: Salt Lake;
    Morgan; Box Elder; Utah; Juab;
    Millard

The faded colors of this pieced quilt provide evidence of important components of this survey: the need for quilts for warmth; the possible use of Utah textile industry fabrics; and the importance of saving treasured heirlooms as clues to the life experiences of ordinary women who settled the Mormon west. The tan pieces, perhaps once a green, were cut from a home-dyed fabric. The 12" blocks are set on point, creating the need for the 6¼" zigzag sashing strips to connect them. The quilt was machine-pieced.

The quilting stitches surround each piece in the pattern block. A gridwork of 1" diamonds in the solid strips hold the batt in place.

———

Lucy Jane Clark Barkdull was the only daughter of the two children born to Samuel and Annie Owens Clark in Theresa, Chautauqua County, New York. Her early training in both farm labor and domestic skills made her equally comfortable working outdoors and as indoors.

The family moved west to Nauvoo where she met Solomon Barkdull. She later married him at Kanesville on August 20, 1848. While living there, they had two children. After they migrated to Utah in 1851, they moved about the valley of the Wasatch Mountain Front Range establishing farms necessary to support the self-sufficient Utah economy. During this time, the couple had

Detail of piecing and quilting

Lucy Jane Clark Barkdull

eight more babies, seven of whom survived.

Lucy was known for her skill in weaving. She purchased a loom while living in Spanish Fork in Utah County, and for fifty-two years, between 1860 and 1912, she provided the families with rugs and carpets for their cabins' bare floors. Her loom and her portrait are part of the Territorial Statehouse Museum in Fillmore, Millard County. Since 1974, the loom has been used to demonstrate weaving and to create yards of carpet for the museum's floors.[32] When her portrait hung in the family home, it seemed to dominate the household.[33]

Full view of Basket Quilt

Quilt: WASHINGTON PLUME
  (II-9)

Category: Appliquéd
Size: 67" x 84"
Date: Mid (1870–1890)
Maker: Matilda Robison King
  (11 March 1811–9 February 1894)
Migration: Montgomery County,
  New York, to Utah
Joined the Church: New York
Year Crossed the Ocean: ————
Ship: ————
Year Crossed the Plains: 1851
Company: Vincent Shurtliff's
  Company
Arrived: October 1851
Came: With husband and family
County Where Settled: Millard; Piute

Border treatment

This is one of four Washington
Plume quilts that surfaced in this
project. Two others were made by
women who were related through
marriage and were members of the
same Relief Society. The fourth was
made by the Hawaiian Saints for
Brigham Young. In each, the large
blocks have four red appliquéd
plumes and four floral buds radiating
from a pieced center pinwheel. While
the others have vine borders, this

quilt has a swag border that adds a
nice frame on three of the quilt's
four sides. Note that the width of
the swag changes from the side
(10¼") to the bottom (7⅜").

The quilting designs of leaves,
hearts, wheels, and crescent shapes
are scattered over the main body of
the quilt. Flowers are placed along
the main seam line. In the border,
the princess feather design empha-
sizes the pieced swag. There is a
heart shape stitched at the point
where the quilting design meets the
base of each swag.

The quilting consists of both double and single rows with six stitches
per inch. The knots show on the top
of the quilt. The cheddar-yellow
binding is continuous around the
edge, curving at the base.

Matilda Robison King was born the
fourth daughter and eighth child of
Joseph and Cornelia Guinal Robison
in Charlestown, Montgomery
County, New York. In 1815, the
family moved to Pennsylvania where
the mother died in 1829. Eight of the
children, including Matilda, were
sent back to New York to live with
their grandmother. Matilda helped
with family expenses by working outside the home. She married Thomas
Rice King on December 25, 1831, in
Cicero, Onondaga County. They
joined the Church in July 1840,
along with his parents and some of
her brothers and sisters. Moving
west, they settled for five years in Lee
County, Iowa, across the Mississippi
River from Nauvoo.

They moved across Iowa in 1846
and settled in Winter Quarters,
remaining behind when the Saints
began to migrate west. Throughout
their lives, they would first attempt
to gather the resources or bring together the support that would allow
them to live in comfort. They then
had the confidence to face the chal-

Thomas R. King

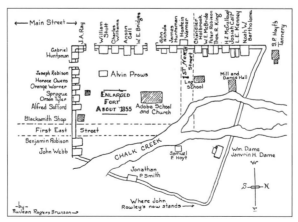

Map of Fort at Fillmore

Matilda Robison King

Full view of Washington Plume Quilt

lenges of pioneer living and of expanding their Church's growth.

Reviewing their histories, a family member wrote:

Thomas writes in his history of raising corn 3 years at Florence so they could immigrate in comfort. Matilda adds that they had three wagons of their own in which to cross the plains. The boys drove the stock belonging to them.[34]

They arrived in Salt Lake in 1851 and joined a company of thirty families colonizing the town of Fillmore in Millard County under Anson Call's leadership. Again desiring to ease their lives, Thomas King was one of the people responsible for bringing the Zion Cooperative Mercantile Institute (ZCMI) to Fillmore. The Kings pioneered again in 1867, moving to the Cove Creek area. Here Matilda had an encounter with Indians that became a traditional family story. Facing the uncomfortable presence of Indians in their Cove Fort housing, Matilda calmed the women by singing a hymn, "O Stop and Tell Me, Red Man."

Soon after the transcontinental railroad was completed in 1869, Matilda and her husband traveled for five months on a "visiting mission" to their non-Mormon family members. The family welcomed them but wished to hear nothing about their religion.

In 1877, they moved to the Circle Valley area of Piute County to found Kingston, the town named in the King family honor. As leaders once again, they led the participation in the "United Order," an economic plan that remained in effect until it was disbanded in 1883.[35]

Quilt: STAR QUILT FRAGMENT
    (II-10)

Category: Pieced
Size: 20" x 22"
Date: Mid (1860–1890)

Maker: Ellen Whittaker Lunt (6 June
    1830–16 May 1903)
Migration: Lancashire, England, to
    Mexico
Place Joined the Church: England
Year Crossed the Ocean: 1851
Ship: George W. Bourne
Year Crossed the Plains: 1851
Company: Morris Charles Phelps
Arrived: September 28, 1851
Came: With parents and family
County Where Settled: Iron;
    Chihuahua, Mexico

Maker: Ann Gower Lunt (10 October
    1843–11 January 1914)
Migration: Staffordshire, England, to
    Utah
Place Joined the Church: England
Year Crossed the Ocean: 1850
Ship: Argo
Year Crossed the Plains: 1854
Company: Joseph Fielding Company
Arrived: Unknown
Came: With her father, stepmother,
    and family
County Where Settled: Salt Lake;
    Iron; Chihuahua, Mexico; Iron

Star Quilt fragment

---

*"This was made by the first and third
wives of patriarch Henry Lunt. . . .
The fabrics were first made into clothes
and then the best pieces were taken
and cut for a quilt block."*[36]

This quilt fragment and its documentation are displayed with a collection of items dedicated to the
Henry Lunt family at the Pioneer
Memorial Museum in Salt Lake City.

In this survey, this quilt is representative of the many Mormon

plural wives who combined their individual talents and abilities to supply their family needs. Ellen Lunt
wove and Ann Gower Lunt spun
both wool and cotton for cloth.
This 21" star has the traditional pattern of quilting lines ¼" from the
seam lines. The fabrics were most
likely home-dyed by Ann, who was
known to use local materials for dye
stuffs.

Ellen Whittaker Lunt was born the
daughter of James and Rachel Taylor
Whittaker in Bolton, Lancashire,
England. The family immigrated to
Parowan in southern Utah in 1851.
In November of that year, Ellen accompanied her father and brother
James as the only woman in the first
company to colonize the area of
Cedar City. On March 25, 1852, she
married Henry Lunt in Parowan and
set up housekeeping in a wagon box
with one chair and a few tin dishes.

She used her domestic skills and natural abilities to enrich their lives. She
served as the family cook. She used
her needle skills to make and sell
straw hats trimmed with the silk and
lace she had brought from England.
She sang in the choir and in 1852
had a leading part in the first dramatic
production in Cedar City.

As the first wife of Henry Lunt,
she accepted sharing her resources
with other wives and children, serving as the role model and leader. Not
having children of her own, she
adopted two Native Americans. As
the children of the Lunt family grew,
she taught them cooking, sewing,
and telegraphy. She was loved and respected by all the family.

When the Deseret Telegraph Line
was brought into Cedar City, she became the first operator in 1866 and
held the job for years, earning
twenty-five dollars a month.[37]

Forced to flee to Mexico in 1889,

Lunt home in Cedar City, c. 1890

she died there after lingering in a long coma during which the third and fourth wives, Ann and Sarah, cared for her day and night.

Ann Gower Lunt was born the daughter of Thomas and Jane Cresswell Gower in Wedensbury, Staffordshire, England. Her father was an iron foundry overseer, managing a work force in Stratford. Her mother was from the English upper class and had brothers serving as officers in the British Army.

After joining the Church, Ann's father was eager to bring his wife and family of three children to Utah. They joined a company going to New Orleans in 1850. The plan was to travel up the Mississippi River to St. Louis where Ann's father would earn enough money in the iron smelters to finance the rest of their journey. Unfortunately, cholera took the lives of three family members, leaving Ann alone with her father. In later years, she remembered being left in the care of neighbors while he worked. She would be locked in their dark attics because she cried so for her mother.[38]

In 1854, after Thomas Gower remarried a young widow with children, he took his family by boat to Council Bluffs. There they acquired an outfit for crossing the Plains, including four oxen and two cows. They settled first in the West Jordan District, but were soon called to go to Iron County where Thomas's skills in the manufacture of iron were needed. The whole family, especially Ann as the oldest child, helped to build the farm and home. She became her father's main help and worked in the field doing a man's work in raising the raw materials for food and clothing. She learned the skills of cloth production from shearing to weaving. Her early dye sources included the tops of rabbit brush and corpus found in the canyon.

On April 11, 1863, she became the third wife of Henry Lunt, a man twenty years her senior who had also been on board the *Argo* in 1850. As a member of his already established family, she continued her role of working both indoors and out to meet their needs. She became the mother of ten children born every two years over a twenty-year period. She also became proficient in braiding and making straw hats, earning extra income and providing the children with Christmas gifts of hand-woven cornhusk baskets.

When the now blind Henry Lunt became ill with cancer, she was the only one he allowed to provide his care. After his death in 1903, she continued to reside in Mexico until 1912 when the Mormons were suddenly forced to leave the country in a political overthrow of Dictator Porfirio Diaz. She returned to Cedar City to the homes of her children and died in 1914.[39]

Quilting Bee at Henry Lunt home in Chihuahua, Mexico.
Ellen Lunt is seated second from the left.

Detail of center block with signature

Quilt: PETER AND PAUL or
   PINCUSHION (II-11)

Category: Pieced
Size: 78" x 89"
Date: Mid (1870–1890)
Maker: Betsy Prudence Howard
   Bullock (23 July 1835–2 June
   1893)
Migration: Bedfordshire, England,
   to Utah
Place Joined the Church: England
Year Crossed the Ocean: 1843 or 1844
Ship: Swanton(?)
Year Crossed the Plains: 1852
Company: Captain James McGaw's
   Independent Company
Arrived: September 20, 1852
Came: Unknown
County Where Settled: Salt Lake;
   Summit

This quilt of illusion creates an interesting figure/ground relationship through the use of two contrasting colors. When one color advances or is predominant, the other recedes to the background. The image appears to reverse as the eye focuses on a different color. The pattern names given are those commonly used in the maker's native England. In America, Robbing Peter to Pay Paul is the generic pattern name.[40]

The "robbing" is created by starting with two squares of fabric of different colors, cutting a curved piece from each side, and exchanging their placement. The finished, hand-stitched 11" squares are set on point block to block. This helps to create an uninterrupted illusionary effect. The use of two colors continues in the quilt's binding, with pink on the two sides and green on the top and bottom.

"We were left strangers in a strange land, but the Lord was good to us. He raised up friends in our behalf...."
   Betsy Bullock[41]

The quilting pattern in the center of most blocks is gridwork or infill encircled by a quilted wreath. In the very center block is the inscription "To —— —— Bullock." The block-style initials are difficult to read because of the quilt's prior use. They may refer to any of the maker's children or to her husband, Thomas Bullock. There are eleven stitches per inch.

The documentation submitted with the quilt reads "Made by Thomas Bullock and his wife, Prudence Howard Bullock during the winter of 1847–1848 in Utah."[42] A study of Prudence Bullock's life and journey reveals an unusual migration and a marriage proposal by a young Mormon woman.

Betsy Prudence Howard Bullock was born the daughter of Samuel Lane and Betsy Pack Howard in Bedford, England. Her family joined the Church in 1837 and crossed the ocean in 1843 or 1844. They had paid passage through to Nauvoo by way of the Mississippi River. However, because the parents became so ill, they were advised to remain in St. Louis, where her mother soon died.

Because of unusual circumstances during her migration, when young unmarried Betsy arrived in Salt Lake, she sought stability for her life. She selected and married Church leader Thomas Bullock as his third wife.

Together they wrote a long letter to her father back east on December 12, 1852.[43] It explains how Betsy had approached Thomas to ask him to marry her about four weeks prior to their December 9th wedding. She had consulted with her family's personal friend President Willard Richards, her guardian Alice Martin, and Thomas's second wife Lucy Clayton Bullock, a sister of her stepmother, Ellen Clayton Howard.

Betsy and Thomas Bullock moved to Summit County in 1862. In 1868, during an outbreak of smallpox, their home was used as a hospital where all with the disease were brought to stay.

Betsy Howard Bullock

Full view of Peter and Paul Quilt

Quilt: STAR (II-12)

Category: Pieced
Size: 85" x 88"
Date: Early (1840–1850)
Maker: Laura Hull Cossitt (20
    September 1782–9 September
    1865)
Owner: Sarah M. Cossitt Mayfield
    Chaffin (1815–91)
Migration: Mercer County,
    Pennsylvania, to Utah
Place Joined the Church: Illinois
Year Crossed the Ocean: ———
Ship: ———
Year Crossed the Plains: 1852
Company: Capt. Henry W. Miller
Arrived: About September 21, 1852
Came: With her husband and family
County Where Settled: Salt Lake; Iron

Sarah M. Cossitt Mayfield Chaffin

According to the accession sheet when the quilt was donated, it was made by Laura Hull Cossitt, mother of Sarah M. Cossitt Chaffin, who brought the quilt to Utah in 1852. The twenty-five pieced star blocks are composed of eight diamond-shaped pieces. Four red and cheddar-yellow diamonds create a traditional floral design in each of the four corners. The blocks are sashed and bordered by green strips varying in size from 4½" to 4¾" wide. The consistent green color throughout the quilt indicates that a better quality of dye stuffs was available in the East at this earlier time than was available in Utah during the territory's period of self-sufficiency.

The quilting in the vertical strips is a herringbone pattern ⅜" apart. The quilting in the other strips and the border is a cable pattern. The red binding completes the design.

———

Sarah M. Cossitt Mayfield Chaffin was born to Epaphroditus and Laura Hull Cossitt in Mercer, Pennsylvania. Her father encouraged her to explore her faith. She had read the Bible three times by the age of fifteen.

After her first husband died young, leaving her a widow and mother at the age of twenty, she moved west to Illinois with her parents and family. She married Louis Rice Chaffin of La Harpe, Illinois, and together they joined the Church. She was the only Mormon in her immediate family, although her father's sister also joined.

The Chaffins were a financially successful and generous couple, respected by Mormons and non-Mormons alike in their community. While Louis Chaffin was on guard duty, a neighbor told Sarah of the mob's plans to kill everyone that would not assist them in driving out the Mormons the next night. Sarah warned her husband and thus helped the Saints to be prepared.[44]

Sarah Chaffin demonstrated a strong sense of resiliency in her ability to recover from unfortunate economic losses they experienced as loyal Saints. This ability is shown in the contrast of her migration experiences. She was forced to flee Nauvoo with a three-day-old baby in an open wagon in February 1846. Yet, for her 1852 journey west to Salt Lake she rode in a horse-drawn carriage with a Miss Pool.

Instead of crossing to Iowa after fleeing, the Chaffin family went to St. Louis where Louis's wealthy non-Mormon brothers operated a mercantile business. Sarah's husband and sons worked there until 1852. During this time, her sons rescued fabric bolts from a fire that damaged the store's inventory. Sarah was given these bolts to take to Utah for distribution there.

Their party of nine traveled in three wagons pulled by oxen with loose stock and a span of horses. They were able to assist two other families by loaning them teams of oxen for the journey.[45]

The hardships of pioneering, however, returned to challenge Sarah after their arrival in Salt Lake. Her husband was called to serve a four-year mission to Australia in 1856, leaving her with the responsibility of caring for the children. At one point, when criticized by the ward teachers for giving away flour, she objected and continued to contribute to others. Eventually, when she had depleted her resources at home, she resorted to taking her own children out into the canyon to live on service berries, a native food stock.

After Louis's return, the Chaffins moved south to help settle Dixie. In Cedar City, they again had to recover from a fire disaster. This time she worked as a cook for the mill hands and taught school for a number of years.

Quilt detail

Full view of Star Quilt

Quilt: FLORAL (II-13)

Category: Appliquéd
Size: 75¾" x 87½"
Date: Late (1890–1910)
Maker: Eliza Melissa Hall (23 July
   1829–31 January 1913)
Migration: Chautauqua, New York,
   to Utah
Place Joined the Church: Utah
Year Crossed the Ocean: ———
Ship: ———
Year Crossed the Plains: 1852
Company: Benjamin Gardner's
   Company
Arrived: September 24 and 27, 1852
Came: With her husband and young
   daughter
County Where Settled: Weber

*Detail of lower left corner including
Sego lily*

Most of this fragile silk quilt's seventy-two 8" blocks contain a different flower or fruit richly embellished with lace, ribbon, embroidery, or crochet. There is a possibility, but difficult to confirm without actual documentation, that the blocks represent each state's flower and tree. The Sego lily is the state flower of Utah and an important food source for early Mormon survival. There are also violets, the state flower of New Jersey, and a sunflower, the state flower of Kansas.[46]

The three borders of pink, white, and green reveal the variations that existed among the available silk fabrics. The deterioration, called "silk rot," is a result of the fabric's having been weighted with lead to meet import standards.

The backing is a surprise. A gauze-like fabric covers the entire surface. There are a few appliquéd flowers scattered under this covering.

The quilting is done in the ditch or seam line between each of the

blocks and the border. In the center of each block, there is either a little quilted circle or a few stitches to secure the top to the backing.

The binding is a ½"-wide pink ribbon, hand-stitched in fine needlework.

———

Eliza Melissa Hall was born the daughter of Hanford and Harriet

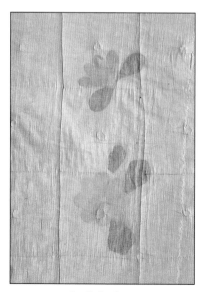

Quilt backing

Sachett Hall in Chautauqua, New York. Her parents were wealthy, devout Methodists who disapproved of her marriage. She married Mark Hall for love on June 24, 1847, in Putnamville, Indiana. Her parents told her she could never return home and they never wanted to see her again. Years later, when she returned east to visit, she stopped to call on her parents. The servant at the doorway told her that they were not at home for her.

With her Mormon husband, she participated in the Mormon migrations and settlement for eleven years before personally joining the Church. After their wedding, the couple immediately left for Nauvoo. In October 1848, they moved on across Iowa to North Pigeon in Pottawattamie County. Here Mark Hall took a major responsibility in the migration preparations. Asked to remain in Iowa to build and repair wagons, they purchased a farm for $400 and set up housekeeping. In June 1852, they started for the Rocky Mountains, suffering the death of their three-week-old baby near the Platte River.

In Utah, the Halls settled in isolated Weber Canyon, later moving for safety into Ogden. They purchased a lot on Main Street and built their home. Here Eliza continued to be generous toward others by sharing their resources. They adopted three children while raising their own ten. When her own last child was less than two months old, she

———

"I spent many happy hours at grandmother's. Her room was like fairy land to me. I remember I was allowed to step in quietly and give her a kiss and stay for a few minutes, but never to touch a thing. She did very lovely hand work, one of her silk quilts is on display in a showcase in our pioneer hall."

*Pearl Jackson Cordon,
her granddaughter[47]*

Full view of Floral Quilt

accepted a deserted, ill, and starving migrant child to care for. The Hall home became a place of respite for immigrant families, who would often stay months at a time. She devoted time to making over clothing for them.

Since there was no public school in Ogden, Eliza taught in her home using a room her husband equipped with a blackboard and child-size tables and chairs. She knew money was scarce and was pleased to be able to contribute to her community in this way.[48]

Item: BABY DRESS (II-14)

Category: Pieced
Size: Child
Date: 1856
Maker: Eliza Dorsey Ashworth (12 May 1821–5 September 1887)
Migration: Yorkshire, England, to Utah
Place Joined the Church: England
Year Crossed the Ocean: 1849
Ship: Argo
Year Crossed the Plains: 1852
Company: Capt. Uriah Curtis 16th Company
Arrived: October 1, 1852
Came: With husband and children
County Where Settled: Salt Lake

Eliza Dorsey Ashworth

This charming pieced baby dress was made in 1856 from a series of pieced blocks. The dress shows the wear of probably many children. Period children's clothes were gender neutral, meaning that both boys and girls wore the same things. Note the sleeve areas where the fabrics would have been rubbed as a child wore the dress. Note, too, the tuck around the skirt. This would have allowed the dress to be lengthened when the child grew or shortened when a smaller child was ready to wear it.

The history told about this woman by her family conflicts with that in one of the standard sources for information on migration companies, *Pioneers and Prominent Men of Utah.*[49] The history presented here follows that of Eliza shared by her family.

Eliza Dorsey Ashworth was born the only child of Stephen and Sarah Firth Dorsey in Bradford, Yorkshire, England. Her father was a professional wool comber. According to her history, she was more fortunate than some. "She attended a Sunday School that taught reading and writing. . . . At an early age she went out to service and learned many little tricks of manners and culture which she later taught her own children. She was very artistic and loved the beauties of nature."[50]

She married Benjamin Ashworth, an iron founder, on June 2, 1839. Their first five children were born in Yorkshire, including a daughter they named Emma Smith after Prophet Joseph Smith's wife.

Eliza joined the Church on July 17, 1842 after the early missionaries visited her home. She often hosted them during their subsequent visits.

The Ashworths' experiences when they attempted to join the Saints in the American West illustrate the reasons that Church leaders eventually developed the highly organized system of transporting Saints to Zion. The Ashworths were finally able to sell their property in England and borrow enough money from the Perpetual Emigrating Fund to be able to travel in 1849. Nine weeks later in New Orleans, they learned that they could journey on up the Mississippi River to St. Louis. There Benjamin found work to earn the additional money to finance the migration's second stage. They stayed in St. Louis for several years, delayed by sickness, death, and hard luck. By 1852, they were financially able and eager to start west.

They arrived in the Salt Lake Valley in October and settled in the canyon near the mouth of the Mill Creek. This rushing mountain

Emigrants gathering at Liverpool

stream brought them even more tragedy. Two small sons, Benjamin Erastus and Charles Alma, drowned in the stream in 1857 and 1862. One, or possibly both, would be the son who wore this dress.

In the early 1870s, the family traded their canyon home to their son-in-law for his downtown Salt Lake home. Here Eliza established a small community-based store that supplied groceries, notions, and con-

fections. She delighted in hosting her friends and relatives for a cup of tea from her collection of dishes while she read the tea leaves. Eliza also served as a midwife in her community.

Full view of Baby Dress

Quilt: STAR (II-15)

Category: Pieced
Size: 70" x 92"
Date: Mid (1860–1890)
Maker: Sage Richards Treharne
    Jones (27 November 1832–
    30 March 1897)
Migration: Carmarthen, Wales, to
    Utah
Place Joined the Church: Wales
Year Crossed the Ocean: 1849
Ship: Buena Vista
Came: With her family
Year Crossed the Plains: 1852
Company: Allen Weeks Company
Arrived: October 12, 1852
Came: With the Evans M. Greene
    family
County Where Settled: Utah; Iron

Cotton mill in Washington

This quilt is made of wool prepared and woven at the Dixie Mills in southern Utah. The Dixie Mills were equipped with machinery brought to Utah earlier, moved to the town of Washington, and placed in full operation in January 1867. It produced both woolen and cotton cloth.

This quiltmaker maintained her pioneer spirit of thriftiness throughout her life. The woolen cloth used here may have been part of entire bolts that the quiltmaker would buy

Detail of quilting patterns

for the plain matching dresses she insisted her grandchildren wear.

In each of the 13" pieced blocks, the center star of diamonds is surrounded by curved triangular pieces creating a circle. In each of the block's four corners is a pieced pattern of four diamonds. The pattern block is very similar to that of Quilt II-12. The blocks are set on point. This creation is complex and visually stimulating to the eye. The design is enhanced by the use of contrasting colors.

The quilting patterns consist of a gridwork in the stars, and leaves and buds in the smaller pieces. In the vertical rows of solid blocks, there is the same design of a vine of leaves around the outside edge. In the two outside rows, the center design is a five-pointed star with two small sprigs of leaves, while in the middle row, the design is a centered star with buds radiating behind it. The binding is of red wool.

Sage Richards Treharne Jones was born the daughter of William and Ann Richards Treharne in Carmarthen, Wales. The family joined the Church and sailed for America together in 1849. They landed in New Orleans three months later. While coming up the Mississippi River, both parents contracted cholera. Sage's mother died on the banks of the Missouri River, and her father died in Kanesville after completing the river

journey. Their children, four young adults, were left without means to finance the rest of their journey. They hired out to work for different families. Sage cared for the Evans M. Greene family when they suffered smallpox because she already had had the disease. They invited her to join them for the migration.

Before leaving Kanesville, she promised to marry Thomas Jones upon their arrival in Salt Lake City. After their marriage, they moved to Spanish Fork for a year. In 1853, they moved to Iron County where they joined one hundred other families living in the "Old Fort." This

Sage Richards Treharne Jones

Full view of Star Quilt

was a one-fourth-mile-square fort with rooms for each family separated by spaces for stock and wagons.

In 1859, while helping to build another fort, Thomas Jones became ill and died three years later leaving her a widow with six small children, including twin babies. She earned a living for her family by doing tailoring and sewing. Later, her children took responsibility for the farm work, relieving her of some tasks.

When her family was grown, Sage became involved in community affairs. She had been taught as a child to read and write Welsh, but only to read English. In order to be able to write letters to her sons, she taught herself to write in English. Soon after, she was appointed postmistress of Cedar City.[51]

Quilt fragment front (left) and back (right)
Size: 9½" by 10½"   Date: c. 1875–1900

Quilt: STRIP QUILT (II-16)

Category: Pieced
Size: 70" x 90"
Date: Mid (1860–1890)
Maker: Christina Erika Forsgren Davis
  (26 April 1820–22 February 1906)
Migration: Sweden to Utah
Place Joined the Church: Sweden
Year Crossed the Ocean: 1852
Ship: Forest Monarch
Year Crossed the Plains: 1853
Company: Capt. John E. Forsgren
Arrived: September 30, 1853
Came: With her brothers John and
  Peter
County Where Settled: Box Elder

The utilitarian quilt and the small preserved quilt fragment were made from homespun, handwoven woolen dresses the quilter produced. They illustrate a classic way to use the strips from the least-worn areas of long skirts and the remnant sections of the fabric after the pattern was cut. The seven different 9¼" strips alternate across the quilt surface, giving a pleasing repeat pattern to the design. The quilting patterns vary from diagonal

Detail of quilt front and back

lines 2" apart on the green and black to a combination of horizontal lines 3" and diagonal lines 2½" apart on the black-and-white check.

Both the use of 9" strips for the piecing and a variation of quilting patterns between the strips are characteristics of the classic "strippy quilt" made in the British Isles.[52] A recent English translation of *Old Swedish Quilts* includes quilts made from the woolen fabrics used in folk costumes. These fabrics consist of strips of cloth pieced together. The strips are large enough to reveal the weaving patterns of these traditional fabrics.[53]

Christina Erika Forsgren Davis was born in Gävle, Sweden, the only daughter of John Olof and Anna Christina Forsgren. Her brother John Erick Forsgren was a Church leader. He had left home to go to sea at age nine. In Boston, he became acquainted with the Latter-day Saints and was baptized on July 16, 1843. John Erick participated in many early Church activities. He was the only Scandinavian member of the Mormon Battalion. In 1849, he was called to serve as a missionary in his native Sweden. Prior to his leaving the United States, he married Sarah Bell Davis, the daughter of Church leader William and Sarah McKee Davis.

According to family tradition, Christina Erika Forsgren had a vision in her Swedish church that a man

would appear with three books and that belief in these books would lead to being saved. When her own long-lost brother appeared with the Bible, the Book of Mormon, and the Doctrine and Covenants, both she and her other brother, Peter, believed in the vision's importance. On August 4, 1850, she became the first Scandinavian woman baptized as a member of the Mormon Church.

On December 20, 1852, with her brothers and two hundred others, she left Copenhagen for the Salt Lake Valley. On their long and difficult nine-month journey they traveled by steamer, train, sailing vessel, steamboat, and wagon train.

Upon learning that his father-in-law, William Davis, had been called to lead the settlement of Box Elder County, John Forsgren took Christina and other Scandinavians there. This was one of the first "inner" settlements (those close to Salt Lake City) to be established in the Mormon Corridor. Christina entered into plural marriage as William Davis's second wife on February 20, 1854. They became the parents of three sons. Their home on North Main Street became the center of community activity in Brigham City. Christina welcomed all by providing food and lodging for travelers. She also produced the items necessary for maintaining a pioneer household, including textiles for clothing.[54]

Full view of Strip Quilt

Mississippi Steamboat by Frederic Piercy

Quilt: CRAZY QUILT (II-17)

Category: Pieced
Size: 66" x 72"
Date: Mid (1885–1890)
Maker: Ann Sewell Hawkins (25 March 1806–16 May 1890)
Migration: Norfolk, England, to Utah
Place Joined the Church: England
Year Crossed the Ocean: 1853
Ship: International
Year Crossed the Plains: 1853
Company: Jacob Gates Company
Arrived: September 9, 1853
Came: With husband and family
County Where Settled: Salt Lake; Tooele; Cache

This Crazy Quilt is one of those commonly referred to as a "contained" Crazy because it is made of blocks that are sewn together, rather than being made as a whole unit. This quilt is composed of sixteen 16½" by 19" blocks of silks and velvets. It is typical of those made in the West because it has fewer or simpler design embellishments. Most of the embellishments appear in the center focal point of four blocks.

This is the one of the survey's few quilts that have a stitched beehive and honeybees, symbols for Utah. The bee was a symbol of the Church's cooperative, communal so-

ciety and industry. The commonly used word "Deseret" is the term for honeybee in the Book of Mormon.[55] Other popular period motifs appear here, including an anchor, a heart, a cross, a horseshoe, and flowers, symbols of security, love, devotion, and luck. The padded flowers were added later after the quilt's completion. The stitches holding them in place appear on the backing.

Susannah Sewell Hawkins was born the daughter of Francis and Hannah Davey Sewell in Little Walsingham, Norfolk, England. She was called either Anna or Ann, both common shortened forms of Susannah. She married James Richard Aucock on May 1, 1843, in Middlesex, England. As a widower with two small sons, he had first hired Ann to be his housekeeper. Earning his living as a cheesemonger, he purchased a factory from a man named Hawkins and decided to change his name. They joined the Church in 1849.

The family started from Liverpool with their six children in 1853, going by way of New Orleans and up the Mississippi River to Keokuk, Iowa. They arrived in Salt Lake in September of that year. In 1855 and 1856, they suffered cold winters, droughts, and the worst grasshopper plagues on record.[56] They were unable to raise any crops and relied on the wild Sego lilies for

food. They also survived the hardships and fears brought on by the advancing Johnston's Army and raiding Indians in the years between 1857 and 1860. When it was safe, they moved to Cache Valley and settled in Maughan's Fort, which was later called Wellsville. After the 1863 Battle of Bear River, the settlers were able to move to construct better individual homes for themselves.

After the sudden death of James Hawkins in 1863, Ann, assisted by her older sons, worked to maintain her family.

Detail of beehive motif

Ann Sewell Hawkins

Full view of Crazy Quilt

" . . . when she came to visit she would ask first thing if Margaret had saved any pieces of cloth for her quilts. She loved to sew and making quilts was one of her hobbies. She made a crazy-patch quilt of silk and velvet pieces, embroidered around each little piece with silk floss in a fancy stitch. Many of the pieces had a flower or design in the center. She entered this quilt in the State Fair when she was eighty-three years old and won a blue ribbon on it. The family was very proud of her."

Ruth Gunnell Victor, her great granddaughter[57]

Quilt: CRAZY QUILT (II-18)

Category: Pieced
Size: 62¼" x 75½"
Date: Late (1898)
Maker: Isabella Calder MacKay (24 September 1833–1 January 1907)
Migration: Edinburgh, Scotland, to Utah
Place Joined the Church: Scotland
Year Crossed the Ocean: 1851
Ship: George W. Bourne
Year Crossed the Plains: 1853
Company: Capt. Moses Clawson
Arrived: About September 15, 1853
Came: With mother, brothers, and sisters
County Where Settled: Salt Lake

This Crazy Quilt was made by Isabella MacKay and her relatives in Taylorsville, Utah, for the marriage of her daughter Jane Calder MacKay to Enos Bennion in 1898. Because each block is constructed on a 16" foundation square, it falls within the category of "contained" Crazy quilts. The rich fabrics with stitched embellishments along the seam lines give the quilt a consistent look and smooth-flowing surface.

As with the Kimball Quilt (II-3), the use of yellow and gold scraps in the blocks and in the 6" flounce adds a sense of brightness. The backing is a soft green wool.

An unexpected surprise is the fabric with the long-tailed red rats woven onto a blue ground in the corner block on the left side. The same fabric appears reversed in the block below. Since most of the fabrics of these quilts were salvaged from other projects by their makers, it leads to delightful contemplation of what the fabric might refer to and how it might have been used.

These special touches of color and fun added to a piece this size would reconfirm that it was used in the Victorian parlor or sitting room of a successful home.

Isabella Calder MacKay was born the fifth child of George and Anne Johnston Calder in Edinburgh, Scotland. Before George Calder died in 1839, he was a ship's captain traveling around the world. His death left Anne Calder a widow with seven children between the ages one to sixteen. She worked as a midwife, assisting many of the city's women in childbirth. The family was considered successful and was able to provide the best education possible for the children.

Emigrating to America in 1851, the family sailed into New Orleans and took a steamboat to Cincinnati, Ohio. The reason for going east on the Ohio River is unknown unless it was to visit family or friends.

Two years later, while migrating west to Salt Lake in 1853, Isabella and a friend became lost while visiting an adjoining camp. Wandering around during the night, she thought she saw a fire but her friend informed her it was only a "Willow of Wisp," the British expression for a delusion to lure one's attention. In the daylight, they discovered camp was not that far away.[58]

Isabella had a relatively easy and carefree experience migrating, as was typical of young single women from wealthier families who did not have

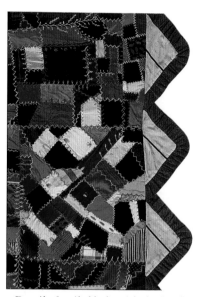

Detail of quilt blocks with the "rat" fabrics

the responsibilities of husband and family.

Isabella married John MacKay on October 6, 1855. Between 1856 and 1877, they became the parents of eleven children. They had a home in Salt Lake and a successful farm in Taylorsville. Isabella was a kind and perfect lady; some called her Lady Isabella. She was respected for her cooking ability. She did a lot of fancy cooking for the Church authorities. As a freighter, John hauled the freight from the Utah Central Depot to the ZCMI, the Church-owned mercantile company, and other uptown warehouses. As a farmer, he was known for his skill in cradling (cutting) grain and was kept busy by all his neighbors. He also worked on all the irrigation projects in the valley west of the river.[59]

Full view of Crazy Quilt

Detail of corner treatment

Quilt: NINE PATCH VARIATION
(II-19)

Category: Pieced
Size: 72⅜" x 88"
Date: Mid (1863)
Maker: Ruth Evan Evans (10 July
1828–3 January 1901)
Migration: Carmarthen, Wales, to
Utah
Place Joined the Church: Wales
Year Crossed the Ocean: 1854
Ship: Golconda
Year Crossed the Plains: 1854
Company: No rosters of the seven
companies crossing that year are
available
Came: With husband and young
daughter
County Where Settled: Salt Lake

This unusual quilt is a treat to study
because of the careful placement of
its fabrics. Although many of these
early fabrics have faded through use,
it appears the quiltmaker made a
conscious decision to place them according to values of intensity, light
or dark. The majority (thirty) of the
forty-two 7½" finished blocks have
one fabric in the center square and

then two others, a dark and a light,
alternating around the rest of the
block.

The blocks are set together with a
4¼" sashing composed of three 1⅜"
strips. Again, the effective use of
striped fabrics in the center sashing
strips and square intersections, especially in the outer ones, reveals a
sense of awareness and sophistication
on the part of the quiltmaker. The
vertical and horizontal placement of
the striped fabric creates a sense of
movement around the quilt. This
placement makes the quilt design
successful without the use of borders
to frame the piece.

The quilting lines are two squares

stitched within each of the pieced
squares. The sashing is quilted ¼"
inch from the seam lines.

The quilt documentation provided
by the quilter's eldest daughter, Ann
Evans Brown, indicates that the quilt
was made by Ruth Evans and her
neighbors in 1863.[60] These women
provided each other with support and
friendship. For this quiltmaker who
resided in Salt Lake the rest of her life
after migration, the neighbors would
have offered a sense of stability.

A faded and worn appliqué quilt
by Ruth Evan Evans is also in the
collection at the Pioneer Memorial
Museum.

Ruth Evan Evans was the daughter
of Walter and Anne Thomas Evan
born in Llanelly, Carmarthen, Wales.
She married Joseph Howell Evans on
December 27, 1848. They had three
babies, two of whom died before the
family left Wales for America. Their
ship with 464 passengers sailed from
Liverpool to New Orleans, where
the Evans family transferred to a
steamboat going up the Mississippi
River. A son, William Howell Evans,
was born on the journey west at the
Little Blue River in Missouri. The
family settled in Salt Lake City. Eight
additional children were born every
two years between 1856 and 1870.

Detail of piecing and quilting

Full view of Nine Patch variation

Quilt: NINE PATCH STAR (II-20)

Category: Pieced
Size: 85½" x 95"
Date: Early (1820–1840)
Maker: Unknown other than the owner's mother[61]
Owner: Sarah Henry Wickle Martin (1824–?)
Migration: Berks County, Pennsylvania, to Utah
Place Joined the Church: Pennsylvania
Year Crossed the Ocean: ————
Ship: ————
Year Crossed the Plains: 1855
Company: Capt. Richard Ballantyne
Arrived: September 25, 1855
Came: With young daughter and the Samuel Martin family
County Where Settled: Salt Lake; Tooele

This quilt of early chintz and calico prints is a treasure. The brown-and-white chintz that predominates is from the early to mid-1800s. The brown was once purple or black. Monochrome prints of this period were characterized by a narrow repeat of the design. The designs often included naturalistic flowers, but had crowded compositions and a lack of contrast and design strength.[62] The use of architectural details in textile prints, wall paintings, wallpaper, and engravings be-

Wagon train crossing the plain

came popular after the excavations at Herculaneum and Pompeii, which also served to spark man's interest in exploration.[63] The use of tendrils or long fingerlike leaves in these prints were popular in the late 1790s and again in the late 1820s.[64]

The hand-pieced 9" blocks are composed of early calico prints, some possibly imported and others early domestic. Note the rainbow print in the center of the pieced block. Its name derives from the vertical stripes in different colors. The colors were blended at the edges with a brush or rubber.[65] The variety and quality of the fabrics reflect their accessibility to the eastern Pennsylvania quiltmaker through the East Coast markets of New York, Philadelphia, and Baltimore.

The 3" squares are either whole or cut into four pieces. The pieces are then exchanged between squares to create an hourglass variation of two light and two dark triangles forming the square. These squares are then placed on opposite sides of the center square. Depending on how the triangles are placed, the arrangement can create a pieced star block. This effect occurs especially when the dominant-colored triangles are inverted on the top and bottom and placed on the sides of the pieced block. This pattern appears in quilts from the early nineteenth century.

The quilting is an all-over square grid of lines 1¾" apart.

Sarah Henry Wickle was born in Berdebra, Berks County, Pennsylvania, where she met and married Harrison Wickle, a Mormon missionary. They migrated to St. Louis and then to Nauvoo, where he died. She and her only child, Sarah Elizabeth Wickle, born on February 21, 1846, in Nauvoo, came West with a man named Martin. The Crossing the Plains Index indicates that traveling in her same party was a widower, Samuel Martin, and his five children. They were later married. They lived in Grantsville, where he built a two-room log house.[66] Sarah Henry Wickle Martin served as a practical nurse.

Detail of rainbow print

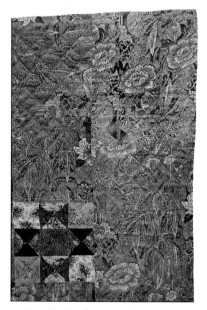

Detail of early monochrome print

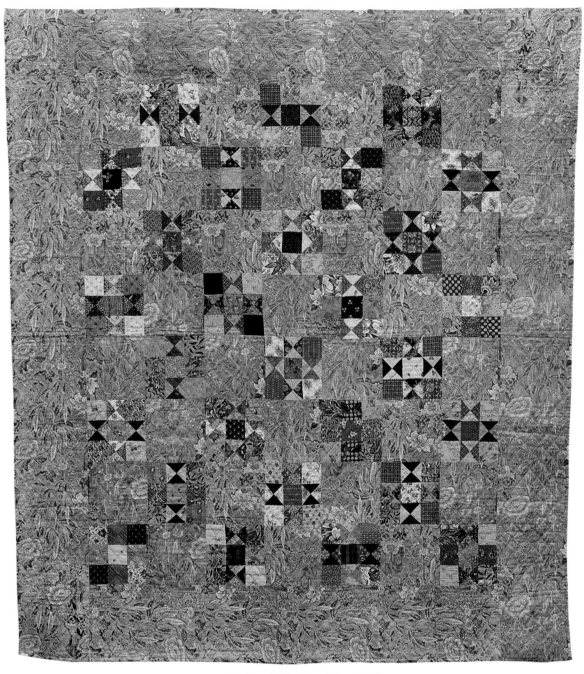

Full view of Nine Patch Star Quilt

Quilt: TULIP (II-21)

Category: Pieced
Size: 62" x 68"
Date: Mid (1870–1890)
Maker: Elizabeth Jones Fox (19 February 1824–26 April 1901)
Migration: Warwick, England, to Utah
Place Joined the Church: England
Year Crossed the Ocean: 1855
Ship: Samuel Curling
Year Crossed the Plains: 1855
Company: Capt. Charles A. Harper 6th Company
Came: Started with husband and family
Company: Capt. Milo Andrus 8th Company
Arrived: October 24, 1855
Came: Arrived with this company after being found
County Where Settled: Salt Lake

At first glance, one wonders why this quilt was constructed the way it appears to have been. On careful examination, one can see that the lighter 5⅜" strip is the same pattern block as the rest of the quilt. The color has greatly faded from the green fabric, however, as a result of laundering or exposure to light. The fading suggests that it was made from a different quality of fabric or that the process of dying used in its construction was different. Since the green print has a more intricate design than had locally produced fabrics, it most likely is a commercially produced fabric from the East, while the light fabric was produced in Utah. It is important to note that the quiltmaker placed this different fabric on the edge of the quilt where it would not be as noticeable when placed on a bed.

The pieced flower blocks, each containing an appliquéd stem and

bud, are set on point, creating an interesting zigzag effect. This is further emphasized by the wide 5¼" sashing strips and the parallel quilting lines. This zigzag effect creates the visual illusion of extra length. The rows of blocks are placed so that the base of each row is oriented toward either side of the bed, three rows in each direction. The use of red in the small bud is unique; usually this piece would be a continuation of the green stem into the flower. Note the red pieced block at the top of the quilt, turned in a different direction. The binding is the white print on the two sides and the red fabric on the top and bottom.

The journey of Elizabeth Jones Fox is the study's most startling and unusual. It was recorded and shared by her family and is an honest description of what happened to some women. Traditionally we hear of either the single "Madonna of the Prairie" young woman blissfully riding in her wagon or else the Mormon Mother driving three yoke of oxen while holding her baby. Elizabeth Fox's experience, however, was probably much more common than generally realized. It was one of a

Detail of edge showing different fabrics

Elizabeth Jones Fox

variety that caused the Church to change their migration structure from a one- to a two-stage process.

Elizabeth Jones Fox was born in Birmingham, Warwick, England, to William and Maria Reid Jones. She married George Selman Fox in 1842 in England. George, Elizabeth, and their five children joined the 581 converts leaving Liverpool on April 22, 1855. Soon after their departure, the ship's passengers were hit by measles and whooping cough. The two youngest Fox children, George and Charlotte, died and were buried at sea. Later, Elizabeth gave birth to a son named Sanders Curling. They named him in honor of the ship's captain, whose name was Sanders, and for the vessel on which they sailed.

Elizabeth did not recover successfully during the six-week journey to St. Louis nor during the extra six-week layover they took for her to regain her strength. Forced to move on, they traveled by flatboat up the Missouri River to Mormon Grove, west of present Atchison, Kansas, to join a westering company. There she became worse, developing "milk

Full view of Tulip Quilt

fever" and losing her nourishment for her young baby. Slowly, he died from starvation and was buried at Mormon Grove.

On the continuing journey west, Elizabeth became delirious and confused. She had to be watched day and night. She seemed to think they had forgotten the baby, and she would try to go back for it. One night, after crossing the Green River in Wyoming, her exhausted husband fell asleep and she left the camp unnoticed. Alarmed and concerned, the company spent two precious days searching for her before limited food and water supplies forced them to move on.

The next company over the route was a freight wagon train of non-Mormons. They found Elizabeth on the opposite side of the river, "eating wild berries and in control of her senses." She told them how she had become separated from her company. They took her to Ft. Bridger, where she stayed to regain her strength. When she was able, a Mormon company took her to Salt Lake City, where she rejoined her family.[67]

After their reunion, the family was asked to take the responsibility for managing one of the Church farms. Later, they purchased their own home near Murray. They may have pioneered again because records show that they lived inside Union Fort. A fort was usually the first living situation when pioneering a new area.[68] Elizabeth Jones Fox died in Jefferson County, Idaho.

PART THREE

1856–1869 WELCOMING THE FAITHFUL

"An emigrant train had just come in, and the bishops had to put six hundred persons in the way of growing their cabbages and building their homes. One bishop said he could take five bricklayers, another two carpenters, a third a tinman, a fourth seven or eight farm-servants, and so on through the whole bench. In a few minutes I saw that two hundred of these poor emigrants had been placed in the way of earning their daily bread."— William Hepworth Dixon, "gentile" observer, 1867[1]

detail from Reunion of the Saints *by C. C. A. Christensen*

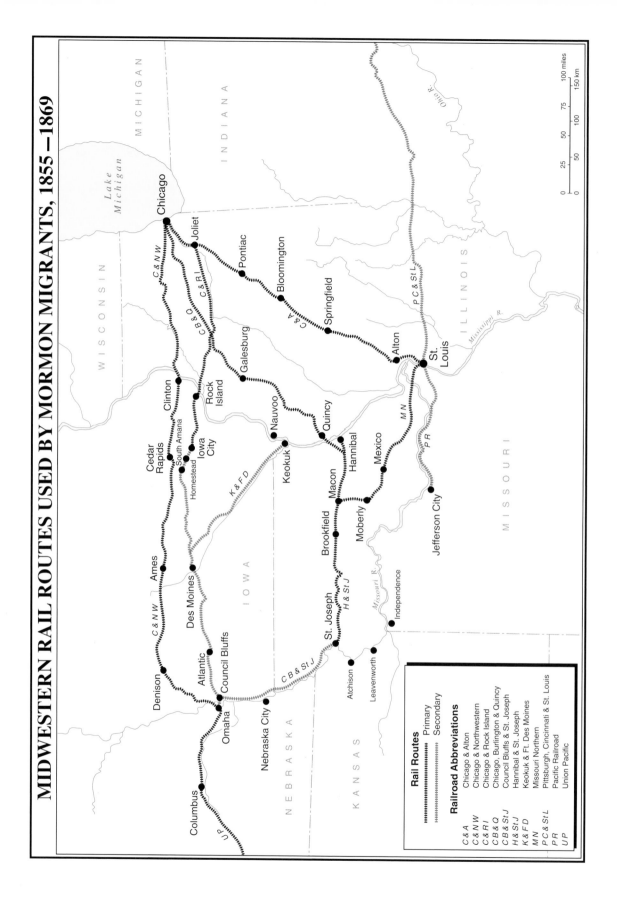

MIDWESTERN RAIL ROUTES USED BY MORMON MIGRANTS, 1855–1869

MICHIGAN

Lake Michigan

WISCONSIN

MICHIGAN

INDIANA

ILLINOIS

IOWA

MISSOURI

NEBRASKA

KANSAS

Mississippi R.

Missouri R.

Ohio R.

Chicago

Joliet

Pontiac

Bloomington

Springfield

Alton

St. Louis

Clinton

Cedar Rapids

South Amana

Homestead

Iowa City

Rock Island

Galesburg

Nauvoo

Keokuk

Quincy

Hannibal

Mexico

Macon

Moberly

Brookfield

Jefferson City

Independence

St. Joseph

Ames

Denison

Atlantic

Des Moines

Council Bluffs

Omaha

Nebraska City

Atchison

Leavenworth

Columbus

C & N W

C B & Q

C & R I

C & A

P C & St L

M N

P R

K & F D

H & St J

C B & St J

U P

0   25   50   75   100 miles
0   50   100   150 km

Rail Routes

Primary

Secondary

Railroad Abbreviations

C & A   Chicago & Alton
C & N W   Chicago & Northwestern
C & R I   Chicago & Rock Island
C B & Q   Chicago, Burlington & Quincy
C B & St J   Council Bluffs & St. Joseph
H & St J   Hannibal & St. Joseph
K & F D   Keokuk & Ft. Des Moines
M N   Missouri Northern
P C & St L   Pittsburgh, Cincinnati & St. Louis
P R   Pacific Railroad
U P   Union Pacific

1856–1869 WELCOMING THE FAITHFUL

THE MIGRATION

DURING THE PERIOD FROM 1856 TO 1869—
Described as a time of "welcoming the faithful"—the Church leaders continued to focus on bringing in new converts from abroad. In addition, they had to develop new colonization plans for the original pioneers and their second generations. The primary need was to conquer the arid land for farming and to work in economic self-sufficient isolation, free from persecution by federal authorities. For many quiltmakers, this time was reminiscent of their pioneering experiences of "seeking the place."

On the international level, the Church was continuing to expand and grow. Its gospel message, disseminated through such communications as the 1853 Church's Ninth Epistle, was reaching beyond the friends and families of the Saints' acquaintances to a more general audience. The new converts were zealous, skilled craftsmen eager to reach Zion, but they were of more limited financial means than earlier converts. Their need for inexpensive forms of transportation from the end of the railroad lines to the Salt Lake Valley led to the experiments with handcarts between 1856 and 1860 and the down-and-back Church trains between 1861 and 1868.

The converts needed to have the Church, as promised, assist them financially in making the transition to Zion. They also needed to have employment opportunities available in Utah so that they could produce needed food, clothing, and shelter. Unfortunately, these needs coincided with a time of increased tension and pressure on the Church in the United States.

Opportunities for building the Mormon economy were slow and costly to develop. Agriculture required taming the land for cultivation and channeling water for irrigation. Production of marketable products required raw materials, equipment, and access to markets. All were difficult to obtain in an isolated pioneering economy. The Church had limited financial resources for

> "Brethren, come home as fast as possible, bringing your poor, your silver, your gold, and everything that will beautify and ennoble Zion, and establish the House of the Lord, not forgetting the seeds of all choice trees, and fruits, and grains, and useful productions of all the earth, and labor saving machinery; keeping yourselves unspotted from the world by the way side."
>
> *Church's Ninth Epistle issued in April 1853[2]*

European city

105

Handcarts

"When we were in Iowa Camp Ground [present-day Coralville, Iowa], there came up a thunder storm that blew down our shelter made with handcarts and some quilts."
Mary Gobel Pay, Handcart Pioneer of 1856 [3]

Handcarts

The handcart mode of transportation was an experiment in transferring a large number of people in a very economical manner with only a few supply wagons pulled by a few animals. The lightweight, inexpensive carts were six to seven feet long and five feet wide. The width enabled them to fit in a wagon track. The shaft on the front extended two to three feet forward with a crossbar on the end. The puller would stand behind the crossbar and push on it in order to move the cart forward. The pusher would apply strength while walking behind the cart. The carts weighed between fifteen and sixty pounds depending on the builder and the materials used. Oak and hickory, the natural woods available in the eastern Iowa area, were used because of their strength and durability.

Only ten companies used handcarts between 1856 and 1860; there were no companies going west in 1858. Of the ten, eight were successful in reaching Zion. The Willie and Martin companies in 1856 experienced a series of problems resulting from poor planning, poor execution, poor health, and bad weather. Poor communication contributed to many of the difficulties. The organizers were unable to correspond swiftly with one another. In addition, the company leaders and immigrants did not know or understand each other's languages.

When the Church leaders announced that the plan to use handcarts would be implemented during the 1856 migration season, everyone enthusiastically endorsed the idea. The promotional pitch used with hopeful converts was that if they believed God and Brigham Young would work in their best interest to get them to Zion, then their faith would pull them through while their bodies pulled the carts. Unfortunately, their physical bodies were not prepared for the challenge of walking twelve to twenty-five miles each day. The hunger, thirst, sore feet, body fatigue, and drudgery of the mundane activity took their toll. "Probably more deaths resulted from privation combined with exhaustion than from actual disease among the handcart people."[4] They faced food shortages when the supply stations that were supposed to restock their meager supplies were shut down. In addition, because of weight limitations, fewer handcarters carried guns and therefore were unable to hunt. When supplies ran low, there was often less than one pint of flour per adult per day.[5]

Dock at Plymouth, 1863

operating all their programs, including the Perpetual Emigrating Fund. Yet many of the new converts could afford only the first stage of crossing the ocean. Needing additional money to fund the migration's second stage, migrants had three choices. First, they could remain where they were until situations improved. Yet often as new members of local Mormon wards, they experienced resentment and isolation from former friends and family.

Second, they could make the first stage of the immigration to America and settle temporarily in an interim location in the eastern states. Often, this choice led to the difficulty of being in an unknown location without assistance while suffering through extreme tragedies. While most Saints journeyed, as recommended in the guide materials, as far as St. Louis—and later Chicago; Iowa City; or Florence, Nebraska—some could not go that far.

The third option was to try to go all the way to Utah. This choice caused strains on resources and led to unfortunate incidents, as reported by quiltmakers who traveled by handcarts.

Meanwhile, a crisis on the territory's home front came to a head in 1857 with the arrival of federal troops, known as John-

The Handcart Company *by C. C. A. Christensen*

ston's Army, and the impending possibility of the Utah War. Misunderstandings about each other's activities in the West had arisen between the Mormons and the nation's leaders. The non-combative military action that followed significantly affected everyone's lives. All migrating women had to remain in crowded conditions in eastern urban cities or in temporary quarters in the Midwest. Women in the West had to return to camping in wagon boxes and tents at safe locations within Utah for safety. When Brigham Young issued a call to everyone to gather together or return to Utah, it effectively ended one era of church migration.

Construction was halted on the network of Mormon Trail stations that were being planned, built, and staffed throughout the West from the Missouri River to the Pacific Ocean. Immigrants en route to Utah were forced to remain in their temporary locations. As a result, in 1858, there were only about 179 emigrants coming from three chartered ships from Liverpool to New York and only about 150 of those traveled in three organized wagon companies from Iowa City to Salt Lake City.

When the conflict was resolved three years later and migration resumed actively, many of those who had been waiting in the

East now made their move. Reports for 1861 show more than 3,900 migrants passing through Florence, Nebraska. Of this number, 1,000 had been organized in the eastern states and 1,900 in Europe; 1,000 more had gathered in Florence on their own. About 1,700 people traveled west on the Church trains. The remainder purchased their own wagons and teams and were assigned to one of the independent companies being led by an experienced captain.[7]

These figures represent the large numbers of people who had been waiting to migrate until relations with the federal government had improved in Utah. They were eager to leave the States because of the increasing threat of a civil war and because of increasing political and social pressure on Mormons to end their practice of polygamy.

The Church had a new transportation system that was both unique and efficient: "down-and-back" or Church trains. This was a transportation plan developed by Brigham Young. It was an alternative low-cost system designed to bring across the Plains those who could not afford the cost of a wagon and team. The Church sent wagons with hired drivers called "Utah boys" and four yoke of oxen each and additional loose stock that could be sold to individuals who were seeking to outfit themselves for the westward journey. Supplies and provisions of flour and meat were deposited at waystations for restocking their companies on their return journey with immigrants. Other extra products that would have a market in the States would also be sent eastward. Young appealed to the Church wards or groups to each contribute one or more well-equipped wagon with two yoke of oxen and drivers. After the first such trains returned to Utah in 1861, the wagons and teams went back to their owners. The Church trains continued to operate until the completion of the transcontinental railroad in 1869.

> "We now contemplate trying another plan. If we can go with our teams to the Missouri River and back in one season and bring the poor, their provisions, etc, it will save about half the cash we now expend bringing the Saints to this point from Europe. It now costs, in case, nearly as much as their teams, wagons, handcarts, cooking utensils, provisions, etc, for their journey across the plains as it does to transport them to the frontiers. We can raise cattle without an outlay of money and use them in transporting the Saints from the frontiers and such freight as we may require."
>
> *Brigham Young,*
> *October 6, 1860*[8]

> "Every Saint who reached Florence, and desired to go home this season, has had the privilege. The sending down of wagons from Utah to Florence is a grand scheme."
>
> *Message sent to Brigham Young,*
> *July 1861*[9]

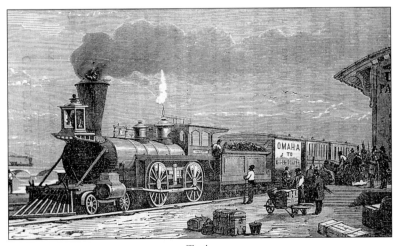

Train

Conquest of Dixie

The colonization of the southwestern Utah area known as Dixie was characteristic of the Great Colonizer Brigham Young's plan to meet the needs of the rapidly growing population. The Mormons needed to become self-sufficient in light of increasing conflicts outside the territory. They needed to have sites for settling new colonies. And they needed a Temple outside of Salt Lake City, offering easier access to the people living in southwestern Utah.

Young began the conquest of Dixie by exploring the possibilities of raising cotton in the semi-tropical climate. At the April 1857 Church conference, twenty-eight newly arrived converts from Texas and the cotton-raising area of the South were called to go to the Dixie area of Washington County.

With the advent of the Civil War in 1861, Brigham Young again saw the opportunity to develop the cotton industry. He had an eye on the eastern markets whose cotton supply from the South would be cut off by the impending war. This time, he issued a call for families to go to Dixie to develop the cotton industry and its necessary support system. For this new agricultural area, the plan was to build a larger town around which the smaller towns already established could centralize.[10]

St. George Temple, built to serve the colonies in Dixie

THE COLONIZATION AND SETTLEMENT IN THE 1860s

Mormon trail encampment

After the military withdrew from Utah in 1860 at the beginning of the Civil War, Brigham Young began in earnest to develop a sound economic plan. It was based on colonizing permanent settlements throughout the congressionally approved Utah Territory according to the existence of natural resources. The cotton and sugar beet industries were established in southern Utah's Dixie area. In its worldwide recruiting and proselytizing efforts, the Church sought those people who were willing to migrate for enhanced opportunities to less populated areas, milder climates, and better agricultural lands. It desired migrants with skills and talents necessary for establishing and securing the group's economic future.

A primary need in these years was to identify water sources in areas in which the Saints could claim the water rights and prevent other settlers from coming in. Harnessing and controlling the water's flow would create viable agricultural land for providing food and clothing. They had learned the necessity of claiming water rights from their previous settlement experiences across the country.

THE WOMEN

The women who came during this third period reflect the vast changes in the migration plans. All were committed to doing what was requested by church leaders, especially Brigham Young. They remained faithful in their goal of gathering in spite of the extended periods of time and the external factors of political disputes, war, and disease. Responsive though they were to Church policy, a number of women made critical decisions affecting their lives in partnership with their husbands or among themselves.

During the entire period of Mormon migrations from 1830 to 1900, the most appropriate and accurate image of a migrating female Saint was that of a woman holding her baby and driving a wagon pulled by multiple yokes of animals. But during the period of 1856 to 1869 the popularly held image of the Mormon pioneer woman pushing her handcart across the Plains with her children by her side eventually evolved to the more appropriate one of a woman riding or walking with a Church train, on which she had purchased passage, and resting at equipped way stations.

"Yet as a company they were meek, they bowed to God's will, trusting His promises, somewhere up or down the line good spirits would break out in song, a foolish marching song that had grown up among them spontaneously, and it would spread until it took them all raggedly in, out of time like the music of a long parade.

For some must push and some must pull
As we go marching up the hill,
As we merrily on the way we go
Until we reach the Valley, oh.
She didn't like the hymn, 'Come, Come Ye Saints.' It brought unhappy memories . . . of the trip across the plains. . . . They sang 'All is Well, All is Well' while people were sick and dying."

Helen Timmons Skidmore, granddaughter of Annie Brighton Thornley, Handcart Pioneer of 1857[11]

Come, Come, Ye Saints

Throughout the migrations, "Come, Come, Ye Saints" provided a source of encouragement and unity among the pioneers with its words of courage and faith. It was first published in the Church hymnal in 1851. The different stanzas gave reasons for the challenges and hardships they faced yet reassured them of the strength of their faith with a promise of the victory in the West. Based on their memories, as revealed in their histories, pioneer Saints responded either tearfully or joyfully to the words. Today, it is commonly known as the Mormon marching song and has continued through its history to be one of the most quoted hymns; it is sung by Mormons and non-Mormons around the world.

William Clayton's migration contributions were significant in their diversity. As a problem solver and inventive thinker, he designed the roadometer to record the mileage covered during the journey. As a writer and recorder, he compiled the guidebook used by many travelers across the Plains before 1869. These were both important tools for reassuring the slow moving companies. As a talented musician and composer, he wrote these words of celebration upon receiving word that his wife Diantha, left behind in Nauvoo, had given birth successfully to a son, Moroni, in April 1846.

Words: William Clayton (17 July 1814–28 February 1877), Locust Creek, Iowa, 1846
*Music: English tune "All Is Well"*12

THE QUILTS

Most of the quilts in this section suggest that these women had flexible time that they could dedicate to quiltmaking. By this period, many women in Utah were living in one location for the duration of their lives. Quilting, therefore, became more of a shared activity as women exchanged pattern designs or hand-quilted their tops together. Individuals could also make labor-intensive masterpieces with intricate piecing and appliquéing and multiple rows of quilting. There is one quilt here marking a period of inactivity in the maker's life after she had suffered through one of the most difficult migrations, that of the 1856 Martin Handcart Company, and before she participated in the difficult migration through the Hole-in-the-Rock in 1879. Betsy Williamson Smith pieced her intricate Star Quilt during a period of invalidism, possibly pregnancy, in the early 1870s (Quilt III-3).

Handcarts across Iowa

Several quilts were made of fabrics and patterns brought from regions outside the Intermountain West after 1890. This indicates the eagerness of these women to be current in their design choices and to use the materials that they had previously been encouraged to boycott.

There are two treasured heirlooms from women's childhood brought with families from abroad. Both these examples were left unfinished, emphasizing their value as visual records of individuals' experiences.

The last four quilts in the section, made by women who shared the commonality of the consistent journeying from Europe to Utah during the 1860s by steamship and down-and-back train, illustrate the uniqueness of this study's quilts and women. The quilts reflect the change in style in the one hundred years between 1825 and 1925. The women reflect the individual backgrounds and experiences that shaped each life.

Looking down the "Hole,"
Hole-in-the-Rock Trek

Quilt: VICTORY (III-1)

Category: Pieced

Size: 74" x 88"

Date: Mid (1860–1870)

Maker: Dorinda Melissa Moody Salmon Goheen Slade (15 January 1808–21 November 1895)

Migration: Iredell County, North Carolina, to Utah

Place Joined the Church: Texas

Year Crossed the Ocean: ————

Ship: ————

Year Crossed the Plains: Started in 1853

Company: Preston Thomas Company

Arrived: September 17, 1856

Came: With third husband and families

County Where Settled: Washington

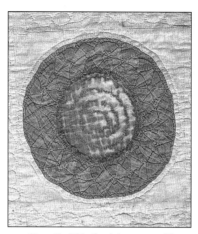

Detail of block with sun motif

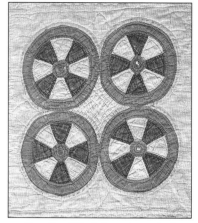

Details of block featuring wheels

This quilt and the next, made by the same woman, are presented separately because they represent different stages in this woman's migration. My interpretation of the quilts and the woman's personal journey suggests a different meaning of the name Victory from that presented by others.

The family's interpretation of the name is as follows: "As Dorinda was quilting on the quilt, word came over the telegraph that Abraham Lincoln was elected President of the United States. Happy with the news, she named her quilt, 'The Victory Quilt'."[13]

This interpretation that the quilt-maker was celebrating the victory of a Republican who sought to eliminate slavery seems to conflict with her family's political and social experience as Southerners, slaveholders, and Saints.* Her own family had benefited economically over the years from owning slaves.

An alternative interpretation would be that the quilt refers to her personal achievement of "gathering in Zion." Her journey marked a period of transition, both mentally and physically, as she demonstrated a steadfast commitment to accomplish her religious and educational goals, to accept her personal life tragedies, and to alter her migration plans by accepting the journey's long layover and added responsibilities.[14]

Two clues that the quilt celebrates her migration appear in each of the twelve 15" pieced blocks. There she made four 6½" circles that look like wagon wheels. In the center of each is Dorinda's signature mark for many of her quilts, a small appliquéd stuffed circle.[15]

At the sashing intersections, there are 7" circles reminiscent of the popular Noonday or Sunburst quilt pattern. This design traditionally symbolizes the importance of sunlight in the lives of pioneering people. For Dorinda, the sun is a common theme: it appears in at least four of her quilts.

The faded green of the 4½"-wide border confirms that Dorinda used indigo grown in southwestern Utah for the blue color. She then overdyed the blue with a yellow made from cedar berries.

The quilting stitches repeat the lines of each piece. The 8" sashing pieces have an original pattern of a central flower, feathered plumes, and a chained edging. The circles in the

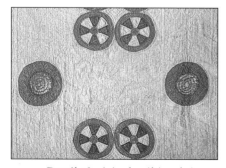

Detail of original quilting design

*A conversation with Church historian Glenn Leonard and a background article by George U. Hubbard from the *Utah Historical Quarterly* entitled "Abraham Lincoln as Seen by the Mormons" provided the following interpretation:

At first in 1861, the Saints disliked Lincoln because his Republican party sought to eliminate the "twin relics of barbarism"—slavery and polygamy—while the Democrats were more open to independence in choosing a lifestyle. Brigham Young and other leaders went on record as strongly opposed to Lincoln. But their attitude toward Lincoln changed over time, beginning when he asked the Mormon militia, the Nauvoo Legion, to help protect the overland mail and telegraph lines against hostile Indians.

The turning point for Mormons came in 1863 when they appealed to Lincoln to oust the oppressing federal officials. His response did not give favors or privileges but revealed a frame of mind that gave hope to the Mormons that they would be free to worship God as they sought. This won the Mormons' respect and appreciation for Lincoln. They saw him as a man who would deal with them justly and impartially.

Full view of Victory Quilt

Dorinda Melissa Moody

intersections each have eight lines of quilting that complete the design. The cheddar-yellow binding is applied by sewing machine.

Dorinda Moody Slade's life and migration journey are described in greater depth in Carolyn Davis's book *Pioneer Quiltmaker*.[16] Dorinda Melissa Moody Slade was born the daughter of John Wyatt and Mary "Polly" Baldwin Moody in Iredell County, North Carolina. As the eldest child, she assumed the responsibility of caring for the younger children and doing household tasks while her mother worked in the fields. This early training would serve her well as she successfully established her own family through two marriages and a migration to Texas. The year 1850 marked a turning point in her life: her only son and her second husband both died, and she and her extended family joined the Mormon Church.

Together this close and supportive family made plans to migrate to Zion. Her brothers took their families and mother up to Iowa by way of the Mississippi River steamboats and then overland to Salt Lake City. Since Dorinda planned to take a herd of Texas longhorns and other livestock, her appropriate choice was an overland route.

In early 1853, as she was making final preparations, she learned her neighbor William Rufous Slade, a recent widower with eight children, was also planning to migrate. The two combined their efforts by marrying on February 20.

As their wagon train headed northwest, illness struck and many in their company died, including some of their family. As a result of this loss, the leaders decided to take refuge in an abandoned army fort in the Cherokee Nation. The location appears to have been near Tahlequah, the capitol of the Cherokee Nation in eastern Oklahoma near the Illinois River.[17] Recent research identifies this location as the staging point of the first migrations over a new route to the gold fields in 1849 and 1850. It was called the Cherokee Trail.[18]

Although the stay was supposed to be temporary, the Slades were there almost three years. The group was organized into the Cherokee Branch under William Slade's leadership, which may partly explain why they remained when others moved on. During this time, Dorinda did unpack her quilting frames and make a quilt in the Rising Sun pattern for Melissa Meeks, a young woman traveling with the group.[19]

Until now, it has been thought that they began their journey in Texas in 1853 and traveled overland through the Cherokee Nation, following the Santa Fe Trail to the Old Spanish Trail, and then headed northwestward to Salt Lake, arriving in September 1856.[20] However, the Old Spanish Trail across southwestern Colorado and southeastern Utah was extremely difficult, if not impossible for wagons to use. This trail was described by Mormon historian Leroy Hafen as "the longest, crookedest, most arduous pack mule route in the history of America."[21] The new research would suggest that they followed the Cherokee Trail along the divide between the Verdigris and Caney Rivers in a northwest direction to join the Santa Fe Trail near McPherson, Kansas. They then headed west to Bent's Fort, again took the Cherokee Trail north along the eastern front of the Rocky Mountains to Ft. Bridger, and then went to Salt Lake by the usual overland trail.[22]

Soon after their arrival, they were called to join the Cotton Mission to develop that industry in southwestern Utah's Dixie. Her life story continues with the next quilt.

Quilt: SUNRISE IN THE PINES
  (III-1a)

Category: Pieced
Size: 85½" x 101½"
Date: Mid (1870–1890)
Maker: Dorinda Melissa Moody
  Salmon Goheen Slade (1808–95)

This is a continuation of Dorinda Slade's story. In 1857, her family was one of the twenty-eight sent to Utah's Dixie to experiment in raising cotton. This was known as the Cotton Mission. This was the earliest settlement there and presented particularly great challenges. The group faced the extremes of heat, drought, bad water, and malaria. But they proved that cotton could be raised, as well as sugar cane and other semi-tropical plants. Fortunately for the Slades, the Church asked them to move again in 1858 to Pine Valley, at a higher elevation, where William was employed as a freighter hauling lumber from the mills. This was the

final move for Dorinda, who was forty-nine at the time. Here she lived with a full zest for life in spite of the many setbacks early in her life.

This second quilt, in comparison to her Victory quilt, marks a period of stability in her life. Like those of most quilters, Dorinda Slade's technical and artistic skills increased over time as her quilts became more elaborate, as her other family responsibilities and ranch tasks decreased, and as her home became permanent. The complexity of this quilt is shown by its more than thirty-four hundred pieces. There are twenty-five pieced triangles in each corner of the twelve finished 16" blocks; on each side of the finished sashing strips; and for the sun in each of the intersecting squares.

The well-planned and balanced design reveals Dorinda's artistic growth. The visually strong pieced borders surround the quilt on three sides of the quilt, creating almost a complete frame. The lack of a border along the quilt's base probably indicates that it was made to use on a footed bed.

The quilting designs are carefully placed. In the many sections of trian-

gles, a single row of stitching in the white piece repeats the template shape. A trefoil or three-leaf pattern is quilted in the red corner pieces. Other designs drawn from nature are quilted in the green sashing strips and white centers of each block. A red binding surrounds the quilt.

According to family history, Dorinda spun, wove, and dyed the fabric for this quilt. This account is probably accurate considering her personal prior connection with the cloth production industry in Alabama and Texas, the 1857 call to the Slades to participate in the mission to introduce cotton raising there, the Church's economic goal to be totally self-sufficient, and the relative isolation of her Pine Valley home from the more urban Salt Lake City.[23] In addition, her daughter Eliza Goheen Lloyd was actively involved in the production of cotton cloth. She owned a small spinning wheel and a company loom and used corn cobs for spindles and reed cane for bobbins.[24]

This particular pattern variation, as well as its name, has been identified as an original by quilt historian Barbara Brackman in the *Encyclopedia*

Detail of Slade Quilt

Detail of Bracken Quilt

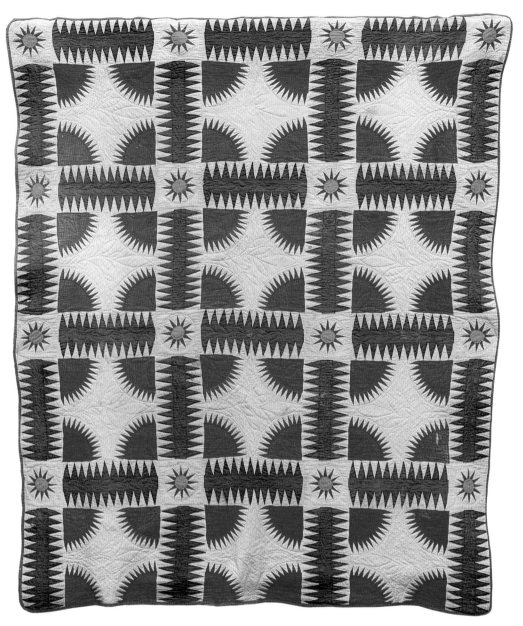

Full view of Sunrise in the Pines Quilt by Dorinda Melissa Moody
Salmon Goheen Slade

of Pieced Quilt Patterns.[25] New York
Beauty is the generic name for this
pattern, as copyrighted by Stearns
and Foster in 1930.

A rewarding discovery was a second Sunrise in the Pines quilt made
by Pine Valley neighbors Sarah

Alzada Bracken Day and possibly her
mother Sarah Head Bracken. It is
included as a confirmation of the
bonds of kinship and friendship
among Mormon women. A comparison of the transparencies for these
quilts shows that they match, thus

confirming that these quilters shared
patterns.[26] For many years, "Sister
Slade's trunk" held Dorinda's collection of quilt blocks. She used these
for pattern references while she led
the Relief Society quiltings in the
Pine Valley Chapel.[27]

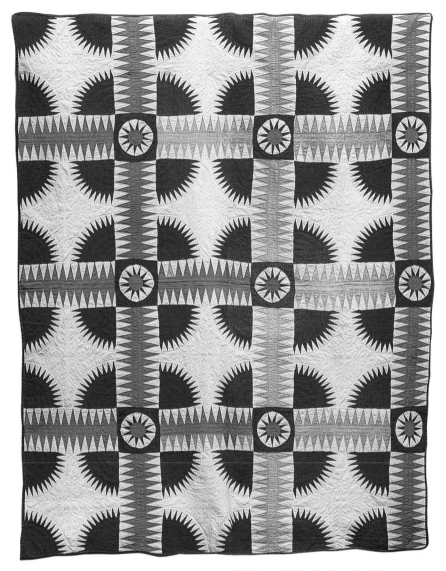

*Full view of Sunrise in the Pines Quilt by Sarah Alzada Bracken Day
and her mother*

Quilt: SUNRISE IN THE PINES
(III-2)

Category: Pieced
Size: 70" x 86¼"
Date: Mid (1870–1890)
Makers: Sarah Alzada Bracken Day
(18 April 1860–18 June 1943)
Sarah Head Bracken (27 February
1817–4 July 1901)

There are two differences between this quilt and Dorinda Slade's Sunrise in the Pines quilt. Whereas Dorinda used the green pieced sashing strips to balance the design, Sarah Alzada placed the sashing strip on only one side. This probably indicates that the quilt's width was her more important consideration. On the other hand, this quilt has significantly more quilt-ing than Dorinda's. The quilting is in double and single rows on either side of the seam created by the piecing in all the triangles. There is also a floral design quilted in the white blocks. The number of stitches per inch varies from ten to eleven. The exten-sive amount of work may suggest that it was the work of more than one person.

Detail of blocks showing different visual effects created by varying fabric placement

Quilt: STAR (III-3)

Category: Pieced
Size: 76" x 86"
Date: Mid (1870–1880)
Maker: Betsy Williamson Smith
   (13 January 1853–28 March 1925)
Migration: Lancashire, England, to
   Colorado
Place Joined the Church: England
Year Crossed the Ocean: 1856
Ship: Horizon
Year Crossed the Plains: 1856
Company: Capt. Edward Martin
   Handcart Company
Arrived: November 30, 1856
Came: With her mother and five
   brothers and sisters
County Where Settled: Iron; San Juan
   and Conejos Counties, Colorado;
   Madison County, Idaho; Conejos
   County, Colorado

This quilt's unique attraction is the piecing and placement of the diamond stars. It is a labor-intensive quilt made by a woman who was often in poor health but who could create effective designs through the use of color. There are 3,980 1½" lozenges in the quilt. Note the different visual effects created by varying the placement of the same fabrics within each star.

To complete the top and square the quilt, the maker split a number of blocks and placed them along three of the edges. The blocks are set on point with the 5¼" green zigzag sashing. The combination of pink and green was popular in quilts of the last quar-

ter of the nineteenth century. The strong contrast in color further enhances the visual length of the quilt.[29]

Betsy Williamson Smith was born the youngest child of James and Ann Aldred Williamson in Lancaster, England. During her life, she was part of two of the most difficult migrations in Mormon history, the Edward Martin Handcart Company and the Hole-in-the-Rock settlement trek. Her father left England for Utah in 1854 to find work and a home. Her mother and the six children followed in 1856. They were members of the ill-fated handcart company that left Iowa City in late July and did not arrive in Salt Lake until November 30. The Church agents in Iowa City had worked to equip three earlier companies of pioneers. But they had not expected such a large company of late arrivals. They frantically worked to supply an additional 146 carts needed to assist 576 people on their journey west. Unfortunately, the hastily made carts broke down, causing losses of precious time for the already weak and hungry group of people. Leaving Iowa late meant they were caught in early snowstorms. Struggling to continue their journey in spite of decreasing supplies and having lost a quarter of their number, the group was finally rescued on Oc-

tober 28, seven hundred miles from Salt Lake. Fortunately, all of the Williamsons survived, including three-year-old Betsy. They were met by their father and taken to their new home in the town of Paragoonah in southern Utah.

In 1873, Betsy married Silas Sanford Smith Jr., a man destined to become one of the remarkable leaders in the settling of the Mormon West. They resided in Paragoonah where their first two children were born.

In 1879, Silas was called to lead one of the last organized colonizing missions in an attempt to settle an unexplored, inhospitable part of the Southwest. Betsy accompanied him

"Betsy walked part of the way. She rode on the Cart sometimes and her brothers and sisters carried her, for she was just a little over three years."
    Arzella Knight Gylling,
       her granddaughter[28]

"There were thirty children in the company and early morning they were sent on ahead of the grownups all in one bunch. Some of them had very little clothing, but they all wore hats. They were driven along with willows and had to keep walking as long as they could. No use to cry or complain, but along during the day when it was hot they were allowed to rest and were given food. They were often two or three miles ahead of us. It was hard for the parents to see their little five and six-year-olds driven along like sheep."
       Theo Dedrickson Sr.[30]

Full view of Star Quilt

on the passage through the infamous Hole-in-the-Rock, considered to be the most difficult geological challenge of all migrations. Having successfully accomplished that journey, the family settled in Bluff, where he served as the first probate judge. He also served as the stake president for this colonization company, called the San Juan Mission.

In 1882, the family moved on to Manassa, Colorado, where Silas served eight years as leader of the San Luis Mission in Conejos County. Here their last four children were born. In 1906, they moved to Rexburg, Idaho, partly in hopes of finding a better climate for Betsy's weak health. In 1911, Silas died and was buried in Rexburg with two of their sons. Betsy returned to Colorado, where she died in 1925 and was buried in Manassa with her two oldest children.[31]

Detail of piecing and quilting

Quilt: FEATHERED STAR (III-4)

Category: Pieced
Size: 78" x 80"
Date: Late (1890–1910)
Maker: Eleanor Jones Young (16 November 1830–3 February 1912)
Migration: Carmarthen, Wales, to Utah
Place Joined the Church: Wales
Year Crossed the Ocean: 1856
Ship: Samuel Curling
Year Crossed the Plains: 1856
Company: Edmund Bunker 3rd Handcart Company
Arrived: October 2, 1856
Came: With her parents and family
County Where Settled: Tooele; Salt Lake; Uintah

This precisely executed quilt is a labor-intensive composition. Its maker was a woman whose life was organized and disciplined. Yet the quilt reveals her unique style. The center stars are pieced of the same fabrics yet vary in their color placement.

The quilting was planned and marked on a block-by-block basis. One can see this because the lines do not match at the seam lines. Across the pieced blocks are straight lines ½" apart radiating out from the center. In the solid-white squares is a section of gridwork surrounded by straight-line infill quilting.

The use of two fabric bindings is unique and shows the maker's continuing attention to detail in perfecting her workmanship.

Eleanor Jones Young, also called Ellen, was born the daughter of Thomas and Ruth Thomas Jones in Pantmour, Carmarthen, Wales. She joined the Mormon Church in 1849. The entire family of ten emigrated from Wales to Utah between April and October 1856. They sailed into Boston in late May and traveled in railroad boxcars to Iowa City, where they had to wait for their four allotted handcarts to be made. They carried one hundred pounds of flour, some bacon, tea, and seventeen pounds of clothing and bedding per person in each cart. Ellen and her sisters Ann, Elizabeth, and Mary, responsible for one cart, reportedly sang songs as they pulled and pushed. They arrived in Salt Lake in October as part of one of the most successful hand-cart companies, suffering fewer than seven deaths.

As with much of the migration, Eleanor, at age twenty-six, was one of the many young, unmarried women. Brigham Young instructed men and insisted his younger brother Lorenzo take additional wives. So Lorenzo chose Eleanor to become his fourth wife. They were married on November 24, 1856, five weeks after she arrived. While Lorenzo and his first wife, Harriet, maintained a home in Salt Lake, he built a home with three apartments for his other wives in Tooele County. The home became the area's stage stop providing meals, overnight lodging, and fresh animals. As a plural wife unable to read or write, Eleanor adjusted to her position by developing her natural

---

"It was very common to see young girls between the age of 16 and 20 with a harness on their shoulders in the shape of a halter, small chain fastened to that, and then fastened to the cart."
Daniel Robinson[32]

Typical homes built in rural areas and early forts

Full view of Feathered Star Quilt

abilities for cooking and raising produce. The hired men and travelers benefited from her talents.

Later, she moved to Salt Lake when Lorenzo became the first Bishop of the Eighteenth Ward in Salt Lake. As his health declined, Ellen assisted him by hosting visitors, who often stayed for long periods of time. She seldom attended church, preferring instead to remain in her kitchen preparing meals for the large family and many visitors. She pre-

pared a feast for three hundred guests invited to double family weddings on November 27, 1879.

Later as a widow she moved to Vernal where her sons had settled, and she earned her living by managing her farm. Among other responsibilities, once a year she plucked the down from her ducks and made fluffy bed ticks and pillows.[33] She died there in 1912 and was buried in her eldest son Edward's family plot.

"Ellen was a natural born cook . . . and it is doubted that she could give anyone a receipt, for she could neither read or write."

*Muriel Colton Johnson,
her granddaughter*[34]

Utah Fort in Provo, "Brigham's shanties at Provo City,"
Harper's Weekly, October 9, 1858

Quilt: FINGER QUILT (III-5)

Category: Pieced and Appliquéd
Size: 72⅜" x 88"
Date: Early (1838)
Maker: Mary Greenwood Giles (24 March 1823–25 March 1913)
Migration: Lincolnshire, England, to Utah
Place Joined the Church: England
Year Crossed the Ocean: 1850
Ship: North Atlantic
Year Crossed the Plains: 1856
Company: Capt. Philemon C. Merrill
Arrived: August 13–20, 1856
Came: With husband and family
County Where Settled: Utah; Wasatch

The name "Finger Quilt" refers to the blue appliquéd strips, which always reminded viewers of a human hand.[35] According to documentation, it was made in 1838 in England, when Mary Greenwood Giles was fifteen. Since the quilt was made during a time before emigration began, it provides a benchmark for studying other quilts. The origin of the fabrics is English rather than American, and the style is an intricate composition that draws one's attention. Pieced block patterns were

Detail of pieced and appliquéd block and corner treatment

made in England in the early nineteenth century but were less common than medallion quilts.[36]

The pieced and curved diamond strips and appliquéd "finger" sections were constructed before the block was assembled. The center fabric is similar in appearance to the floral-trail prints described as being popular, and particularly suitable for women's dresses, in England from the late eighteenth century on.[37]

The color of the sashings used to set the blocks together changed from a "nice" green to blue when the donor washed the quilt for the first time.[38] This verifies that the maker used a two-step dye process of blue and yellow to achieve green. The vertical sashing runs the length of the blocks, indicating it was attached after the blocks were stitched in strips.

The appliquéd border shows the creative use of the square and diamond geometric templates to create the leaves and buds along the vine.

Mary Greenwood Giles was the daughter of George and Elizabeth Greenwood born in Owmby, Lincolnshire, England. She married George Giles on June 1, 1847, in Lincoln, England.

The Gileses' journey to Zion took place in two stages over six years. Theirs became the pattern of many

Saints coming from abroad with a strong commitment to reach Zion, yet lacking the funds necessary for completing the journey in one year. This need to generate additional funds in order to continue, as well as continuing to supply food, clothing, and shelter in the interim, became the typical experience of many foreign Saints. Most traveled from England by sailing ship and to mid-America by Mississippi River steamboat. Like the Gileses, most early migrants would travel northward toward Mormon settlements along the Mississippi River. The Gileses went to Burling-

Mary Greenwood Giles

Full view of "Finger Quilt"

ton, Iowa, where they could lay over with assistance from other Mormon families and missionaries. Two children were born to them there between 1852 and 1854.

Continuing west in 1856 to Salt Lake, they settled first in Provo, where two more children were born. They very likely were directed to Provo when they arrived as the Church tried to gather the Saints in a safe place south of Salt Lake City in anticipation of the arrival of Johnston's Army the following year.

Their last two children were born in Heber City in Wasatch County, where the Gileses resided the rest of their lives.

Quilt: NINE PATCH VARIATION
  (III-6)

Category: Pieced
Size: 72" x 90"
Date: Early (1840–1850)
Maker: Elizabeth Carter Flahrity
  Whitmore (11 February 1827–
  24 November 1892)
Migration: Morgan County,
  Alabama, to Utah
Place Joined the Church: Texas
Year Crossed the Ocean: ————
Ship: ————
Year Crossed the Plains: 1857
Company: Homer Duncan Company
Arrived: Between September 14 and
  September 20, 1857
Came: With husband and four small
  sons
County Where Settled: Salt Lake;
  Washington; Salt Lake

The set, or way the blocks are
arranged, of this Nine Patch quilt is
truly intriguing because of the placement of the early printed fabrics.
The brown was originally purple and
the pink was originally red.

The on-point set of the blocks and
the contrasting triangles of dark and
light fabrics create a strong direc-
tional flow from right to left. Yet the
effect of the fabric's fading is that
the viewer has difficulty identifying
whether the quiltmaker wanted her
design to read from left to right, as
would seem more natural, or from
right to left, as is currently more
strongly indicated. The blocks are
consistent in their piecing pattern of
squares and triangles but not in their
placement within the quilt. The effect is to capture the viewer's attention and interest as one attempts to
interpret the design.

The pieced triangle border, as it
appears, successfully frames the

quilt. The elbow pattern quilting
is in clusters of four curved lines
placed ¼" apart with an inch between the clusters.

———

Elizabeth Carter Flahrity Whitmore
was born the fourth child of Richard
and Elizabeth Lonas Carter in De-
catur, Morgan County, Alabama. Her
early life's experiences reflect a sense
of partnership yet a strength for self-
sufficiency. Her family moved to Texas
when the government offered free
land to settlers. They became successful cotton and cattle raisers through
hard work and dedication.

She continued this work during her
first marriage to a man named
Flahrity. Together they established a
successful four-hundred-acre farm on
Waxahachie Creek in Ellis County.
After his untimely death from yellow
fever, she managed the farm by herself
until her marriage to James Montgomery Whitmore, a druggist knowl-
edgeable in the care of animals.

The Whitmores were introduced
to the Mormon religion by missionaries in Texas. By opening their
home to these missionaries, they became social outcasts and soon de-

Elizabeth Carter Flahrity Whitmore

cided to leave their Texas ranch for
Utah. Theirs was a well-supplied
company with herds of cattle and
mule-pulled teams. Elizabeth drove
one of the light wagons.

Arriving in Salt Lake six weeks
ahead of Johnston's Army, James
Whitmore joined the effort to keep
them from advancing into the Valley
while Elizabeth worked behind the
lines to carry supplies to the men
through that winter.

While in Salt Lake City, James
became a partner and co-owner of the
pioneer mercantile company Staynes
and Needham. The company was
known for freighting merchandise between the Missouri River and Salt
Lake City and on to San Francisco.

The Whitmore family's knowledge
of raising cattle and cotton made
them one of those called to migrate
to southern Utah's Dixie for the
Cotton Mission of 1861–62. James
traded his share of the mercantile
business for Church livestock. The
family established a farm near St.
George to raise grapes, apples, and
peaches, and to run cattle on the
open range. In 1866, James was
attacked and killed by Indians while
he and a companion were herding

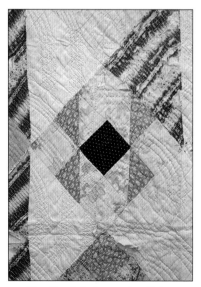

Details of piecing and quilting

Full view of Nine Patch variation

cattle near Pipe Springs in what is now Arizona.

As a widow with nine children under the age of twelve, Elizabeth demonstrated a keen ability to adapt by continuing to manage the farm for seventeen years. Utilizing her management and financial skills, she also served as a director of the Ladies Co-op in St. George during its existence between 1875 and 1880.[39]

In 1883, she returned to Salt Lake City where she resided until her death on November 24, 1892.[40]

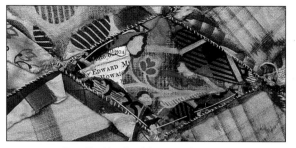

Detail of back with paper fragment

Quilt: PIECED DIAMONDS
    SEGMENT (III-7)

Category: Pieced
Size: 17½" x 17½"
Date: Early (1823)
Maker: Hannah Lawrence Rawlinson
    (22 February 1817–15 June 1865)
Migration: Essex, England, to
    California
Place Joined the Church: South Africa
Year Crossed the Pacific Ocean: 1857
Ship: Vaquera
Year Crossed the Plains: ———
Company: ———
Recorded: ———
Came: Husband and son brought
    quilt segment to Utah
County Where Settled: San Mateo,
    California

As a memento of early childhood, this section of pieced fabric lozenges or diamonds brings to life an unusual story of a family's migration and the memory of a young mother.

"Lozenge" is the term used to identify this shape in England, the maker's native country.[41] The 2¾" by 2" diamonds were pieced by Hannah in 1823 at the age of six while she lived in England. This documentation is confirmed by several factors. One is the lack of attention to detail and precision in template placement and precise piecing. Second, the fabrics were mounted on paper and whip-stitched by hand with dark and light threads in the style of traditional English piecing. Third, many diamonds feature the early polychrome roller-printed fabrics of the early 1800s. These fabrics feature a fine ground design and an overprint of green, blue, or red. Several of the prints are of the same design in different colors. Being able to make a variety of prints from the same engraved cylinder with different colors of ink was a revolutionary development made by the textile industry between 1810 and 1815.[42]

Hannah Lawrence Rawlinson was born the daughter of Thomas and Elizabeth Appleford Lawrence in West Ham, Essex, England. She married Charles Rawlinson on February 11, 1840. He was a talented carpenter who had been asked to carve the wooden banquet tables for Queen Victoria's coronation in 1837. As a young woman, Hannah was recognized as gentle, refined, and skilled in all kinds of artistic needlework.

They first learned of the Mormon Church while living in London. They did not join, answering instead the British government's call for people to go to South Africa to colonize the region in exchange for free passage. Five years later, in 1853, they again heard the Mormon missionaries preaching. They joined and decided to leave for Zion in Utah. But, like many Saints, they lacked the money for the journey, so they lived and worked along the way. They went first to Australia where they stayed for four years at Port Adelaide. Charles operated a sawmill and Hannah made their home available to the church elders.

In 1857, they sailed from Melbourne for San Francisco on the two-masted sailing ship *Vaquera*. The journey took two months with part of the time being spent in the Sandwich Islands awaiting ship repairs.

They settled in the Bay Area where Charles worked cutting timber for ship-building and tending a chicken ranch. Here Hannah suffered an accident in her buggy and died ten weeks later on June 15, 1865. She was buried in the Canada de Remondo cemetery in West Union.

Charles and their son, Charles Jr., left for Utah the following year, arriving in Salt Lake City on September 24, 1866. They brought with them this pieced treasure and other special mementos of Hannah's life, carefully tucked away in a small black box to preserve her memory.[43]

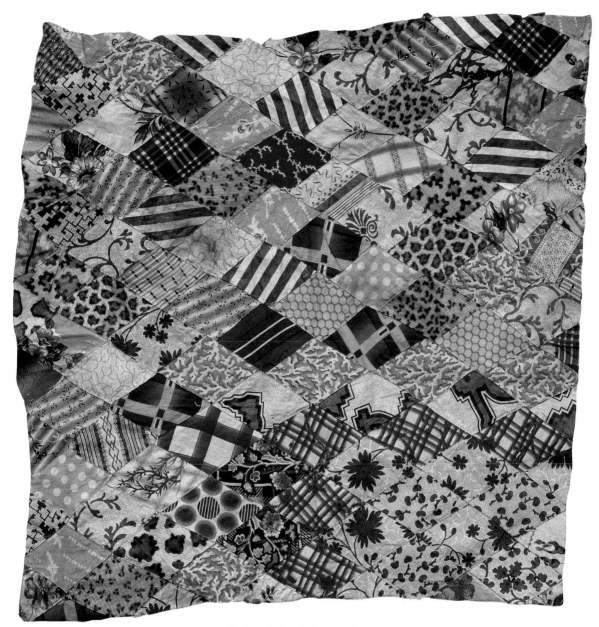

Full view of Pieced Diamonds segment

"Note: It was a deep love and an incurable sorrow in the heart of Charles Rawlinson for his lost girl-wife which prompted him to fold away and keep these pitifully inadequate mementos. Catherine, his second wife, respected that love and never showed jealousy over it, but cherished and protected the few keepsakes which have come down to us in the little black box, now in the possession of the Walter W. T. Rawlinson family. In that box also are a newspaper clipping of the christening of Charles William Hames Rawlinson, in the St. Stephens Lutheran Church in Cape Town, Cape Colony, and a bit of exquisite petit point representing a bouquet of violets, beautifully shaded and in stitches too tiny, almost, to see."

Jane Rawlinson Geertsen[44]

Quilt: OAK LEAF AND REEL
(III-8)

Category: Appliquéd
Size: 81" x 98"
Date: Early (1845–1855)
Owner: Sarah Dall Weech (21 April 1849–7 November 1939)
Migration: Cambridge, England, to Utah
Place Joined the Church: England
Year Crossed the Ocean: 1855
Ship: Chimboraza
Year Crossed the Plains: 1857
Company: No rosters available
Came: With parents and family
County Where Settled: Utah; Graham County, Arizona; Wallowa County, Oregon; Salt Lake; Graham County, Arizona

This traditional masterpiece-quality quilt was the Arizona Quilt Project's most historically significant find in the Safford area. The find confirms Mormon settlement in that southern region.

The hand-stitched quilt contains sixteen appliqué blocks and a continuous appliquéd vine in the border. The quilt contains three different green prints and a single solid-red cotton. In the nineteenth century, an oak leaf signified courage and strength.[45] In

quilt symbolism, an unbroken vine in a quilt's border could carry the meaning of a continuous life. Note the ease in identifying the beginning and end of the vine. There are many rows of fine hand quilting, each spaced one-half inch apart.

There are some discrepancies about this quilt and when it was made. It is doubtful that Sarah Dall Weech made the quilt around 1850. The dates and events of her life do not correspond with the time and talent required to produce such a labor-intensive quilt, even though she was quite resourceful and had a great sense of pride in her accomplishments.

A stronger possibility is that the quilt was a family treasure made or acquired during their journey. There is a report that the family received dress fabrics from the wife of the Mississippi employer of Sarah's father. This quilt may have been a gift from a woman who valued fabrics and needle skills.

Sarah Dall Weech was born the fifth child of Henry David and Rebecca Carrier Dall in St. Tanious-the-Less, Cambridge, England. They joined the Church while in England. They sailed for New Orleans in 1855. After landing, the family spent two years in Philadelphia, Mississippi, where her father found work and saved money to complete the journey.

Once they had arrived in Utah, the family settled in Pleasant Grove. Sarah's father traded those dress pieces they had received earlier for their first livestock of a milk cow, two pigs, and four sheep.

Typically Sarah was expected to help improve the land, harvest the crops, and fight the crickets and grasshoppers. When the bugs appeared, everyone worked to kill them by driving them into either water or fire.

On November 12, 1866, Sarah married Hyrum Weech and settled in Payson. Over the next twelve years, he worked as a teamster, miner,

Hyrum and Sarah Dall Weech

steelworker, and farmer to eke out a living for their family.

Tiring of the cold winters in Utah's high desert climate and hearing much about the Mormon settlements in Arizona, the family joined with the families of several of Sarah's brothers and sisters. In September 1879 they started the three-month journey south.

In Arizona, they faced rustlers, Indians, and Mexicans as well as invasions by snakes, centipedes, scorpions, and tarantulas. When Hyrum traveled back and forth to Tucson for supplies, Sarah was never sure if she would see him again. Establishing the area's first store at one end of their log house,

Detail of appliquéd block and quilting

Detail of corner treatment

Full view of Oak Leaf and Reel Quilt

she clerked and helped the area's women to "club together" to make purchases they could share. She also served as a Relief Society teacher for a number of years before being chosen president in March 1898.

The Weeches became the parents of fifteen children, two of whom died in infancy. Theirs also became a plural marriage when Hyrum took a second wife, Mary Taylor, in 1885.

After living in Arizona for twenty-four years, they decided in 1893 to move to the area near Elgin in northeastern Oregon, where Mormons were beginning to settle. Hyrum Weech, who had become frustrated over the amount and distribution of water in Arizona, said of Oregon: "The Lord made it rain enough there for both the just and unjust."[46] As leaders in this new settlement, Hyrum served as the local Church leader or bishop and Sarah as the first counselor in the Pine Grove Relief Society. During their eight-year stay, she wove carpets, drawing on her previous years of experience weaving cloth. She and her son John and daughter-in-law Myrtle wove nearly five hundred yards, including thirty for the church house's aisles.

The couple returned to live in Salt Lake City in 1911 and then moved to Pima, Arizona, in 1918 to be near family.

Quilt: WILD GEESE (III-9)

Category: Pieced
Size: 70" x 73"
Date: Mid (1860–1870)
Maker: Eliza Spencer Moses (15
    June 1813–15 December 1874)
Migration: Trumbull County, Ohio,
    to Utah
Place Joined the Church: Ohio
Year Crossed the Ocean: ———
Ship: ———
Year Crossed the Plains: 1861
Company: Thomas Woolley (probably)
Arrived: September 16, 1861
Came: With husband and extended
    family
County Where Settled: Salt Lake

This quilt's history reveals the impact that an influential and impressive leader can have on a young woman. According to the donor, a dress of the lilac fabric in the quilt was made by Eliza Moses for her seventeen-year-old daughter, Martha. When Martha, who was raised on the East Coast, arrived in isolated Utah and wore the dress, which was in the latest fashion, she was told it was inappropriate. Brigham Young admonished her that the dress was not modest enough. The sleeves were too short and the neckline was cut too low. Hearing this, she refused to wear the garment again. When her mother suggested remaking it, perhaps for a younger sister, Martha again refused. To avoid wasting the fabric, they compromised by using it to make a quilt.

Brigham Young was indeed conscious of women's fashion for two reasons. In order to promote self-sufficiency, he wanted to discourage women from buying supplies from outsiders. He wanted the women to

avoid extravagance, stressing frugality instead.[47] In addition, he was concerned about their modesty; anything less than four full widths or yards of fabric in a skirt was considered immodest for Mormon women to wear.[48]

By refusing to wear the dress and ultimately agreeing to its being remade as a quilt, these two women showed their allegiance to the Church and to leader Brigham Young.

On the quilt, the pieced 3" triangles represent the geese. This popular pattern, often seen in the pioneer American West, represents themes of nature and outdoor living, including migration.

The quilting pattern in the solid blocks, viewed in detail from the back of the quilt, shows one large 6⅝" circle and four smaller 3¾" circles quilted in double rows. Between them are simple petal-shaped designs. The quilting lines in the pieced strips are angled double lines that complete a square with the fabric triangle. This is an unusual plan that connects the piecing and

quilting steps of construction into a unified design.

Eliza Spencer Moses was born the daughter of Solomon and Martha Jones Spencer in Johnston, Trumbull County, Ohio. The story of her life prior to arriving in Utah reveals a long loyalty to the Church. After her father's death, she and her mother joined the Church despite the strong opposition of Eliza's three brothers. She was forced to cut herself off from her own family. From Ohio, she went to Missouri and then to Nauvoo. There she married widower James Moses on October 17, 1839. This marriage caused her to permanently estrange herself from her family. The couple had two children born in Nauvoo, one son who died and daughter Martha born in 1844. The family migrated west to Kanesville in western Iowa where three more children were born between 1848 and 1853.

They always remained in contact with the Moses family back in Connecticut. The senior Moses was

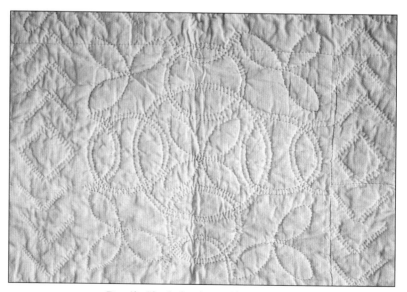

Detail of back showing quilting patterns

Full view of Wild Geese Quilt

eager for his son to return there to live after the other brothers and sisters had gone. After seeking counsel from Wilford Woodruff, who had known the senior Moses, the family returned to Connecticut to live until the father's death.[49] In

1861, with their extended family, they traveled from New York to Florence, Nebraska. On their journey they suffered a measles outbreak and threatened attacks by Civil War soldiers.

Arriving in Salt Lake City in

1861, the family settled in the Cottonwood area. Eliza Spencer Moses died in Holladay in Salt Lake County in 1874. Daughter Martha, who never married, became a schoolteacher in the Big Cottonwood Canyon area.

Harvest Time in Ephraim by C. C. A. Christensen

Quilt: NINE PATCH (III-10)

Category: Pieced
Size: 66¾" x 77"
Date: Late (1930–1935)
Maker: Mary Ellen Salisbury Parsons
(19 November 1852–21
November 1936)
Migration: St. Louis, Missouri, to
Utah
Place Joined the Church: Missouri
Year Crossed the Plains: 1861
Company: Job Pingree Independent
Company
Arrived: August 23, 1861
Came: With parents and family
County Where Settled: Weber; Salt Lake

This quilt reflects the variety of fabrics and the commercial patterns available to a Salt Lake City quiltmaker long after the period of normalization brought on by the 1890 Manifesto (see page 154.) and the 1896 declaration of statehood. These supplies were produced elsewhere in America. The quilt suggests that its maker was a woman living successfully in an urban environment. She showed her pride in her family by making a quilt for each grandchild.

The twenty 10" blocks and the 5½" sashing strips consist of two matching prints and a third fabric. Such coordination of fabrics indicates that the maker planned the quilt and acquired fabric specifically for its construction.

The quilt's unique feature is the repeat of the block size and quilting pattern in the horizontal sashing, creating a very symmetrical balanced presentation. The straight quilting lines across the sashes repeat the quilting lines of the pattern's rectangles.

The quilter may have taken the idea from the published pattern in Ladies Art Company, an early mail-order pattern source that printed its first catalog in 1898 and a second in 1928. Nine Patch is the pattern name used by Ladies Art Company.[51]

Mary Ellen Salisbury Parsons was born in St. Louis to Thomas and Eliza Knowles Salisbury. Her parents had emigrated in 1851 from Preston, England. That their journey took place in two stages over a ten-year period illustrates the commitment these people had to gathering in Zion. They had joined the Church in 1837 during the first missionaries' journey to England. When George Greenwood, a wealthy suitor of Eliza's younger sister Mary, offered to finance the journey for the entire Knowles family, the eager family journeyed to St. Louis. At the time this had become the site for orchestrating all Mormon migrations.

It took ten years until the Salis-burys were able to finance the second phase of migration. Even then, the equipment they acquired was poor and they were forced to trade their cookstove for a healthy ox.

Arriving in Utah, the family was instructed by Brigham Young to go to Slatersville, a town near Ogden. They spent the winter in a dugout, using sheepskins for blankets. During the first years, Mary Ellen spent much of her time, as most pioneers did, gleaning the wheat fields for grain and flailing the grasshoppers. After her mother died when she was twelve, she hired out for three dollars a week doing washing, ironing, cleaning, pasturing, and milking the cows.

In 1875, she met and married non-Mormon Arthur Parsons, "a handsome dude from England," who had come

"Mary Ellen was always busy with household duties, but she also made many quilts for the family. They were utilitarian rather than works of art and many were made from fabric scraps rather than new materials. She made a quilt for each of her grandchildren."

*Margaret Noall,
her granddaughter*[50]

Mary Ellen and Arthur Parsons

Full view of Nine Patch Quilt

to visit his aunt. He joined the Church and became an American citizen.

Although she had limited formal education, Mary Ellen combined her own skills with those of her college-educated husband to establish a school in Salt Lake City. Like other pioneers who took similar steps, they were trying to achieve financial success in a non-farm institution. She taught the younger children in the two rooms on the main floor. Her husband taught the older students in the two rooms upstairs. Later, Arthur be-

came the credit manager for ZCMI, the Church-owned department store. This was a position of importance in Mormon society because of the compassion and understanding required in handling financial matters for the many destitute converts.

During their sixty-one-year marriage, they became the parents of seven children, six of whom lived to adulthood. Mary Ellen died at age eighty-three on July 15, 1936, surrounded by her family members at her Marmalade District home.[52]

"She had a great sense of humor and loved 'Amos and Andy' and the movies, and a caramel sundae at Keeleys. We grandchildren used to take her. Grandfather was not entirely in favor of these outings, but he couldn't resist us. One time when the family took her on an outing to Saltair he proclaimed to us all that 'no good woman stays out till after 10 P.M.'"
                    her granddaughter[53]

*Detail of center block
with extensive floral stitchery*

Quilt: BASKET WITH FLORAL
    STITCHERY (III-11)

Category: Pieced and Appliquéd
Size: 71¾" x 75"
Date: Started 1851
        Completed 1860s
Maker: Elizabeth McKay Treseder
    (19 November 1811–
    21 November 1891)
Migration: County Cork, Ireland,
    to Utah
Place Joined the Church: Isle of Jersey
Year Crossed the Ocean: 1855
Ship: Chimborazo
Year Crossed the Plains: 1862
Company: William Godbe Freight
    Company
Arrived: October 14, 1862
Came: With husband and family,
    including her daughter Elizabeth
    Treseder Chandler Williams
County Where Settled: Salt Lake

This quilt and the next are especially significant as treasures of Mormon migration available today in Utah. As part of Jean Christensen's quilt collection, they are valued as important artifacts of the lives of her pioneer family. They are the separate works

of a mother and daughter who journeyed together and whose quilts and stories reflect their different ages and individual experiences. This quilt by the mother represents the transition from British to American quilting styles: the maker created the blocks in the British style and then used American products to finish the quilt.

According to family history, the embroidered floral blocks were stitched while en route by ship to America and while living in the East for six years. Each of the eighteen blocks has a different floral motif, including fuchsia, lily of the valley, Christmas cactus, and bleeding heart. Each is created with yarn and bits of wool cloth, reminiscent of English crewel work.

The presence of the pieced cotton-print baskets may indicate the influence of American patchwork. However, the basket pattern was popular in Britain because "it provided the opportunity to combine appliqué with patchwork techniques."[54] The basket in this quilt is probably British in origin since the red print is an early Turkey red that the maker brought with her from England. There the commercial production process for this cloth was done extensively. This cloth is known to have been weakened in the dye process; this could explain some of its deterioration when compared with the blocks.[55]

The consistent shade of green fabric and the wool batt suggest the maker completed the quilt after she arrived in America and Utah. She most likely acquired the green cloth while on the East Coast because the quality of the dye process was not so successful in Utah. The wool batt could easily have been produced in the West.

Note two other significant features. The finished 11½" blocks are set on point to read from either side of the quilt. The most richly embellished block is placed near the center.

The quilting designs in the blocks

are the classic infill patterns from England of the shell, which is the width of a woman's finger, and square-diamonds.[56] These designs would be easy and quick to mark if time and space were an important consideration. The quilting started at the base of the basket and worked toward the top. A vine is quilted in the sashing following the same pattern as the seam lines for the strips. The long vines are in the longer unbroken strips and the broken vines are in the shorter strips.

Elizabeth McKay Treseder was born the daughter of Thomas and Elizabeth Holland McKay in

"I think she was probably more experienced with embroidery and appliqué than she was with quilting, which would figure, wouldn't it? Because I don't know how many quilts she might have attempted to make in the Isle of Jersey before she came, but I think she was strongly influenced to use flowers which she had loved. You know, when she came to this country it would have been pretty dreary compared to the Isle of Jersey, so why not put it in a quilt so it connects you to home, so to speak."

*Jean Christensen,
her great-granddaughter*[57]

Elizabeth McKay Treseder

Full view of Basket with Floral Stitchery Quilt

Queenstown, County Cork, Ireland. She married Richard Doughty Treseder on November 4, 1833. They lived on the Isle of Jersey and became the parents of eleven children, nine of whom survived to emigrate with them in 1855. Their ship sailed from Liverpool to Philadelphia, Pennsylvania. Their three oldest sons purchased their own way direct to Utah. The rest of the family remained in the East in Philadelphia and New York until 1862 when they had enough money to continue their journey. Taking the train to Florence, Nebraska, they traveled west with a freight wagon train.

They settled in Salt Lake, where Elizabeth fed the poor and cared for the sick. She provided a home for two young orphan boys. Her warm personality and keen mind gave her a reputation of integrity, tolerance, and sympathy. When she died it was stated, "a pioneer is gone."[58]

Quilt: LOG CABIN (III-12)

Category: Pieced
Size: 67½" x 73¾"
Date: Late (1890–1930)
Maker: Elizabeth McKay Treseder
    Chandler Williams (18 January
    1848–24 November 1936)
Migration: Isle of Jersey to Utah
Place Joined the Church: New York
Came: With family, including her
    mother, Elizabeth McKay Treseder
County Where Settled: Salt Lake; Weber

Detail of fabrics and piecing

*Elizabeth McKay Treseder
Chandler Williams*

The quilt made by the daughter of this traveling pair represents their settling in the resource-deprived territory of Utah and adjusting to a life of self-sufficiency and thrift. This Barn Raising variation of the Log Cabin pattern builds on the concept of concentric squares radiating from the center. Figuratively, it represents the difficulty of acquiring logs to build cabins and barns in Utah's high, dry climate.

Visually, the design and construction are compact and complete with two full squares of dark fabrics. Both indicate the maker's knowledge and sophistication about the use of fabrics. The dark points on the squares touch the quilt's edge on three sides. The fourth has an extra row of blocks to provide the length needed to cover the bed. In answer to the question of which end was the top or bottom, the owner remembers that her grandmother used a large pillow laid over the top of her quilt on her beds. Thus, the quilt could be placed with the dark points defining the edge of the bed.

The center squares of the 8½" blocks are velvet and wool, while the strips or logs are cotton, wool, and silk. This quilt indicates that textiles

of different fibers can be mixed effectively in quilt construction.

The quilt is backed with a rich green fabric that is brought to the front for the binding. It is quilted with a dark thread around the outside edge of each block.

Elizabeth McKay Treseder Chandler Williams was born the ninth child of Richard and Elizabeth McKay Treseder on the Isle of Jersey. Six of the couple's twelve children had their mother's maiden name as their middle name. She emigrated with her family to America in 1855 where she was baptized in the Hudson River. She thought her 1862 wagon journey to Zion was wonderful. In later life, she enjoyed telling her family members about her experience.

In 1874, she married Calvin H. Chandler and moved to Granite, where two children were born before he died in 1881. She moved to North Ogden where she married L. W. Williams, a widower with six grown children. A son was born to them in 1886. She served as a teacher in the Relief Society for ten years in the Ogden area. In 1904, she helped to raise the funds and supplies to build the Ogden Relief Society Hall.

Both her second son and husband had died by 1910. She had to adapt to living as a widow the last twenty-six years of her life.

" . . . when you think how many years it must have taken to collect these, and I don't think there was a new fabric in it. I think they were all recycled, so to speak. She did like to tell us about some of the places that she came up with that little velvet piece. I believe if you'd have visited her with a velvet dress you might have lost some of the inner seams. She was like that, very resourceful. She told about taking the hat band out of a hat that someone had finished wearing. When you look at them, you see that it was difficult for her to find those pieces. The prettiest one of all is right smack in the middle."

*Jean Christensen,
her granddaughter*[59]

Full view of Log Cabin Quilt

Quilt: FRAMED CENTER
     MEDALLION TOP (III-13)

Category: Pieced
Size: 78½" x 76½"
Date: Early (1822)
Maker: Elizabeth Bell Barton (21
     December 1814–19 April 1896)
Migration: Lancashire, England, to
     Utah
Place Joined the Church: England
Year Crossed the Ocean: 1862
Ship: Manchester
Year Crossed the Plains: 1862
Company: Captain Ansel P.
     Harmon's Ox Train (4th down-
     and-back train)
Arrived: October 5, 1862
Came: With her husband and family
County Where Settled: Davis; Salt
     Lake

Detail of corner

This is an outstanding example of the
rich piecework heritage among English Mormon pioneers, especially
those coming later when they were
able to carry more with them. It is
one of several preserved pieces that
women made when they were children. The documentation on the quilt
says it was made in 1822 when the
maker was eight years old. The careful
planning and execution indicate that
this child, who was raised by her
grandmother, had adult supervision.

The fabrics and style of construction are typical of quilts made in England in the early 1800s.[60] The center
medallion fabric is an early roller print
from the period from 1820 to 1825.
This floral-trail print is similar in scale
to those used for early nineteenth-
century dresses.[61] Notice that the
prints in the opposite corners of the
first inside border match.

Left unfinished, it has greater
meaning and value as an artifact of
the maker's early life than it would
if it were completed.

Elizabeth Bell Barton was born the
daughter of William and Margaret
Martlew Bell in Upholland, Lancashire, England. Both her father and
baby sister died in 1816. As a young
widow with a two-year-old daughter,
Margaret Bell returned to her mater-
nal home in Pemberton. After her
mother remarried, Elizabeth contin-

ued to live with her grandmother
until her 1835 marriage at the age
of twenty-one to John Barton.

They resided in Lancashire, where
their seven sons and one daughter, including twins, were born between
1836 and 1855. Following the model
under which she was raised, she
taught all her children the skills
needed to produce bed linen and
clothing. When it was necessary, the
punishment in the household was to
knit a few rounds on the stockings.[62]

She became acquainted with the
Latter-day Saints in 1840 or 1841
and began taking her young family
to their meetings. She was baptized
on June 27, 1847, at Liverpool.

While most Saints were encouraged to emigrate as soon as they
could, she remained a loyal member
of the St. Helens Branch, active after
many members had left. She often
served as the host for visiting missionaries. She performed an important role for the Church, serving
as a constant presence in a period of
change and growth. William, one of
her eldest twin sons, became an elder
at the age of twenty and served in
Newton Branch of the Liverpool
Conference.[63]

Emigrant Ship, 1867 *by C. C. A. Christensen*

Full view of Framed Center Medallion Top

In 1862, after four of her children had emigrated to America, the rest of the Barton family joined them. They sailed from Liverpool to Castle Garden in New York and then traveled on by railroad and down-and-back Church train. They settled in Kaysville, Utah, and their home was the first brick house in town. After her husband died in 1874, Elizabeth spent a great deal of time with her family, living the last eleven years of her life with her son William.

Her pattern of living in one location and providing assistance to Church leaders continued throughout her life. Elizabeth felt highly honored to have two of her sons and a grandson serve as bishops, and one son as a bishop's counselor. At the time of her death in 1896, four of her grandsons were serving missions in New Zealand, Samoa, Switzerland, and Germany. All were following her role model by serving the people in their respective home areas.

Quilt: ROSE OF SHARON
VARIATION (III-14)

Category: Appliqué
Size: 62" x 77¾"
Date: Late (1920–1935)
Maker: Eliza Jane Eynon Ricks (7
    September 1856–21 June 1939)
Migration: Cardiff, South Wales, to
    Oregon
Place Joined the Church: South Wales
Year Crossed the Ocean: 1863
Ship: Linnershore (not listed on
    regular list of ships)
Year Crossed the Plains: 1863
Company: Captain Rosel Hyde (9th
    down-and-back Church train)
Arrived: October 13, 1863
Came: With mother and sister and
    brother
County Where Settled: Tooele; Cache;
    Tooele; Teton, Idaho; Wallowa,
    Oregon; Bannock, Idaho; Union,
    Oregon

This quilt represents the new direction in quiltmaking in the twentieth century and is a bright compliment to this woman's difficult and challenging life. The color choices and design style are those commonly seen at this time when women were either marketing or purchasing completely designed kits of patterns and fabrics. It is difficult to tell if this is a kit quilt because there

Immigrants arriving at New York

are none of the usual signs of pre-stamped cutting or quilting lines.

The six 16" blocks contain the balanced stylized roses. The interior border is 2½" wide. The white 13" border is divided by a machine-appliquéd scallop border. The binding is a repeat of the orange fabric. The quilting pattern is an all-over grid design of parallel lines one inch apart with seven stitches per inch.

Eliza Jane Eynon Ricks was born the daughter of John and Eliza Lewis Eynon in Cardiff, South Wales. Her parents joined the Church of Jesus Christ of Latter-day Saints in 1859. Her parents were eager to come to Zion, but her father had recently apprenticed himself for seven years on a man-of-war ship. So in 1863, while he still had three years to serve, Eliza's mother and the three young children came alone. The challenges were great, the struggle incredible. Not only did all of them suffer from seasickness, the mother also gave birth to a baby boy who died and was buried at sea. They landed at New York's Castle Garden and then traveled west by train and steamboat through the Great Lakes to Florence, Nebraska.

There they waited six weeks for the Church train to come from Utah. After crossing the Platte River, the two-year-old brother died and was buried on the Plains. When they arrived in Salt Lake City, there was no one to meet them.

After Eliza's father arrived, the family lived in Tooele for four years and then pioneered in Cache Valley. Life was a constant struggle as they endured illness, weather, and insects. To help support her family, Eliza worked outside the home.

She married Jonathan Ricks on January 3, 1875. They had nine children during the nineteen years they lived in Tooele County. Life continued to be a challenge as they tried to establish farms in the high fertile valleys of Utah, Idaho, and Oregon.

Detail of appliquéd block and quilting

Each time the cold weather took its toll on the family's health or on their farm crops. Commenting on their years in Idaho's Teton Valley, she said, "We never raised our bread in all the fourteen years we lived there."[64]

During the winter of 1893, eight of the children suffered diphtheria. Three of the children were sick for three months. One young daughter died in February and one son was left with heart damage. His health continued to drain their finances. After they recovered, the family had to burn everything, including all the clothing and bedding. They were

---

" . . . and not a soul to meet us, so we sat on our sacks until nearly dark and mother cried all the time for we thought we were left and had no place to go. But the teamster with whom we had come had forgotten his whip and when he came back for it and found us there he took us home with him. . . . We lived that first winter on a few carrots made into molasses. Mother had a silk dress which she sold for 10 lbs of cornmeal. We did not like it, and mush was like sand in the mouth and that is why I cannot eat cornmeal to this day."

Eliza Jane Ricks[65]

Full view of Rose of Sharon variation

forced to sell the farm to pay the medical expenses and to acquire needed clothing and household items.

They moved to LeGrand, Oregon, in 1917 and were beginning to be prosperous when their youngest son was drafted into the Army. In addition, within one week in May 1921, three loved ones died of the flu.

Yet through it all, Eliza Ricks demonstrated, in her writing and quiltmaking, a seemingly amazing ability to adapt to life's challenges:

We have had 12 children all of them good to their parents. 34 grandchildren and 2 great grandchildren. We have cared for 4 grandchildren and 5 not our own. It has been harder for me than for some better prepared for I was never in school in all my life. all I know I have taught myself. But you children know I can sew, spin, knit, weave and do every kind of work inside and out. With my husband I have helped to pay on all the Temples making quilts, carpets, rugs, knitting socks and mittens for me and my children and have paid our pennies to the Canadian and Hawaiian Temple. I have crossed the Atlantic Ocean and the American Continent to the Pacific ocean. I am 5 foot 4 inches tall, grey eyes, hair now grey but originally dark brown. weigh 180 and in good health.[66]

Quilt: TRIP AROUND THE
        WORLD (III-15)

Category: Pieced
Size: 84" x 78"
Date: Late (1890–1910)
Maker: Elizabeth Jane Rogers
        Shepherd (7 October 1829–
        17 August 1912)
Migration: Hampshire, England, to
        Utah
Place Joined the Church: England
Year Crossed the Ocean: 1866
Ship: Caroline
Year Crossed the Plains: 1866
Company: Capt. John D. Holladay's
        Ox Train (down-and-back train)
Arrived: September 25, 1866
Came: With husband and children
County Where Settled: Utah; Juab

Detail was important to this quiltmaker, as indicated by the stitching
in red thread on the quilt back:
"Elizabeth Jane Rogers Shepherd,
Pioneer of 1866, 10,513 pieces."
Placed in seventy-two rows are different printed cottons cut in squares
smaller than ¾". They represent a
span of time and place from the
maker's early years in England to
about 1880 in America. For a while
in Utah, her husband, John Shepherd, operated a store from which
she was able to get calico cloth
scraps for her quilts.

The attention to detail continues
with the careful placement of her
template on the fabric to center the
most important design element in
the finished square.

The quilt's style is typical "English piecing," a reflection of the
maker's British heritage. It uses
pieces of one size in a single geometric shape or template pattern, varying from triangles to hexagons.
Although the style of template piecing was common, "quilts made from

square patches only are rare—probably because the severe outline is not
sufficiently inspiring and also it is re-
markably difficult to make patches
which are perfectly square."[67] The
squares are stitched together into
strips using a whip stitch. These
strips are then assembled around a
center, creating a framework.[68]

The quilt edge is a self-finished
treatment in which the back and
front pieces are folded inside and
hand-stitched. The resulting saw-
tooth appearance accentuates the
use of the square template. This
work was done by Emily Lafont,
the ninety-year-old grandmother
of Lenore Romney, wife of George
Romney, the former governor of
Michigan.[69]

Elizabeth Jane Rogers Shepherd
was born the daughter of George
Augustus and Jane Lunt Rogers in
Southampton, Hampshire, England.
She joined the Church in 1848, two
years before her marriage to John
Worlock Shepherd. Between 1850
and 1866, he worked as a chief stew-
ard for the Peninsula Oriental Company, traveling the world while she
lived in an apartment in Southampton. During this time, they had
eleven children, including a set of
triplets. Only five children survived
to emigrate with their parents.

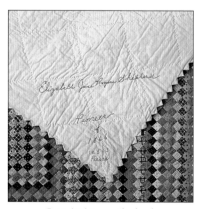

Inscription on the back

Detail of the quilt's center

Their 1866 journey to Utah
took five months. They left Liverpool on May 5 and arrived in New
York City on June 11. From there,
they traveled by train and steamboat to Wyoming, Nebraska, arriving on July 19, 1866. This was
the western end of the railroad at
that time. The final segment of
their journey was by Church train.
They arrived in Salt Lake on
September 25, 1866.[70]

The family first settled in
Springville, Utah County, where another baby was born. In 1868, they
moved to Levan in Juab County
where their first home was a dugout
smoothed and plastered with native
white clay. Their first bed was a
wagon box. Here four more babies
were born, two of whom died quite
young.

Elizabeth lived by the motto
"Waste not, want not" and used
everything, such as rags for carpets
and tallow for candles. She taught all
her children, boys as well as girls, to
sew and knit in an effort to teach
them to care for their belongings.

Eager to learn and adjust to her
surroundings, Elizabeth tried many
recipes brought by people from
many European countries. She made
candy—pink musk, peppermint
sticks, and coltsfoot sticks—to sell in
their store.

Full view of Trip around the World Quilt

"While in England, Grandmother started a pieced quilt made of tiny diamonds and sewed together by hand. Grandfather had made a brass pattern from which she cut pieces of paper to be covered with calico or other cotton material. I am sure she had each of her children start one of these quilts, because from her Bible she gave me a small one started by my father and it is the center of the one I am working on now. She also gave me a brass pattern. I think each of the girls had one and I have the one she made for Ellen, who reared me when my mother died. Ellen had no children of her own and her quilt is the only one not worn out."

Ruby Shepherd Karpowitz, her granddaughter[71]

Quilt: STAR (III-16)

Category: Pieced
Size: 77½" x 78"
Date: Late (1890–1930)
Maker: Christina Maria Christiansen
    Lund Jensen (21 May 1861–
    28 February 1951)
Migration: Viborg, Denmark, to Utah
Place Joined the Church: ———
Year Crossed the Ocean: 1868
Ship: Either the *John Bright* or the
    Emerald Isle
Year Crossed the Plains: 1868
Company: Capt. John G. Holman's
    Ox Train
Arrived: September 25, 1868
Came: With parents and family
County Where Settled: Sanpete
    County

This large single-star design quilt was called a "camp quilt."[72] It is a type of utility quilt used by families in camps during early settlements, temporary mining camps, or cattle camps. In later years, they were used in cabins and cottages near lakes and mountains. The donor, who is no longer living, remembered sleeping under it as a child.

The quilt's front and back are cotton flannelette or outing flannel, a yarn-dyed, light- to medium-weight fabric with brushed nap on both sides.[73] The diamond segments are each 14" by 5". The use of yellow and blue as strong contrasting colors creates an interesting visual effect. The repeat of the center's red stripe fabric at the outer points ties the design together.

The quilting lines repeat the diamond shapes and star pattern. The lines are placed at three-inch intervals. The batt is wool.

Christina Maria Christiansen Lund Jensen was born one of a set of twins to Christian Peter Christensen and Marie Pedersen Lund in Aarup, Denmark. Little is known about her early life and emigration except that the family traveled on one of the last two wagon trains to arrive in Utah in 1868. Their wagon journey from the end of the railroad line at Benton, Wyoming, to Salt Lake was short: twenty-six days.

Detail of piecing and quilting

She married Frederik Jensen in Salt Lake on January 6, 1880. They lived in Manti in Sanpete County their entire lives and raised nine children.

"Down-and-back" church train and railroad, 1869

Full view of Star Quilt

PART FOUR

1870–1900
SETTLING THE INTERMOUNTAIN WEST

"Quoting from one who has lived all her life in Dixie, 'Of all the territories colonized by the Mormon Church, this Dixie Mission was by far, the most difficult. Of all the God-forsaken lands that any human beings were asked to carve a town from, it was a hole bounded on the north by red sandstone cliffs, on the east and west by hills of black lava rock, and on the south by the muddiest, dirtiest river imaginable, a river that meanders its muddy, lazy course part of the year and becomes a ferocious, raging torrent sweeping everything before it the rest of the time. The country was hot and dry. The temperature from April to October ranged from 80 to 112 and 116 degrees. The floor of the valley was red sand and alkali over which hot dusty winds blow. The only plant life was cactus, mesquite, and sagebrush. The animal life consisted of rattlesnakes, lizards, gila monsters and coyotes.'" — Beatrice Winsor, granddaughter of Erastus Snow[1]

detail from Crossing the Missouri River *by C. C. A. Christensen*

MORMON COLONIZATION, 1847–1900

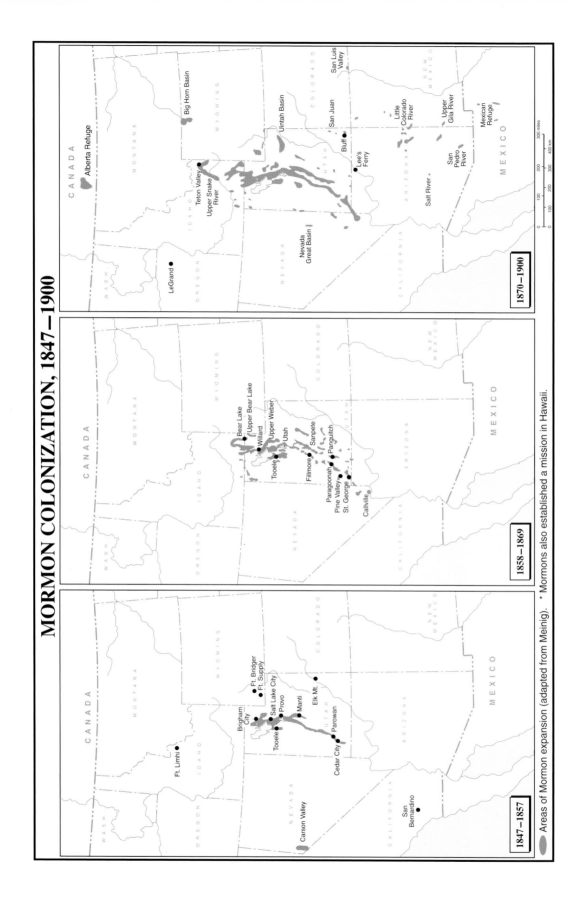

1847–1857

Ft. Limhi

Ft. Bridger
Ft. Supply
Brigham City
Salt Lake City
Tooele · Provo · Manti
Elk Mt.
Cedar City · Parowan

Carson Valley

San Bernardino

WASH · OREGON · NEVADA · CALIFORNIA · IDAHO · CANADA · MONTANA · WYOMING · UTAH · COLORADO · ARIZONA · NEW MEXICO · MEXICO

1858–1869

Bear Lake
Upper Bear Lake
Willard · Upper Weber
Tooele · Utah
Fillmore · Sanpete
Paragoonah · Panguitch
Pine Valley · St. George
Callville

WASH · OREGON · NEVADA · CALIFORNIA · IDAHO · CANADA · MONTANA · WYOMING · UTAH · COLORADO · ARIZONA · NEW MEXICO · MEXICO

1870–1900

LeGrand

Alberta Refuge

Big Horn Basin

Teton Valley
Upper Snake River

Uintah Basin

San Luis Valley

San Juan
Bluff
Lee's Ferry

Little Colorado River

Upper Gila River

Mexican Refuge

San Pedro River

Salt River

Nevada Great Basin

WASH · OREGON · NEVADA · CALIFORNIA · IDAHO · CANADA · MONTANA · WYOMING · UTAH · COLORADO · ARIZONA · NEW MEXICO · MEXICO

300 miles
400 km
0 · 100 · 200 · 300
0 · 100 · 200 · 300

Areas of Mormon expansion (adapted from Meinig).   * Mormons also established a mission in Hawaii.

THE MIGRATION

THE COMPLETION OF THE TRANSCONTINENTAL railroad on May 10, 1869, brought significant changes to the Utah Territory. The International Society of Daughters of Utah Pioneers recognizes it as marking the end of the Pioneer Period, as do others responsible for maintaining that part of their heritage. It was the end of one era and the beginning of another. Travel which previously had taken weeks was accomplished in days. It ended the region's social and political isolation and the Saints' sense of security in which they had practiced their faith. It opened new economic opportunities for Utah products, and it brought new ventures into the area by non-Mormons. It created new political challenges as Utah repeatedly sought to become a state of the Union yet remain in control of its own government. It brought new waves of persecution as federal authorities clamped down both on the religious practices and on the connections between the Church and local government that existed in Utah.

In the years after 1869, migrants were able to travel from New York to Utah using a system that became so routine, safe, and efficient that plans could be made in advance with amazing confidence and trust. While agents were available in Liverpool, New York, and Chicago to plan and assist with travelers' arrivals and departures, much of the previously required assistance was no longer needed.

Such developments, as well as a number of other factors, led to the Church's decision to withdraw from active involvement in planning, financing, and overseeing either the migration within the United States or emigration from abroad.

One key factor in this decision was the tremendous debt (about $1.6 million in 1880) in the Perpetual Emigrating Fund that was not being repaid by those already in Utah because of continuing limited finances. New converts were still coming,

Pioneers on the Mormon Trail

averaging about 1,740 a year. The number of people still seeking financial help ranged from 20 to 50 percent of the emigrants. The majority continued to be from Great Britain and the Scandinavian countries, with a few from Germany, France, and Italy.[2]

A second factor was that the employment opportunities generated by the traditional method of colonization were exhausted, as farms and commercial enterprises were already well established. The new employment opportunities that arose were needed by maturing sons and daughters who were already in Utah.

The Church changed its policy so that it continued to welcome those who came, but stipulated that they must accomplish the journey by themselves. Individuals of limited financial resources eager to be in Zion sought help from friends, relatives, private sources, or the few labor contracts that existed, such as coal mining. Other individuals were able to personally finance their journeys.

THE COLONIZATION IN THE 1870s AND 1880s

With increased pressure from federal authorities to prosecute practitioners of polygamy, two plans, defined by Brigham Young before his death in 1877, became major focuses for colonization. One was to create a corridor to Mexico where polyga-

Wickiup home in southern Utah near the Colorado River, c. 1873–74

mist families could live in peace outside of federal government jurisdiction. The other was to settle in the high plateau river valleys of southeastern Utah and southern Colorado. These isolated valleys within the rugged mountain terrain were extremely difficult to access. The people who went there had to repeat their pioneering experience of traveling by wagon over rough terrain to access the valley, grubbing the land, building the irrigation canals, planting the crops, and praying for the results. For many people, the journey was equivalent to the last days of their original migration experience, during which they endured tough ascents and descents over the Wasatch Mountains. This still-current memory gave many the confidence that they would overcome even this new physical challenge.

Action to achieve statehood continued. The Church's political party was eliminated and a move made toward the Republican National Party. Utahans wrote a state constitution that specifically prohibited polygamy and ensured separation of church and state. On January 4, 1896, Utah became an official state of the Union.

THE EMIGRATION AND COLONIZATION AFTER 1890

Internationally, the Manifesto of 1890 created new roles for the Saints throughout the world. Now faced with global eco-

nomic depressions and pending global political confrontations, converts were encouraged to remain where they were already settled, secure their futures there, and when able, visit Salt Lake City's Temple Square, the "Crossroads of the West."

After 1890, second- and third-generation pioneers needed to establish themselves. These young families were discouraged by the continuing difficulties of farming Utah's marginal land and the scarcity of adequate commercial jobs. Many now sought land on which they could use their agricultural skills. They also sought to claim the 1862 Homestead Act allotment of 160 free acres per individual.

Manifesto of 1890

Significant changes for all Saints came on October 6, 1890, when the Church approved the Manifesto announcing that the practice of polygamy would be discontinued. This decision was announced publicly on September 24. President Wilford Woodruff, the man who succeeded John Taylor as president, had spent considerable time discussing with leaders the issues of statehood and the Church's political and financial burdens in light of the federal laws. Meeting with the Council of the Twelve, he announced "in broken and contrite spirit, . . . he had sought the will of the Lord, and it had been revealed to him that the Church must relinquish the practice of plural marriage."[4] This announcement became the official recognition that the Church would obey the federal law banning the practice.

Spiritually, the current economic situation had another effect on the Church's emigration program. From the beginning of the Church sixty years earlier, one firm belief had been that they were chosen people, Saints, destined to proselytize their message to others and gather them to Zion to establish the Millennium, the second coming of Christ. Now, leaders realized that for those already present in the Mormon West in Utah to survive, the Church had to change its belief to one of serving people in their present locations.

By approving the Manifesto and being willing to live by laws set by the federal government, the people within the area changed the internal and external attitudes toward the Saints and their faith. It opened a new era of cooperation and understanding around the world. Families who practiced polygamy before the Manifesto were allowed to continue living together, though formally the practice was outlawed. Amnesty was issued by President Grover Cleveland in September 1894 to all men arrested for polygamy.

Pioneer colony on way to the Big Horn Country

After the issuing of the 1890 Manifesto, however, Church officials feared that if individuals moved away the sense of community among their members would diminish. To help alleviate possible problems, the Church announced plans to colonize in the areas of the Big Horn Basin in Wyoming; the Grande Ronde Valley in Oregon; and Alberta, Canada.[5]

THE WOMEN

For the quiltmakers and owners, the completion of the transcontinental railroad offered new opportunities. For those in the West, it allowed them to reconnect with the eastern states, both for visits with family and friends and for exposure to a greater variety of material goods, especially after 1890. For those women interested in coming west, the journey was significantly easier. A young child traveling with strangers or single women traveling independently would be able to accomplish the trip more easily.

During this period other adult women, who had come as children or who were born in the West and now were wives and mothers, assisted in colonization efforts to better the opportunities for their families. Many took leadership roles in women's organizations. They also helped in industrial and technological community development.

Silk workers in St. George

THE QUILTS

These seven quilts represent the communal nature of quiltmaking, either in the contributions of fabrics, the process of making, or the celebration of people and events. Three quilts brought by women coming west during this time were made earlier and serve as visual records of family history and quiltmaking. Treasured by their owners, they are now part of the museum collections within Utah. The remaining quilts are from areas beyond the borders of Utah. They either were made in these outlying areas or were taken there as the Church reached out to serve a broader geographic area. All are now located outside the traditional central repositories identified with the Church's organization. They were discovered in small museums through this project's survey or in private families through personal referral.

Two quilts found in Wyoming tie directly to colonization efforts during this final period. Both are stitched in what was considered the current style and record the experiences of their makers. One is the richly embellished Crazy quilt stitched by Agnes Bell Cunningham during her three oceanic and continental crossings in one six-month period (Quilt IV-3). The other is an organization's celebration of the members' shared support (Quilt IV-5).

Two others were shared by Joyce Peaden, a Mormon quilt historian from Utah who settled in Washington (Quilt IV-2 and 2a).

Missionary home, Laie, Hawaii

These last three quilts draw attention to an interesting dimension in migration history: Sometimes parents sent their young children first in the company of an older woman or family, possibly even someone unfamiliar to the child. This practice indicated the family's trust in the migration system and their faith in getting to Zion later themselves. It also shows that the Church had established a successful organizational structure and schedule for migrations by the years after 1861.

The last quilt marks the new direction for the Church's missionary program after the 1890 Manifesto (Quilt IV-6). At this time, the Church actively began again to reach out beyond its borders to new converts. Missionaries with special talents were sent to help establish the Church near the new converts' homes within a specified geographic region. This traditional Hawaiian-style quilt was made before 1900 for Libbie Noall by the native Hawaiian Saints.

Detail of quilting design

Quilt: GRAPE WITH FLOWERS
(IV-1)

Category: Appliquéd
Size: 81¾" x 83"
Date: 1860–1865
Maker: Mary Elizabeth Lusk Coray
(4 April 1833–30 March 1909)
Migration: Indiana to Utah
Place Joined the Church: Utah
Year Crossed the Ocean: ———
Ship: ———
Year Crossed the Plains: circa 1870
Company: ——
Recorded: ——
Came: By herself on the
transcontinental railroad
County Where Settled: Salt Lake;
Costilla, Colorado; Salt Lake

This and the following quilt are the two masterpieces made in Missouri during the Civil War and brought to Utah by Mary Elizabeth Lusk Coray. Both exhibit skillful construction, consistent workmanship, and well-executed design composition. The quilts were most likely a shared project of Mary Elizabeth and her mother Cynthia Beeler Lusk. Their history reveals they had the available time to devote to such labor-intensive quiltmaking. The documentation indicates that seventeen-hundred yards of thread were used in the twelve-stitches-per-inch quilting of the Peony quilt and one thousand yards in this quilt.[6] The difference in the amount of thread consumed is the number and closeness of the rows. In this quilt, the rows are spaced ⅜" to ½" apart, while in the Peony, they are ⅛" to ¼" apart.

Other commonalities between the quilts include the on-point block set, the gridwork quilting, the leaf quilting pattern, and the size of the borders. Note how the leaf pattern radiates toward the corners. Note, too, that the leaf pattern is perfectly split to complete the design between the triangles and the border. The border sizes vary because the maker wished to square the quilt.

This quilt's unusual feature is that the center block is composed differently from the other eight. It is significant that this different block is

Detail of center block in middle row

placed at the very focal point where the viewer's eye is naturally drawn first. Among other things, note the following differences: the number of grape clusters and leaves; the varying shades of grape colors and floral prints; the varying lengths of stems; and the execution of the chain stitch. Note how the flowers in full bloom droop as if under their full weight, and how the grapes are attached at the ends of the stems. This all indicates perhaps that the quiltmaker of the center block was more attuned to the fine points of recreating floral inspirations from nature. It further suggests that this block was used as the pattern and perhaps was from an earlier time or a different maker.

The other unusual feature is the set of the blocks, reading from right and left rather than bottom and top. Considering that the other quilt has a row of peonies upright along the base in addition to the left and right presentation, such a placement would be the arrangement of choice for these quiltmakers. This placement would also have been appropriate for use on a typical period bed, which had both head and footboards.

Full view of Grape with Flowers Quilt

Second Quilt: PEONY (Quilt IV-1a)

Category: Appliquéd
Size: 74" x 74"
Date: 1861–1865
Maker: Mary Elizabeth Lusk Coray
(4 April 1833–30 March 1909)

Mary Elizabeth Lusk Coray was born the daughter of John Nicholson and Cynthia Ann Beeler Lusk in Johnston or Bridgeport, Marion County, Indiana. Her parents had

"She was a beautiful woman of 39 . . . appearing not over 25 . . . with curly black hair, sparkling black eyes, and naturally rosy cheeks and lips. Howard was instantly attracted to her and they were soon chatting, as if acquainted for years. Thus began a romance that met the established conditions and nothing happened to frustrate their plans for marriage in the Endowment House. In 'unity of mind the purpose' the disparity in their ages was ignored and together they weathered the trial and tribulations of pioneer life in Utah and Colorado for 35 happy years."
Edna Coray Dyer,
her daughter[7]

married in Butler County, Ohio, in 1823. They settled in Indiana for a time before moving to Schuyler County in northeast Missouri. Her family were not members of the Church, but two sisters had married Mormons and gone west to Utah prior to 1870.

The quilts were made during the Civil War when Mary Elizabeth and her mother were together in Missouri. Her father had died in 1857 and her widowed mother lived until 1885.

Mary Elizabeth remained a single woman who resided with her parents in the Midwest before an 1872 visit to Utah. She was able to visit her sister Julia Maria Roberts because of the completion of the railroad in 1869. While there she met and married a young Mormon, Howard Coray.

Howard had recently returned from a mission and was visiting old friends and relatives in Provo when they met. He was nine years younger than Mary Elizabeth. His parents, Howard and Martha Jane Knowlton Coray, had served as scribes when Joseph and Lucy Mack Smith dictated the histories of the Prophet.

Their life together of pioneering would be considered a struggle with advantages. The couple lived in Salt Lake City where their only child, Edna Coray Dyer, was born in 1875. Around 1879, the family left to colonize the San Luis Valley in the southern Colorado mountains. They

established a ranch near Ephraim and later lived in Sanford. Here, along the headwaters of the Rio Grande River, the Mormons established five settlements. They featured fine Victorian homes, good schools, and an active community life of the arts. Music was an important component in the lives of many citizens, including the Corays during their twelve-year stay.[8] Their organ is now part of the Pioneer Memorial Museum in Salt Lake.

Returning to Salt Lake City in 1891, Mary Elizabeth died in 1909.

Detail of quilting design

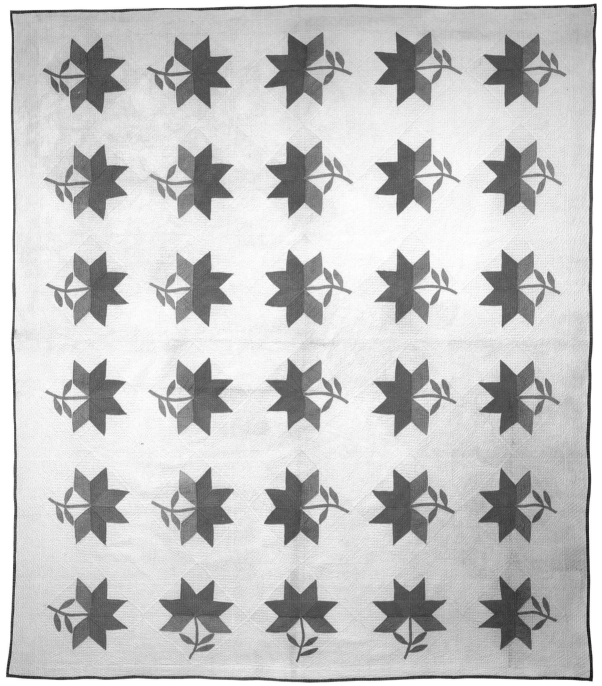

Full view of Peony Quilt

Quilt: CRAZY PATCH I (IV-2)

Category: Pieced
Size: 70½" x 78¾"
Date: Late (1913–1921)
Maker: Mary Mortensen Bjork (5 July 1869–30 October 1951)
Migration: Ålborg, Denmark, to Utah
Place Joined the Church: Denmark
Year Crossed the Ocean: 1876
Ship: Idaho
Year Crossed the Plains: 1876
Arrived: July 1876
Came: With Lars Larsen and family
County Where Settled: Utah; Salt Lake

The next two "contained Crazy Patch" quilts were made in an ongoing project by Mary Bjork and four of her five children. They worked together to create one for each of the children before their marriages.

The finished size of each of the four sections is 35" by 37¾". Each section was begun in a structured manner so that when assembled, the pieced segments would match to form a framed center medallion. Beyond that, each section is free-formed in the usual Crazy quilt style. Some pieces are laid down and stitched in place whereas others are laid right sides together, seamed, and folded over to form a more finished edge. Some are top-stitched by sewing machine. The wool fabrics used are of both dress and upholstery weight.

Mary Mortensen Bjork on afternoon of interview by granddaughters

The 23" by 24" medallion features the typical western American treatment of a single floral motif made of a three-ply wool yarn. The scale of yarn and stitch size are appropriate to the overall scale of the quilt. The various regular and double herringbone, feather, cross, and straight stitches are evenly spaced at 1" apart and vary to about ¾" in size. Some follow the seam lines while others serve to enrich the fabric surfaces. These features show the maker's flexibility and sense of creativity.

The quilting lines are 16" sweeps in the elbow style at varying distances apart. A row of quilting ½" from the top and bottom edges completes the design.

———

Mary Mortensen Bjork came to Utah after the defined Pioneer Period. The circumstances of her journey and her life in Utah were impressive influences on the lives of her family, especially her granddaughters Joyce Bennion Peaden and Dorothy Bennion Potter.

For this project, the two shared their quilts that had been made by their grandmother, their pictures, and the history they wrote after a 1949 visit to her old farm in Holladay, Utah. On that summer afternoon, Mary had recalled the events of her life. The granddaughters took notes and later wrote the history together for a Church school project. Joyce was inspired to continue working with quilts and family history. She has become a nationally recognized quiltmaker and author researching and publishing Mormon quilt history.

Detail of front and backing

Full view of Crazy Patch I Quilt

Quilt: CRAZY PATCH II (IV-2a)

Category: Pieced
Size: 68" x 76"
Date: Late (1913–1921)
Maker: Mary Mortensen Bjork (5
    July 1869–30 October 1951)

Crazy Patch II follows the same format with only slight variations. The
sections are smaller, 33" by 33¾".
The fabrics include woven and sin-
gle-knit wools and velvets.

The elbow quilting is done on a
slightly smaller scale with a sweep of
11". A quilting line forms an inner
border 4" from the edge around the
entire quilt. The finished edge treatment is a self-binding with the raw
edges turned inward and finished with
a herringbone stitch in brown yarn.

Mary Mortensen Bjork was born
the daughter of Peder and Ane
Dortea Justsen Mortensen in Ålborg,
Denmark. She lived with her grandmother until she was five. Then she
lived with her parents in a rented
two-room cottage. Her mother
helped to support the family by
weaving cloth from her clients' yarn.
Her father was the first to join the
Church and offered to serve as a
local host for Church missionaries.

Like most, her parents were eager
to emigrate. In order to achieve this
expensive goal, they agreed to send
their children ahead individually and
travel separately themselves over a
seven-year period. Sending children
ahead to the Zion in America was
thought to be a way for the children
to better their lives. Within the Mormon community, these children were

raised by childless couples or widowed women in exchange for help
and work. Many could not overlook
the offer of assistance in going to
Utah that the Mormon missionaries
brought, no matter the financial
obligations and cultural expectations.
Mary, at age six, was the first to emigrate. Traveling in a company with
her mother's male cousin Christian
Anderson, she was placed in the care
of a widow, Mrs. Larsen.

Upon leaving Denmark, Mary's
mother, grandmother, and aunt gave
her special treasures, including her
mother's string of crystal and pale-
blue beads. These became very
meaningful to her as she traveled,
lonely and scared, across the ocean
and continent to Zion without those
who loved her. An incident occurred
on the train that has always been
part of the family migration lore.
One day, as little Mary's neck was
being washed, her attendant's hand

Detail of front and backing

became caught in the necklace. As
she pulled back her hand, the string
broke, scattering the precious beads
everywhere with most of them falling
through the open cracks between the
car's floorboards, gone forever. Yet
Mary overcame the negative experiences of her journey and grew to respect and care for the elders who
cared for her. In fact, when her
mother finally arrived seven years
later, Mary chose to remain with Mrs.
Ingree Peterson in Pleasant Grove,
who had provided a home for her.

On June 26, 1889, she married
John Gustaf Bjork. They lived in a
log cabin in Linden, now Orem,
for nine years and had four children. Then they moved to a farm
in Holladay where another girl and
boy were born. The boy lived only
ten days.

Mary Mortensen Bjork's special
contribution was as a role model for
her family, especially her two granddaughters.

*Mary Mortensen, her grandmother
Else Marie Jacobsen, and sister
Amalia, c. Spring 1876*

Full view of Crazy Patch II Quilt

"When we were in our early teens we picked fruit, and especially strawberries, for Joseph Bjork, her son who had taken over the farm. We started as soon as it was light, and worked until around ten in the morning, by which time we would be tired and hot. Yet I felt I must stifle my own complaints and not be weak, because Grandma had worked earlier than we had, and would continue through the day, and be out at the field with the first pickers in the afternoon, and she did not complain. This has prodded me on to work harder and more persistently all my life. The thought always comes to my mind, What would Grandma think of me?"

Joyce B. Peaden,
her granddaughter[9]

Quilt: CRAZY QUILT (IV-3)

Category: Pieced
Size: 82½" x 82½"
Date: Mid (1879–1890)
Maker: Agnes Bell Cunningham
    (2 October 1843–23 November
    1924)
Migration: Glasgow, Scotland, to
    Wyoming
Place Joined the Church: Scotland
Year Crossed the Ocean: April 1879
Ship: Wyoming
Came: With her husband
Year Crossed the Ocean: October 1879
Ship: Arizona
Came: With her children
Year Crossed the Plains: Three times
    in 1879
County Where Settled: Cache;
    Sweetwater and Uinta Counties,
    Wyoming

This richly embroidered Crazy quilt
of velvets, silks, and satins represents
the very peak of this style of work.
It also reflects the adaptation of the
maker to her surroundings. In a
Crazy quilt at this level of decoration, the images are usually created
by a variety of techniques, including painting, embroidery, and
appliqué stitchery with embellishments of beads, buttons, ribbons,
and braids. On this quilt, only embroidery is used, no doubt an indication of the materials available to
this Scottish emigrant as she moved
westward. The combination of the
brilliantly colored fabrics and embroidery floss makes the overall
appearance one of intense color and
brightness—something that was
appreciated in a Wyoming home on
a dark winter day.

The stitched images on the 14½"
by 14¾" blocks reveal the transition of
this quiltmaker's life from one coun-

try to another. Two American flags
are near the quilt's center while the
British symbols of thistles, heather,
and Celtic knots are scattered over
the surface. The embroidery stitches
overlapping the patchwork pieces are
similar to those found on other Crazy
quilts of British origin.[10] The amount
and style of embroidery stitches along
the edges of the pieces are similar to
those illustrated in the British *Wel-
don's Practical Publications* in 1885.[11]

Yet, several images reflect the
maker's knowledge or impression of
life in western America. The woman
with the washtub symbolizes the
ever present dust and the endless
task of laundry, especially in a large
family. The flowers worked with
their bulbs included indicates an important message about life in the
West: the necessity to pack and carry
one's own nourishment. Bulbs grew
well and were able to sustain themselves and survive through the extremes of the climate.

Detail of quilt block with flower

Research into 1879 migration experiences yields a more accurate picture of how and where the quilt was
made. By this date, the modes of
transportation were steamship and
the transcontinental railroad. The
European Emigration Index indicates that in 1879, Agnes Bell Cunningham first traveled with her

husband, Thomas, sailing from
Liverpool on April 19 aboard the
Wyoming. Then she returned to
Scotland to bring her eight children
ranging in age from two to fifteen
years old. She sailed a third time
with them, leaving Liverpool
aboard the *Arizona* on October 18.
Considering that the journey from
Liverpool to Salt Lake took three
weeks, she would have spent nine
weeks aboard ship and railcar over a
twenty-eight-week period. This was
sufficient time for a traveling
woman with few responsibilities
and tasks to work on a quilt, as the
documentation states. The surprise
validation on the quilt is a small
woven label reading "water proof
clothing."

The usual practice when traveling
on ships and trains was to stow the
majority of the passengers' baggage,
allowing each person to retain their
hand luggage with supplies needed
for daily routines. Scraps of fabric
would have been very easy to pack
and carry. This was a standard practice among women who transported
their needlework with them. Piecing
and stitching were socially acceptable
tasks to be done in public.

"Water Proof Clothing" label

Agnes Bell Cunningham was born
the daughter of John and Margaret

Full view of Crazy Quilt

Brush Bell in Glasgow, Scotland. She married Thomas Syme Cunningham on December 31, 1862, in Carmuith, Scotland. They joined the Church in 1878 and migrated in 1879. Their settling first in an established area made her transition to America relatively easy compared with others. She was willing, however, to face the challenges of pioneering in the rugged, isolated, and cold areas of southwestern Wyoming.

Their first eight children had been born in Scotland. Another daughter, Mary Campbell, was born in 1880 in Mendon in Cache County, Utah. Later, in Rock Springs, Wyoming, two more daughters were born: Elizabeth in 1883 and Susan in 1885. Thomas worked as a coal miner for the Gunn Quaely Mine Combined Company before he died in 1897.

After his death, Agnes kept ho-

tels in Smith Fork and later in Lyman to support herself and her family. She provided beds and food to those settlers coming into the area or those people, mostly men, who were temporarily in the area. She lived the last seven years of her life with her daughter Jessie Cunningham Kidman in Lyman. A devoted member of her faith, Agnes planned her funeral service and burial.

Quilt: BUTLER ALBUM (IV-4)

Category: Pieced
Size: 84" x 102"
Date: 1845–1855
Maker: Unknown
Owner: Maud May Babcock (2 May 1867–31 December 1954)
Migration: New York to Utah
Place Joined the Church: Utah
Year Crossed the Ocean: ———
Ship: ———
Year Crossed the Plains: ———
Company: ———
Recorded: ———
Came: By herself
County Where Settled: Salt Lake

Maud May Babcock

This classic album quilt was made in New York State where the twenty-four friends and relatives of the Butler family named here resided. Butler was the maiden name of Maud May Babcock's mother. The quilt is a family keepsake brought to Utah by the owner after 1890. It serves as a visual record of her ancestors, but it also is a link to a young woman who was drawn to the Intermountain West for reasons other than Mormonism.

The dates of 1849 and 1850 written next to the family names coincide with the period of the eight different Turkey-red prints. The county names include Montgomery and Otsego in south central New York and Cattaraugus in the southwestern part of the state. The names appear to be written by one hand and some include an unusual mark, perhaps a hand.

Maud May Babcock was born the only daughter of William Wayne and Sarah Jane Butler Babcock in East Worcester, New York. Her name is well-recognized as the first woman professor at the University of Utah, head of the Department of Speech and Drama, and the "First Lady of Utah's Dramatic Arts."

As a young educated woman, Maud May began exploring opportunities to improve her physical health. In 1885, she found that the Delsarte method of using light calisthenic exercises combined with oratorical work helped her tremendously. While teaching a class combining physical activity and

voice lessons at Harvard University at the University's gymnasium in 1891, she met Susa Young Gates, daughter of Brigham and Lucy Bigelow Young. Susa encouraged Maud May to consider Utah as a teaching site.

Susa, an active civic and church leader, worked to promote Maud's professional opportunity for teaching physical culture. Maud May came to Utah to teach one year at the University of Utah at a salary of five hundred dollars. Her work of blending voice and physical activity became so successful that it evolved to be the first university theater program in the United States.[12]

Leaving her East Coast upbringing behind, she saw the opportunity to combine her professional interests with the physical environment of Utah's outdoor world. Coming as she did in 1893, she is symbolic of the major transformations of the time: the end of isolationism and the practice of polygamy, and the offering of statehood. She was an outsider but she had the advantage of being sponsored by Brigham Young's daughter. Quickly, she made her transition complete by joining the Church within four months of arriving. She stated: "I have never regretted my choice."[13]

Inscription: Mr. Howard Halls Ville 1849 unidentified mark

Inscription: George David Roxberry 1849 unidentified mark

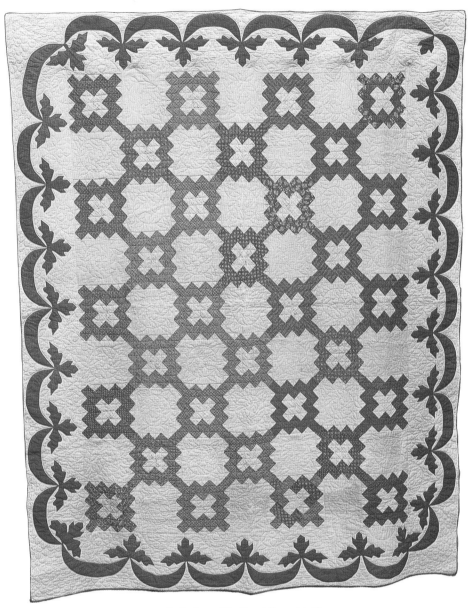

Full view of Butler Album Quilt

"She [Susan Young Gates] gave the most wonderful descriptions of the land among the mountains, the beauty of its scenery and the intelligence of its people. Above all, this charming woman spoke of the intense need of physical culture and elocution, and that one coming here now would be as it were, a missionary or chief reaper in this field already white for the harvest."

Maude May Babcock [14]

Quilt: FRIENDSHIP CRAZY
    QUILT (IV-5)

Category: Pieced
Size: 72" x 72"
Date: Late (1903)
Maker: Byron, Wyoming, Relief
    Society
Owner: Byron Museum

Wagon train preparing to leave for Big Horn Basin

Between 1900 and 1903, eight companies of pioneers mostly from Morgan, Iron, and Davis Counties gathered to build the Sidon irrigation canal and to lay the Burlington railroad tracks into the Big Horn Basin of northern Wyoming for settlement by the Mormons. Mormons also settled areas in Arizona, southern Colorado, northeastern Oregon, and southern Idaho. This Crazy quilt, dated 1903, marks the celebration of the efforts of the women who settled the Big Horn Basin.

Each of the thirty-six 11" blocks contains the name of one member. Each woman made or designed her own block. In the center blocks are the names of both the Woodruff Stake Branch Relief Society's first leaders from May 28, 1900, to May 25, 1901, and those of the Byron Ward Relief Society, organized in 1901. The names indicate the organizational structure of the Church. The group was from the Woodruff Stake in Utah. Comparing the names on the quilt with the Byron Relief Society membership lists indicates that some members but not all are included on the quilt. Considering the extreme conditions under which they strived to survive in this remote area those first years, it is not surprising. They may have either died or become discouraged and left the area.

During this time of canal and community building, the Relief Society cared for one another and their families and helped to maintain their church building. Many people became ill as a result of trying to stay warm in the cold, wind-battered tents. Many suffered from frozen hands and feet, colds, pneumonia, croup, and sore throats as a result of hauling water from a distance in the cold weather. Many died from typhoid, smallpox, and cholera. The Relief Society helped to dress and bury the dead.

The following are a few of the migration stories of Relief Society members who contributed blocks to the quilt.

Author's Note: It is an honor to share the stories of the grandmothers of three families whose paths crossed mine while I was doing research. Louis and Zelda Jones Moore, granddaughter of Samantha Nelson Johnson, initially shared the quilt in Cody, Wyoming, as they were making plans to display it at the new Byron Museum. Later, in Salt Lake, I met award-winning quiltmaker Cody Mazuran, named for her birth location of Cody, Wyoming. For her, we made the especially rewarding connection that her grandmothers shared her passion for quiltmaking. Cody and her parents Edwin and Jeri Neville shared the histories of Anne Neville and Julia Ann Denney. Then later in St. George, Utah, Cal and Geraldine Jones, a grandson of Samantha Nelson Johnson, worked to locate family pictures while sharing their artistic interests and the beauty of southern Utah.

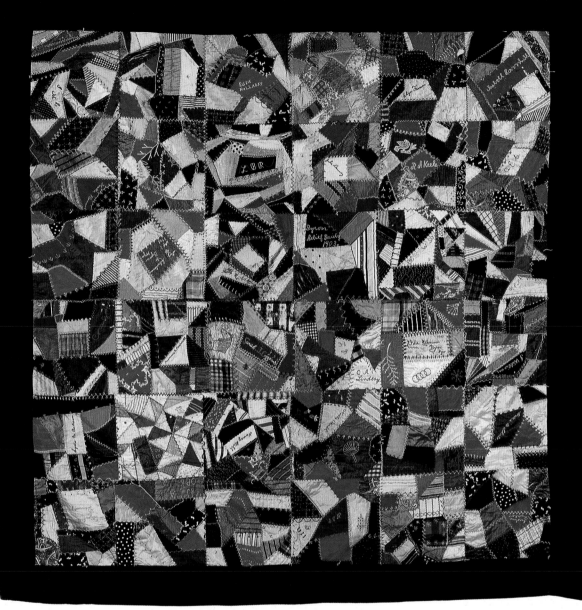

Full view of Friendship Crazy Quilt

Ann Lydia West Neville (1 May
    1856–14 July 1930)

Migration: England to Wyoming
Place Joined the Church: England
Year Crossed the Ocean: 1862
Ship: William Tapscott
Year Crossed the Plains: 1862
Company: Joseph Horne 3rd Church
    train
Arrived: October 1, 1862
Came: With her older sister in the
    care of James King and family
County Where Settled: Utah; Salt
    Lake; Weber; Rich; Utah; Big
    Horn, Wyoming

Ann Lydia West Neville's name appears as initials in one of the center blocks because she served as secretary of the first Woodruff Stake Relief Society.

She was born the daughter of Charles Henry John and Eliza Dangerfield West in London, England. Her parents joined the Church and were eager to go to Zion. Her father was a vellum binder of books, earning a good living but not enough to pay for the journey.

At the encouragement of Elder John Brown, who was staying with the family, the parents agreed to send their two young daughters

Ann, age six, and Caroline, age ten, with James King and his family. The promise was that if they remained faithful, the elder would see that the family would follow the next year. The European Emigration Index has a separate entry for the two children indicating they sailed on May 14, 1862, aboard the *William Tapscott.*

Ann wrote in her reminiscences that their journey was difficult and long, especially after the deaths of their caretaker's wife, mother, and baby on the Plains. Their journey took eight weeks on the sea and twelve weeks on land. The two sisters sang to escape from the poor food and living conditions, and from their poor care. They had sung in public before leaving England and soon realized that if they sang, they were treated to better food on the ship and to rides in the wagon.

Arriving in Salt Lake City, they had no one to care for them. Brigham Young called on Provo Bishop William Miller, who agreed to welcome them into his home. "One of his wives, Sarah, took me as her girl and the first wife took Caroline as her girl."

Reunited later with their parents and brothers and sisters, their struggle continued as they tried adjusting to a new lifestyle, finding a secure start, and getting ahead financially.

At sixteen, Ann married a professional bricklayer and plasterer, Joseph H. Neville. They had ten children as they followed the building trade to new settlements in northern Utah and Idaho. He was specifically called to do the canal leveling for the Sidon project by leader Byron Sessions. In the end, Joseph trained Sessions to do the leveling while he did the blacksmithing.

After living in a tent for seven months, the family moved into a

Wedding portrait, 1872

four-room house with nice large windows. Ann considered the house "a palace." Their home became the post office and the location for the town's one telephone line. Ann "took care of all the calls and the money from them." She also served as a midwife.

Years later natural gas was discovered on their property in what was considered to be the largest flow to date in the area. Selling it for a good price, they built a ten-room house. After Joseph died, Ann continued to live in the Byron area surrounded by her family members.[15]

" . . . we paid our debts, and built us a very nice house and grist mill, 10 rooms, large basement and bathroom and had it well furnished. Porch all around the east and south side and everything modern. Hot and cold water, bath and toilet, and we sure enjoyed it."

Ann West Neville[16]

Julia Ann England Denney
(19 January 1873–13 September 1969)

Migration: Utah to Idaho
Place Joined the Church: Utah
Came: With her husband and children
County Where Settled: Tooele; Big Horn, Wyoming; Oneida, Idaho

Julia Ann England Denney's name appears in a block above the center, while her sister-in-law Elizabeth Denney has one in the lower left corner. Julia Ann was born the sixth of twelve children to John and Eliza Kennington England at Tooele, Utah. Her parents had come to Utah in 1856 as handcart pioneers. She married Edward Denney on December 5, 1894, in the Salt Lake Temple. Their first three children were born in Utah before they an-

swered the call for pioneers to settle the Big Horn Basin in 1900.

During the first year in Wyoming, their home consisted of two tents, one for sleeping and one for cooking and eating. While her husband helped build the railroad, she cooked for the men on the crew. Seven more children were born in Byron. Julia Ann England Denney brought joy and encouragement to the local people by growing flowers and providing lovely bouquets for Church conferences and for friends. Her flowers became one of the symbols that their efforts to make the land productive would pay off.

The typical housecleaning routine for a Byron woman in the early years of settlement was difficult.

Each woman did a complete, systematic housecleaning every spring and fall. Those who had woven rag carpets took them up and thoroughly cleaned them. The floor was scrubbed and covered with clean fresh straw. If a mouse hole was found in the floor, a lid off a tin can was nailed over it. Then the carpet was put down over the straw and tacked around the edges. The walls were cleaned and repapered with newspapers or whitewashed. Sometimes thin white cloth, factory, was tacked on the ceiling. The stove and stovepipe were cleaned and polished with stove blacking. Actually, the stove received this kind of attention every week. The wooden bedsteads were taken apart and cleaned with scalding soapsuds and fresh straw was put in the bed ticks. The cupboards were thor-

Julia Ann England Denney

oughly cleaned. Everything was clean and lovely until the next dust storm left a layer of dust everywhere, or until the next rain caused muddy water to leak through the dirt roof and run down the walls and stovepipe.[17]

Eventually, the Denneys acquired enough land to try subsistence farming. They sold honey and butter to help cover their expenses. In 1921, they moved to Marsh Valley, Idaho, in hopes of finding better quality land. Julia Ann continued her interest in gardening and raising flowers and houseplants. She died in Idaho on September 13, 1969, at the age of 96.[18]

Permelia Jane Smith Johnson (12 July 1850–5 November 1919)

Migration: Utah to Arizona to Wyoming to Utah
Place Joined the Church: Utah
Came: With her husband, his wife Samantha, and their children
County Where Settled: Coconino, Arizona; Big Horn, Wyoming; Kane, Utah

Permelia Johnson's name appears on the quilt in the lower-right quadrant. She was born the daughter of Jonathan and Nancy Jane Taylor Smith in Farmington, Utah. She married Warren Marshall Johnson in Salt Lake City on October 4, 1869. Warren operated the important ferry crossing on the Colorado River along Honeymoon Trail between 1874 and 1894. They became the parents of ten children born mostly in odd-numbered years between 1872 and 1891. In March 1875, he moved her to the Lee's Ferry crossing on the Colorado River upriver from the Grand Canyon.[19]

A terrible tragedy struck her family while living at the isolated Lee's Ferry crossing. Although the large Johnson families lived there permanently isolated from regular contact with other children, they were regularly visited by those passing through. In May 1891, a family traveling from Richfield, Utah, to Tuba City, Arizona, spent the night. They told the Johnsons they had just buried a child on their journey who had died very suddenly of an unknown ailment. Four days later, a Johnson boy was stricken with a sore throat and fever. Diphtheria had in-

Permelia Smith Johnson with grandchildren Ruanna Judd, Joseph Cook, and Edna Johnson

vaded the family. Before it was over, three of the daughters and the son of Permelia and Warren Johnson had died between May 19 and June 5. Three others became ill and recovered. Fortunately, a number of the children were away at boarding school in Kanab, Utah. The visiting family had not recognized the illness and had not disinfected themselves and their belongings.[20]

Samantha Nelson Johnson (28 October 1853–7 October 1922)

Migration: California to Utah
Place Joined the Church: Utah
Came: With her husband, his wife Permelia, and their children
County where Settled: Coconino, Arizona; Big Horn, Wyoming; Kane, Utah

Samantha Nelson Johnson's block is in the top row, second from the left corner. She was born the daughter of Price W. and Lydia Ann Lake Nelson in the Mormon community of San Bernardino, California. She married Warren Marshall Johnson as his second wife on October 28, 1872, in Salt Lake City. They became the parents of ten children born mostly in even-numbered years between 1874 and 1895. She moved to the Lee's Ferry location early in 1876.[21]

Like women in all large Mormon families in the West, the Johnson women faced a challenge in washing their clothes.

Wash day was far from a pleasure in those days. A barrel of water would have been hauled the previous day. Or, if water was running down the ditches, a barrel would have been filled the previous evening so it would settle by morning. Some people put prickly pears in the water to help it settle. The woodbox was filled with firewood. A boiler of water was put on the stove to heat. However, if the boiler had small holes in the bottom, from long use, rags were put in the larger holes and the smaller ones were patched with a paste made of flour and water. In the winter when ice was used, it took much longer to melt the ice and heat the water until it boiled. When the water boiled, it was put in the washer, which looked like the lower half of a wooden barrel with four legs. A batch of clothes was put in the washer and someone, usually one of the older children, began to turn the washer. That is he turned a wheel on the side of the washer. This operated the mechanism on the inside. This mechanism consisted of four wooden pegs which turned back and forth, swishing the clothes in the water until they were clean. This continued for ten minutes with each batch of clothes. There might be eight or ten batches. Then all the clothes had to be washed again in a "second water." All this was hard work for the one turning the washer.

Samantha Nelson Johnson

The mother still had to rinse all the clothes, starch part of them, hang them out to dry, gather them in again, sprinkle them, and iron them with old style flatirons which had to be heated on the stove. Of course, everyone did not do the washing in this manner. Many of them had no washers, so they had to scrub all the clothes on the washboard. That was much harder work.[22]

Leaving there twenty years later, the Johnson families moved to the Byron area. While planning the move, Warren was permanently paralyzed in a farming accident. This made their life particularly difficult. Unable to survive the harsh experience, he died in Byron in 1902. The two wives and most of the children returned to southern Utah, where they lived out their years.

Quilt: HAWAIIAN
PRESENTATION (Quilt IV-6)

Category: Appliquéd
Size: 98" x 86"
Date: Late (1894)
Maker: Hawaiian Saints
Owner: Libbie Noall (11 November
1864–21 March 1897)
Migration: Utah to Hawaii to Utah

Libbie Laker and Matthew Noall

This quilt is included as typical of those made by or for Mormons as part of the Church's worldwide missionary outreach. It represents the change in focus after 1890 from gathering in Zion to serving the people in the locations where they lived. Quilts similar to this had been presented in the past within the Hawaiian culture and in exchange between the Hawaiian and American cultures.[23]

Missionary Libbie Noall received this quilt in 1895 at the conclusion of her family's second stay in Hawaii in acknowledgment of her guidance as a teacher, manager, and midwife in spite of her own failing health. Libbie and her husband, Matthew, served two missions in Hawaii in the mid-1880s and the early 1890s. As a talented young couple, they successfully managed the mission program. Among other things, they learned the unusual and difficult language as directed to do by the missionary program. Libbie was special, being one of only two Mormon women to master the language at that time.[24]

The Hawaiian makers expressed their respect and appreciation for her in the quilt's design and presentation. It contains the significant design elements seen in other historic Hawaiian quilts. The center medallion eagle with flags signifies the sharing of two cultures at the time of

the overthrow of the Hawaiian monarchy in 1894. Afterward, the Hawaiians were not permitted to fly their flag, and many turned to making quilts to demonstrate their loyalty to the royal family. The repeated images are reminiscent of the designs they stenciled on their tapa cloth coverlets. It is known that Hawaiian women gathered together to quilt in bees, using low "horses" to facilitate their sitting on the ground.[25]

The "Aloha 'oe Libbie Noall" is interpreted by family members to mean "In appreciation of Libbie Noall." The words also have the meaning of a greeting or a farewell. The "M. H. 1894" refers to the Mission House constructed under Matthew's leadership as a professional builder during this second mission.

The split border is intricately cut and appliquéd in two distinctly different patterns. At first glance, they appear to be alike and then close inspection reveals that they are not. This is a further example of the Hawaiian quiltmakers' desire to be creative and personalized. One tradition of their quiltmaking is to create patterns that could not be easily copied. Another typical style is the "echoing" quilting, with lines moving away from each design element.

Before their departure, the Hawaiians recognized Libbie's "straight for-

ward kind words of help and good, . . . her forward leadership."[26] In their traditional love of pomp and show, they staged a special event in the Mormon chapel. Although the quilt is not mentioned specifically in Matthew's description, it was most likely presented at this special occasion:

> When the congregation was assembled, and my wife and I and our children were seated as guests of honor, a procession started up the west aisle of the chapel with several committeemen alerted to the spirit of the occasion, either leading or following the procession. The center of interest was a chaise intricately loaded with a maze of vines, ferns, flowers and wreaths, arranged with such care and beauty that it was a marvel to behold. Topping all these were two miniature canoes with riggers, paddles and sails. One was carved of sandal wood and the other of koa. These canoes were carrying many scrolls, each expressing confidence, trust, and love for myself and my wife. There was one from each of the several Church organizations, such as the Relief Society, Sunday School, and Mutual Improvement Association. The testimonials came from the saints of Laie and Honolulu as well as many private Church members. . . . The care and execution of the details of this pageant, the speeches and sentiments expressed, were indeed masterpieces in their line; and the love expressed both by the promoters and us recipients will live on and on in my memory.[27]

Full view of Hawaiian Presentation Quilt

Elizabeth De Ette Laker Noall was born the daughter of Lashbrook and Annie Bryceson Laker in St. Charles, Bear Lake County, Idaho. At sixteen, Libbie Laker first met Matthew Noall. Their courtship bloomed between 1882 and 1883 while she boarded at his parents' home while attending the University of Utah. They were a romantic young couple; she wrote him a love poem and he created for her a lady's work box with over one thousand pieces of inlaid wood.

In 1884, while she taught school in Round Valley in rural Bear Lake County, he constructed his bride's house. It was a three-room brick house with detailed handmade moldings, carvings, and panels, adjoining his father's home in Salt Lake City. Married after the school year ended, they had been settled for only four months when they received the call to go to the Sandwich Islands (now Hawaii). Libbie remained at the mission site at Laie, thirty-seven miles north of Honolulu, and served as Relief Society president, while

Matthew traveled for extended time periods. In 1887, they transferred to Honolulu for a much larger responsibility. As a young twenty-three-year-old mother, wife, and missionary, Libbie became the resident caretaker of the mission house Auwaiolimu, providing for all visiting missionaries and their wives. Returning to Utah in 1888, they were called again to head the mission program in 1892. Returning to Salt Lake, Libbie died of pneumonia on March 21, 1897, at the age of thirty-two.

CONCLUSION

THE MIGRATION

THE MIGRATION AND SETTLEMENT STORIES OF these nineteenth-century female Saints can be summarized as ones beginning with profound difficulty and displacement, though sustained by religious and social commitment. Their lives then transitioned to become more normal, as that could be defined in the arid, isolated Intermountain West.

To some degree, all of these women experienced the difficulty of being a part of a new social organization during its period of discovery and definition. This began during the "Second Great Awakening" when many traditionally educated women and men were encouraged to search for new beliefs. Yet many others felt threatened by these new social and religious movements and tried to defend their own beliefs and economic values. The resulting conflicts challenged much of the whole nation throughout a large part of the nineteenth century.

This turbulence and its shifting alignments (immigrations and migrations) created new lifestyle opportunities. A wide range of Mormon women studied here made the individual or family choice to associate with others of common beliefs and vision. Their stories show how their choices played out in their own lives and faith.

For example, the Book of Mormon had specifically directed the Saints to reach out to the Native American peoples. They thus had a special interest in each new tribe they encountered as they began their westward migrations and mission outreach. This attitude led to the general, yet unofficial, Mormon approach of being good neighbors without causing confrontation.

Once in Utah, this special interest between Indians and Anglos was mutually shared as they continued to live their parallel lives. Often curiosity led to responses of calmness or of surprise and alarm on either's part. In an 1854 letter to her family, Susan Mandeville Fairbanks wrote:

"While I am writing an old squaw stands looking in the windows she wants to know what I am doing I told her in this way, niny maunch togeme niny mamaco reheny niny pica. It is this my Father is a great ways off and wants to see me. The children all talk Indian."[1]

The Mormons' ability to gather together repeatedly, in spite of the human and environmental challenges that they encountered, demonstrates their leaders' extraordinary ability to organize and facilitate large groups of people and to adapt to changing circumstances. Once having settled together finally in Deseret, they then demonstrated sufficient flexibility to be able to protect their accomplishments by changing some of the most fundamental components of their faith. They continued to build a membership of strong, capable individuals and normalized their relationships with their neighboring Americans.

THE COLONIZATION AND SETTLEMENT

In general, studies conclude that most nineteenth-century women in the American West desired to return to the cultural norm of being a wife, mother, and housekeeper once they became securely established. Women within each geographic settlement area, however, had their individual perspective. For example, the women in Oregon's Willamette Valley, who owned their land jointly with their husbands, were reluctant to relinquish the role they had established on the trail of being partners with their husbands. Women viewed their homes as part of their farm's work environment.[2]

The experience was much the same for many early Utah pioneer quiltmakers who migrated before 1853. They established their role as partners while on the trail. Once settled, this role continued and expanded as they often became the sole support of their families. For those coming in the more general migration, individual women found that taking on some role helped them to adjust. They might become a friend, helper, hired hand, or plural wife; often they joined with someone of the same native origin. Assuming these roles within established homes and families helped them to bridge the challenges, confrontations, conflicts, and conquests necessary to survive in the West and to dissolve the demographic complexity of their new society.

For the general agricultural migration to the West, economic development would take place in two stages. The first stage was a survival period of usually two to five years when the concern was to establish the home and to farm land in order to support the family. The skills developed during the migration would serve the pioneer woman well as she made this transition. This adjustment period would be repeated by each new arriving group but with varying degrees of difficulty. For women coming early, the resources were rare and primitive. For those coming later, developed communities were available for support.

The second stage of economic development would evolve from the first. People would seek to build a community by interacting socially and by establishing schools, churches, and governmental units.

For members of the Latter-day Saints, women and men alike, their transition to established security and economic opportunity in the West was different. To begin with, the Church specifically sought out people of various trades and skills in Europe and brought them to the territory. Their migration journeys were made easier by the Church-staffed commercial ventures and agencies established along the way. Arriving in Utah, the homes were grouped together as in Europe, first in forts and later in villages centered on networks of stakes and wards. Because of this grouping, the migrants' time to recover and establish themselves was substantially shorter than for other populations. In addition, the same experienced pioneers were repeating the survival period of conquering the land and building the communities again and again. The number of counties where these women lived during their lifetimes is evidence of this repeated pioneering. Mary Young Wilcox and her family answered the call to colonize six different times (Quilt I-6).

Repeated colonizing also meant that less transition time was required before being able to provide the needed community support services. Converts were already in communities established by the Church—namely, their migration companies either in the Midwest or in Europe. At times, a company arriving in Salt Lake City would be directed to settle together in a particular area, or they would be sent to locations where citizens with the same ethnic backgrounds already lived.

THE QUILTS

Note: A detailed analysis of the quilts appears in Appendix A.

These stitched treasures are a visual microcosm of the rich legacy of textiles either brought to the American West from the eastern United States and Europe, or produced locally for an extended period of economic isolation within the territory. Many contain clues to the textiles, dyes, and resources available; the climatic conditions of agriculture and settlement; and the social and economic opportunities provided to women through their evolving roles in Mormon families, communities, and organizations. They provide background information to the owners' geographic places of origin, as well as the locations of their pioneering. The collection gathered here allows one to observe these people's twenty years of turbulent search (1830–1850), forty years of self-sufficient isolation (1850–1890), and the subsequent years of accommodation (1890 and following).

These quilts are a unique collection representative of the great complexity of demographics that brought women together from North America, the British Isles, and Northern Europe. They individually symbolize the women's desire to retain their initial cultures as part of their heritage, while blending into a social and spiritual movement. While only a few quilts survive that were brought with the early pioneers, others indicate the ideas and concepts that came in their minds and hearts. Some reflect the diverse traditions of styles and construction methods, while others contain special fabrics or references to individuals and events.

Two quilts commemorate the successful achievement of the individuals' migration and gathering in Zion. One is the Victory quilt (III-1) by Dorinda Moody Slade celebrating her personal adventure. The other is the 20th Ward Relief Society quilt (I-4) with the patriotic symbols referring to the makers' homelands: Ireland, Scotland, Denmark, Britain, and America. The quilt's written phrases and verses also refer to emigration and its spiritual nature: "The Gospel Power Is Strong," "It Gathers from Every Land." Other messages relate to Zion and carry political overtones, such as "Our Mountain Home and Celestial Marriage," "Woman's Rights in Utah," and "United We Stand."[3]

There are few quilts—mostly preserved fragments and unfinished tops—remaining from the most active pioneering and community building period. The reasons for this scarcity include the unsettledness brought on by repeated pioneering; the chaos of political threats interrupting the otherwise steady maturing of their lives; the natural challenges of unexpected drought and insect invasions; and the imposed economic isolation of the middle years.

The quilt fragments are remnants of the many quilts known to have been made entirely by hand for warmth and protection within the people's homes. Women often worked together to make them because of necessity and a desire for shared experiences.

The unfinished tops by Sarah Pea Rich and Elizabeth Ashby Snow, both from traditional New England families, represent an interest in quiltmaking beyond the basic purpose of providing bedding (Quilts I-2 and I-12). The red and green Star patterns speak of the personal satisfaction and enjoyment that nineteenth-century women received from quiltmaking. These two women were unable to complete their quilts because they were busy filling leadership roles for their extended families and communities, and did not have the repeated pioneering experiences.

The majority of quilts, including these tops, were made just prior to and after 1890. These treasures represent their makers' final work, often their last quilt or most important quilt. They are symbolic of the transition to normalcy for both the women and their Church's society. This was the time when settlement had stabilized and statehood was reached, and the segregated order for self-sufficiency was reduced. Women could now create quilts expressing their own individuality by drawing on the new fabrics, patterns, and supplies available to them. Thus most of these quilts shown here were the last or finest quilts that they made because the design and construction of early ones had been dominated by use, practicality, and necessity.

Reunion of Pioneers of 1847

Some quilts were made by women who resided in Salt Lake City their entire lives. They preferred the social and economic advantages of urban life. Many reflect a skillful mastery of the techniques and design concepts of quiltmaking.

THE WOMEN

Thus, these Mormon women, brought together spiritually by a common faith, found that their lives were defined and determined by the organization and structure that the Church needed for its survival.

In the early years, the husbands were often away for extended periods of time fulfilling Church or community obligations or their other families' personal needs. In later years, because of polygamy, the husbands were often in prison in Utah or in exile elsewhere. The wives were left alone with their children to find their own financial, physical, emotional, and mental support.

As concluded by several Mormon historians, women's writings indicate that "women lived much of their lives in a subculture separate from men. It was a culture whose chief occupations were nurturing and housekeeping and whose primary rituals centered around women's relationships with other women, children, and men."[4] The women lived separately from their husbands, yet they were influenced and directed by the actions of the male-dominated Church leadership.

Women's roles in the earliest years of Mormon settlement and resettlement, were driven to a great extent by the strictures of the church, not only in matters of faith, but also in matters of logistics and family structure. This differs significantly from the independence among individuals and family units of the other overland trail migrations to the West in the mid- to late nineteenth century. Whether it was a matter of accepting polygamous marriage and the "wife order" within that structure, or a role in the women's relief organization, or a specific task assigned by church leadership to manage a hotel, to start a cotton industry, or to build a canal, the women took roles from authority figures who sought to shape their lives to fit the need of a larger social order. Only as the years went on, bringing the stability of settlement and statehood, did these women come into their own individuality. Later after 1870, moving towards the period of stabilization, women's roles began to differentiate, individualize, and become more artistically expressive well toward the end of the community-building era in Utah.

Of primary significance for these quilt owners was the life

they shared with others through polygamy or plural marriage. The quilts indicate mutually supportive relationships and an ability to accommodate to such a living situation. Yet the practice and its acceptance varied with each individual. A number of these women were the first wives of plural marriages and thus had the opportunity to reside in one location, often Salt Lake, without the ongoing responsibility for their husbands. For others living together, polygamy provided the opportunity to have help in producing and maintaining food, bedding, and clothing in order to meet the Church's goal to develop a home-based, self-sufficient economy, from raw material to finished product.

Among the women of this study, the practice of polygamy was more widely accepted than in the population as a whole. Among these quilt owners thirty-five families (54 percent) were monogamous while twenty-eight (43 percent) were polygamous; for two, information is unavailable. Polygamy was never widely practiced among Church members, in spite of the notoriety it brought to the Mormons. Approximately one-fifth of the Church population lived in polygamous families.[5] It was the custom of only a small group of Church leaders and their hand-picked representatives. Of these, only a very few, Prophet Joseph Smith and President Brigham Young in particular, had large numbers of wives. Only one woman in this study was directly connected to these two men: Zina D. H. Young was married a second time to Joseph Smith in 1842, and a third time to Brigham Young on February 2, 1846, as his twenty-second wife (Quilt I-13). This was just four days before the Saints were forced to flee Nauvoo. For her, the marriage offered a sense of family security as they headed off into the unknown of a westering experience. Later in Utah, because of the household arrangements, she was free to pursue work with the Relief Society, becoming the leader of the silk industry promotion and eventually the third general president.

The "wife order" of the women in this study who were in polygamous marriages is also balanced, with twelve (43.7 percent) being the first wife and sixteen (57.3 percent) being second, third, or higher in order of marriage. These figures correspond to the percentages in the larger population who practiced polygamy. The practice must be considered within the framework of time, place, and existing conditions.

The first factor was the large number of early members who accepted the doctrine only after "prayerful study and thought," as demonstrated by Prophet Joseph Smith. Many of these women personally knew and trusted him. It is known he and his own family had extreme difficulty with this practice. It is one of the reasons his wife Emma did not continue as a member

"The dear old lady's rambling talk threw strong side lights on the way in which she took up this new life, accepting uncomplainingly all that was strange and hard; bravely carrying the burdens of her whole family; and going out to minister to her neighbors whose sufferings were greater than her own. . . . 'I never could have borne it all if had not been for my hope, my great hope.'"
A Mormon grandma described by Florence A. Merriam, 1894[6]

of the Church after his death. She chose instead to follow her sons and become a member of the Reorganized Church of Latter Day Saints, the group not practicing plural marriage. Brigham Young actively encouraged the practice because of the people's social and economic needs during the years he was president between 1845 and 1877.

A second factor was that many were a part of the relatively peaceful period between 1840 and 1857 in Nauvoo and Utah, when they felt a sense of freedom, safety, and security to practice their faith without intervention by governmental authorities.

Third, polygamy offered an instant solution to the problems of where to live and who to befriend for the high number of single women who migrated to Utah by choice or with adult family members. When they arrived, these young women often would be welcomed into someone's home as an extra pair of adult hands in exchange for bed and board. She then had an opportunity to view the family situation, develop a friendship with the husband, and decide to "accept her fate" that she had been directed to this home.

Older women who had lost their first husbands also felt a sense of security in plural marriages. By marrying another husband, perhaps that of a sister or other close relative, women would be provided a home and family for shelter and support. In the family of Cherrel B. Weech, her great-great-grandfather married his brother's widow in order to provide a home for her and her children. In the large complex of relatives that resulted, Cherrel asked her grandfather Ammi John Curtis to clarify the connections between the siblings, the half-siblings, and the cousins. His response was "Honey, I have never seen any half people. They are all my brothers and sisters."[7]

The Saints have long used terms of kinship to address each other, such as "Sister" and "Brother." Friends and relatives alike commonly called older women "Grandma" as a name of respect. This was a common practice, however, among many people in nineteenth-century America.

Historically, after the arrival in Nauvoo when the practice of polygamy became more visible, the name "Aunt" was used by wives and children to refer to the other wife in plural marriages. Younger wives would often call the first wife "Ma" as a sign of respect for her position in the family. Often, the first wife's role would be similar to that of Sarah DeArmon Pea Rich (I-2), who served as stabilizer, counselor, and comforter. Another example is the role of Ellen Lunt (II-10), who supervised raising and educating the multiple numbers of children in the extended family.

"Many may think it very strange that I wuld consent for my dear husband, whom I loved as I did my own life and lived with for years, to take more wives. This I could not have done if I had not believed it to be one principle of His Gospel once again restored to the earth, that those holding the Priesthood of Heaven might, by obeying this order, attain to a higher glory in the eternal world. By our obedience to that order, we were blessed, and the Lord sustained us in the same . . ."

Sarah DeArmon Pea Rich
(Quilt I-2)[8]

Another aspect of the friendship and kinship in these women's lives was their relationships with their children. Many women mentioned the support they received from their children. When they were young, both boys and girls helped in maintaining the farms. Often the daughters were sent out to work for others. Later in life, many women visited or lived near an adult daughter or son and eventually were buried beside them. These women strengthened family relationships and received respect as honored elders in return. As Amanda Barnes Smith (II-5) wrote: "Alma was a great source of comfort to his mother and while yet a boy, helped make a home and provide for the younger children."[9]

One quilt in particular, the Crazy quilt by Lydia Rebecca Baker Johnson (I-10), illustrates the bond of kinship and friendship as a predominant theme among the Mormon people. The quilt's centered documentation of "1841 Mother 1915" reveals the important connection between this woman and her son.

An interesting feature of these marriages was the relative ease of gaining a divorce, which could be requested from and granted by Church authorities. Amanda Smith (II-5) sought a divorce from her second husband after arriving in Utah. Ann Mariah Bowen (Call) Loyd (II-1), as a second wife, obtained a divorce from her husband. Matilda Ann Duncan Winters (I-16) was married in polygamy for a time to Charles Henry Stoddard before divorcing him in favor of monogamous marriage.

Another example of kinship and friendship among these women was their particpation in the Relief Society. Many, like many other Mormon women, had either leadership positions within the organization or responsible teaching positions, conducting classes for all ages of people. These assignments were often taken on for long periods of time, as demonstrated by Dorinda Moody Slade (III-1).

Other tasks that women performed for each other rather commonly in Utah included teaching school, dressing the dead for burial, aiding the sick, and serving as midwives.

For all these women, these stitched treasures of transition contain the message that their lives were ones of accomplishment and personal achievement, as they survived the challenges of joining a new religion and adjusted to living in the arid desert of the Intermountain West.

"Her life was one of service and sacrifice, both for the Church and for the people who were to follow after her to make a better place for us all to live in."

Leona George Smith and Hilda Mann Condie, granddaughters of Ann Mariah Bown (Call) Loyd[10]

Mormon Washday *by William Henry Jackson*

APPENDIX A

QUILT ANALYSIS

Note: A list of quilts and their page numbers appears on page 202.

GENERALLY SPEAKING, THE TEXTILES AND TECHniques the Saints used in making their quilts, and the traditions they maintained, followed the same rags-to-richness pattern as their migration experiences. Yet these women, like most others, were influenced in their choices for quiltmaking by their exposure to new ideas, conditions, and resources. Therein lies these quilts' uniqueness as a body of work expressing themes of women's experiences living in the American West.

For their initial migration, if they had the opportunity, they brought with them a special completed quilt or segment of unfinished handwork. But more often, these women arrived in Utah with more dreams than personal belongings. From the pioneering period, the existing recycled pieces or remnants of quilts represent the women's personal desire to be responsive to the Church's directives for self-sufficiency and economic boycott. The quilts of the later period, on the other hand, contain fabrics and designs that represent an underlying desire to be current in taste and style with the mainstream of American culture. This cultural contact came through increased travel and communication. It occurred to a limited extent after the completion of the transcontinental railroad in 1869 and more significantly after the Manifesto of 1890 and the normalization of relations with others outside Utah.

Noting the continent of origin for both the quilt and the owner draws attention to the contributions these diverse women made to Mormon quilt heritage. The quilts were from either North America, the British Isles, or the Scandinavian countries, as were the majority of Saints. They represent the history of European-American quilts during the nineteenth and early twentieth centuries. The sharing of these quilts found in the Intermountain West will add to the growing awareness of how quilting traditions migrate across continents and oceans. At this time, emerging new research is providing evidence that definitive statements of quilt design and construction made previously are no longer accurate.[1]

Although meager numbers of Saints migrated from France, Italy, and Switzerland, no quilts have surfaced from any of these national backgrounds. The lack of a quilting heritage within these areas may help to explain this absence. Thus far, the textile traditions of these countries have not revealed any quilts or textile sandwiches among the social economic groups who joined the Church. The second reason that the U.S. descendents of Swiss Mormons, in particular, do not have heirloom textiles is that most of them pulled handcarts, with only enough space for bare essentials and a minimum amount of extra weight.[2]

The charts that follow are intended to help the reader compare the quilts in order to be able to note similarities and differences in styles and textiles among quilts from different categories. The reader is encouraged to refer back to the photographs of the quilts. Studying the quilts in this way can enhance one's appreciation of them as visual records of women's work. To avoid confusion in interpreting a chart, when a quilt may qualify for several categories within the same field or when a question exists, a footnote is included.

TEXTILES

The chart on the following page presents the textiles according to the possible place of origin and the study's specifically defined time periods of early (1800–1850), mid (1850–1890), and late (1890–1935).

In general, the textiles represent the period from the late 1700s through the early 1900s. They reflect the rapidly expanding production made possible by the new developments resulting from the Industrial Revolution in Europe and America. The fabric weaves range from the simple domestic handloomed to the complex industrial machine-produced. The design images and colors illustrate the evolution printing techniques and dye processes.

The fabrics also represent the Utah textile industry of cotton, wool, and silk production as it evolved during the time period of 1860 to 1900. The 1860 date was chosen because prior to this the Mormons were focused on building shelter, conquering the land, and providing food. The years from 1857 to 1860, with the federal military presence and the threatened Utah War, forced an interruption in their planned agricultural production. The date 1900 was chosen because it marked the end of their silk industry. By this time, the period of normalization was also well underway, with greater use of outside resources. The same range of finished textile goods existed here as on the national scene but with a lesser degree of sophistication. Current studies have not yet produced results that determine conclusively whether a textile was made in a Utah factory. Much of the evidence is hearsay and is receiving further evaluation.

An interesting finding was that no quilts exhibit the predominance of the American, factory-produced cotton prints so overwhelmingly popular throughout the country between 1870 and 1890. Specifically, there are no quilts of red, white, and blue fabrics and no commemorative prints for the 1876 Centennial. Nor are there any of the gray-appearing mourning prints of black and white. The obvious reason was the economic boycott.

Origin and Time Period of Textiles in Representative Quilts in This Study

Origin / Time Period	EUROPEAN			NORTH AMERICAN			UTAH	
	Early 1800-50	Middle 1850-90	Late 1890-1935	Early 1800-50	Middle 1850-90	Late 1890-1935	Middle 1860-90	Late 1890-1935
TEXTILE FABRIC								
Woolen								
Imported		Cunningham (#IV-3)[A]						
Domestically produced								
Home				Lathrom/Young (#I-13)	Smith (#II-5)[B]		Davis (#II-16), Dalton (#II-6), Lunt (#II-10)	Jones (#II-15)
Factory								
Cotton								
Imported	Fairbanks (#I-8)[C], Barton (#III-13), Rawlinson (#III-7), Chase (#I-11), Harris/Bankhead (#I-30), Unknown/Martin (#II-20)[D]	Tresder (#III-11)	Shepherd (#III-15)[E]					
Domestically produced								
Home				Heward (#I-14)				
Factory				Butler/Babcock (#IV-4), McArthur (#I-15), Whitmore (#III-6)	Moses (#III-9)	(Call) Loyd (#II-1), Winters (#I-16), Parsons (#III-10), Ricks (#III-14), Jensen (#III-16)	Barkdull (#II-8)[F], Sunrise in the Pines (#III-1a and 2)[G]	Butterfield (#II-4)
Silk								
Imported[H]		20th Ward R.S. (#I-4)	Kimball (#II-3)[I], Bybee (#II-7), Hall (#II-13), Byron R.S. (#IV-5)					
Domestically produced								
Home								
Factory								Carter (#I-5)[J]

A Other fabrics are imported silks and satins brought with her from Scotland.

B The textiles are both North American factory and Utah home products.

C The center fabric may have been either imported or produced in an early American printworks.

D The fabrics are either imported or early domestic.

E This quilt most likely contains both European- and North American-produced fabrics.

F These fabrics were probably factory produced and home dyed.

G The dyes used to make green involved a two-step process of overdying blue with yellow. The yellow faded away leaving the remaining blue. Elsewhere in the world of dyestuffs, by 1850 there was sufficient technology to have created a fairly successful green dye without having to use the two-step method. This presence of the remaining blue is the indication of the imposed isolation and of the predominance of indigo as a

H May contain silk from both international and domestic markets; specific information is not available.

I These quilts may contain Utah-produced silk.

J This one quilt may definitely contain Utah silk because it is known Sophronia Carter was actively involved in the southern Utah silk industry.

Another quilt, popularly thought to be made of Utah silk from women's dresses, is at the Museum of Church History and Art, made by Anne Leaver Musser. However, research by Jan Fletcher disclosed that Musser had passed away before the time the first dress from Utah silk fabric was made in 1877. Sources: Ida Sheets Adamson, "History of Ann Leaver Musser," Manuscript Collection, ISDUP Pioneer Memorial Museum, Salt Lake City; and Jill Mulvey Derr, Janath Russell Cannon, and Maureen Ursenbach Beecher, *Women of Covenant* (Salt Lake City: Deseret Books, 1992), 105.

Frequency of Quiltmaking Techniques
According to Origin of Maker
(Total Number of Quilts: 65)

Origin of Maker	EUROPEAN	NORTH AMERICAN	BOTH[A]	UNKNOWN
TECHNIQUES				
Format				
Pieced	19	42		3
Appliquéd	1	4		
Both	1	1	1	1
Whole Cloth		2		
Crazy	5	1	1	
Unknown		1		

[A]Group quilts with contributers from both continents.

TECHNIQUES

The numbers in the chart above yield several interesting comparisons between quilts made in or brought to Utah and those quilts made elsewhere.

Of the project's total number of quilts, the pieced far outnumber the appliquéd. The small number of appliquéd quilts (eight) is interesting. All of them were made either before the owner came to Utah (four, including one by an unknown maker) or after her life had achieved a level of stability (four). The small number of appliquéd quilts can be attributed to the economic isolation and repeated labor-intensive pioneering for most Mormon quiltmakers.

In North America's more settled areas during the corresponding forty years after the 1830s, red-and-green appliquéd quilts were especially popular.[3] Sufficient amounts and variations of quality fabrics could be purchased for creating the more laborious appliquéd designs. Also time- and labor-saving domestic tools and machinery were being invented, and women eagerly acquired them so that they would have more discretionary time in their routines.

Of the four appliquéd quilts that were probably brought to Utah, three were made during the height of the style's popularity, the 1850s and 1860s (III-8, IV-1a and 1b). Family tradition states Mary Greenwood Giles made her pieced and appliquéd "finger quilt" in England in 1838 (III-5). Of the others, two were probably made after the completion of the transcontinental railroad in 1869: one by Matilda Robison King after a visit back East in 1869 (II-9), and the other by a plural wife, Rebecca Burton Jones, who lived in urban Salt Lake City while her husband worked as a territorial colonizer (II-2). The seventh was made late in Eliza Hall's life after her family had become well established in their Ogden home (II-13). Eliza Ricks made the last one in the 1920s or

Styles and Traditions of Representative Quilts in the Study
According to Origin of Maker

Origin of Maker	EUROPEAN	NORTH AMERICAN	UNKNOWN
STYLES			
Construction			
Whole cloth	Lathrom/Young (#I-13)		
	Chase (#I-11)		
Single template			
Diamond/Lozenge	Rawlinson (#III-7)		
	Jones (#II-15)		
Square	Burton (#I-19)	Kimball (#I-30)	
	Shepherd (#III-15)		
	Bullock (#II-11)[A]		
Rectangle/Logs	Williams (#III-12)	Butterfield (#II-4)	
Set			
Framed center			
medallion	Barton (#III-13)	Smith (#II-5)	Fairbanks (#I-9)
	Bjork (#IV-2)		
Strips	Davis (#II-16)	Whitmore (#III-6)	
Block to block	Bullock (#II-11)	Hall (#II-13)	
Block to block			
with sashing	Evans (#II-19)	McArthur (#I-15)	
	Treseder (#III-11)		
Blocks			
alternating	Young (#III-4)	Jones (#II-2)	
pattern and plain			
TRADITIONS			
Condition of Textiles			
New	Shepherd (#III-15)	King (#II-9)	Unknown/Martin (#II-20)
Remnants	Jones (#II-15)	Butterfield (#II-4)	
	MacKay (#II-18)		
	Barton (#III-13)		
	Bjork (#IV-2)		
Recycled	Williams (#III-12)	Smith (#II-5)	
	Davis (#II-16)	Moses (#III-9)	
Craftsmanship			
Piecing			
Simple	Barton (#III-13)	Winters (#I-16)	
Complex	Smith (#III-3)	Slade (#III-1)	
Appliquéing			
Simple	Giles (#III-5)		
Complex		Coray (#IV-1)	
Quilting			
Simple	Ricks (#III-14)		
Complex			Mormon Mothers (#I-20)
		Bracken (#III-2)	
		Lathrom/Young (#I-13)	
Decorative			
Stitching			
Simple	Bjork (#IV-2)		
Complex	Cunningham (#IV-3)	Johnson (#I-10)	
	Tresedar (#III-11)		
Design			
Unique			
Pieced	Smith (#III-3)	Whitmore (#III-6)	
Stenciled		Heward (#I-14)	
Appliquéd	Noall (#IV-6)		
Quilted	Jones (#II-2)		Mormon Mothers (#I-20)

[A] The construction format used here is one of exchanging segments of cloth cut from squares to create two-color blocks.

1930s, possibly from a kit, long after a period of normalization in both her own life and the Mormon economy had been reached (Quilt II-14).

When one considers the quiltmaker's origin, one discovers almost equal division between the numbers of North Americans and Europeans who chose pieced block patterns. Elsewhere in North America, pieced patterns were the choice of many quiltmakers, who used both available scraps and the vast array of new textiles produced in the Mid-Atlantic and New England mills from about 1830 until the end of the century. British Isle quiltmakers of the nineteenth century also chose to use pieced patterns such as the star and the basket.[4]

Several quilts may represent a crossover between European and American styles, possibly attributable to interaction among the Mormon women, as well as the influence of their environment. The Treseder quilt (III-11), made by a British quilter, has traditional English crewel embroidery work and a style of British quilting called "infill." Family tradition indicates it was completed in the West where its wool batt was acquired. The Smith quilt (II-5), made by a North American, has the framed center medallion and repeated borders commonly seen in British quilts. The Cunningham Crazy quilt (IV-3), made in transit by a Scottish woman, has traditional embroidery patterns available in Scotland, yet includes stitched images associated with the American West.

STYLES/TRADITIONS

The styles of the seven Crazy quilts represent the two variations in this category: embellished ornamentation and practical fabric recycling. Both were popular trends in the world of late-nineteenth-century quiltmaking. The choice of fabric and the amount of stitched detail reflect the lives of the women who made the quilts. Generally in the United States, the elegant embellished style reached its peak of popularity in the 1880s within the urban, populated areas, while the more practical rural or country style of using up fabric remnants continued over a broader time span. An extensive amount of stitching indicates an increased amount of discretionary time or limited physical activity. Small pieces of rich fabrics such as silks and velvets reveal greater accessibility to these resources. Less detail and larger pieces of remnant fabrics indicate less available time, a greater need to supply bedding, and less emphasis on detailed design and construction.

Of this study's four embellished Crazys, only the Cunningham quilt (IV-3) dates to the time of peak popularity. Agnes Bell Cunningham was traveling outside the territory during the time she made her quilt in 1879.

The other three, made after the 1890 Manifesto, reflect these women's desires to be fashionable, to mark special events, and to use the limited available resources in their ongoing lifestyle. The Byron Relief Society silk quilt (IV-5) was made of their best fabrics in order to record, in a public visual medium, the fellowship of these women who survived the harsh pioneering and contributed to the success of northern Wyoming. The MacKay silk wedding quilt (II-18), with its elegant

border and wool backing, would have added brightness and warmth to the young couple's Victorian Salt Lake parlor in 1898. The Johnson quilt (I-10), made in 1915, was a celebration of the maker's needlework ability and her son's special interests in America and Abraham Lincoln.

Although the other three Crazy quilts are more utilitarian in style, they reveal the quiltmakers' continuing desire to make special quilts. The Hawkins quilt (II-17) was made before 1890 from scraps salvaged from family and friends. Mary Bjork's quilts (IV-2 and IV-2a), made with her adult children as their wedding quilts in the decade following 1910, reflect her life's pattern of recycling and re-using.

FEATURES OF QUILTS MADE IN UTAH

SET OF BLOCKS

Once blocks are constructed, the quiltmaker makes decisions about their placement that affect the completed quilt's visual presentation. Three arrangements appeared more commonly than expected. Although these are not unique to quilts in Utah, each merits further study as an indication of the women's relative isolation from other evolving styles and design decisions, the influence of their early needlework training, and the possible sharing of quiltmaking within the territory.

The "on point" set of the blocks appears in fifteen of the thirty-two quilts known to have been made in Utah. The blocks are set on the corner of the square rather than flat on a horizontal edge. For visual reference, compare the Rebecca Jones quilt (II-2) with the King quilt (II-9).

Since other nineteenth-century quiltmakers used the on-point set, it cannot be identified as uniquely Mormon. Quilts using this block placement have surfaced in the American state projects in New York and Ohio; North American women originally came from or passed through both these areas on their way west.[5] This set was also used in mid-nineteenth-century England; it therefore could have been familiar to British converts such as Elizabeth Treseder and Elizabeth Fox (III-11 and II-21). Quilts with this set have been published in studies by British quilt historians Averil Colby and Dorothy Osler.[6]

QUILTING PATTERNS

The styles in quilting patterns again represent the breadth of these women's backgrounds and experiences. Of those quilts known to have been made in the West, the balanced distribution of quilting patterns reflects the change in the time women had available to devote to their quiltmaking. The earlier quilts, made during the pioneering periods, have the elbow and straight line designs. The later ones, made during and after the period of normalization, have the more labor-intensive patterns of separate designs or quilting around individual pieces.

The most commonly produced patterns are the straight lines and the elbow or fan, both understandable for these western pioneer women.

Frequency of Features of Quilts Made in Utah
(Total Number of Quilts - 32)

BLOCK PLACEMENT

With blocks set "on point" or diagonal	15 17
Block set flat or horizontal	

QUILTING PATTERNS

	7
Around each piece	8
Overall elbow/fan sweeps	8
Overall straight lines and/or gridwork	7
Defined pattern in separate block	1
In the seam line	2
Infill	1

Since available time and living space were limited, these patterns could be quickly and easily marked and quilted. The straight lines were marked perhaps by a chalked or spice-powdered string "snapped" in place on the surface. The fan or elbow pattern was also easy to mark. A series of points were placed at equal distances apart on a board which was laid on the quilt. Then the quilter would place her elbow as the pivot point on one of the board's marks, and swinging an arch with her arm and hand, mark the curved line with her needle or marking tool. It is usually easy to identify the corner of the quilt where she started by the sweep of the curves. This process would be repeated until all the lines were marked within a given distance.

One classic European quilting style appears in the Davis quilt (II-16), which has a different pattern in each of the woolen strips. Another is the "infill" quilting used in the Treseder quilt (III-11). Both were made during the isolation period relatively early in the women's years in Utah and thus probably honestly reflect their native quiltmaking heritage. Another with the infill pattern is the quilt by Eleanor Jones Young, who came as a young Welsh woman pulling a handcart (III-4).

There are three quilts held together in unique ways. Lydia Johnson embroidered an outline drawing of Abraham Lincoln on the back of her Crazy quilt (I-10). Anna Hawkins placed extra padded flowers on the front of her Crazy quilt that were stitched through to the back after the quilt was completed (II-17). Elizabeth Williams quilted around the outside edge of each Log Cabin block with a dark thread (III-12).

ADDITIONAL FEATURES

CENTER BLOCK FOCUS

Repeatedly, the quilt's most important theme or design element was placed directly in the center. This indicates the maker's desire to focus the viewer's attention on a very particular feature. The effort was successful, for as the current keeper of the Treseder Quilt (III-11) exclaimed, "The prettiest one of all is right smack in the middle."[7]

While this center focus may stem originally from British quilts with a framed center medallion, it appears in quilts by makers of all native origins. For comparison, view the different featured centers in the following quilts: the 20th Ward Relief Society quilt (I-4), where the most significant centered square has the group's name and honoree stitched with traditional American patriotic symbols; the Bullock quilt (II-11), where the owner's name is barely visible in the center square; the Johnson quilt (I-10), where the maker proudly referenced her title and her age at the time the quilt was made; the Fairbanks quilt (I-8), where the special fabric is preserved; the Cunningham quilt (IV-3), where the small woven label and the symbols of her native and adopted countries are carefully stitched; and the Coray Grape quilt (IV-1), where the one varying block is centered.

ORIENTATION OF THE QUILT'S BASE

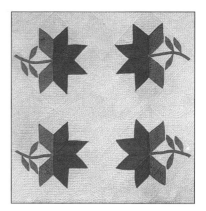

The orientation of a quilt's design reflects the maker's intention for how the quilt would be placed on a bed or displayed in another space. The question is which edge is the base or foot of the quilt. This determines how the maker oriented her blocks to be read, from the bed's foot or from either side. It is an important consideration in how a quilt is viewed during study. Sometimes, in the absence of the maker's spoken or written word, this question becomes a puzzle for the viewer to solve.

Most often, length and width are clues to the answer. The long side of the quilt runs the length of the bed as in the King quilt (II-9). However, this rule becomes complicated when quilts are square, as in the Coray quilts (I and Ia). Here, the clue is revealed in comparing both quilts—an advantage of seeing more than one quilt by the same maker. The Peony quilt (IV-1a), with its additional defined base row, provides the answer for reading the Grape quilt (IV-1).

A third clue may be the maker's signature. For example, in the Rebecca Jones quilt (II-2), her signature appears in a white triangular piece used to square the quilt. If the signature is to be read from the base of the quilt, as was common, than the rows of blocks would read from either side. If it is to be read from the upper right side, an unusual place for a signature, then the rows are oriented two to the bottom and one to the top. Following the more common trend, it would appear she intended the quilt to read from either side.

THEMES

QUILTS AS VISUAL RECORDS OF WOMEN'S LIVES

Quilts can provide important clues in the study of women's history, especially when the goal is to explain the significance of the activities and values of ordinary women in their daily lives.[8] It is widely accepted in the study of quilt history that women made some quilts to mark the significant events in their families' lives. These are broadly categorized as life's passages of birth, childhood/education, coming of age, marriage, and death, as well as important values such as friendship/community and religion.

These Mormon quiltmakers were no different. Some of the early pieces, representing both early American and British origins, were made by mothers, sisters, and aunts who did not themselves choose to join the Church and emigrate; others were made by the women themselves as part of their needlework education as young children. Those that were brought today show signs of use and wear, but they served as visual records of family and friends before the days of photography. The quilt brought by Susan Mandeville Fairbanks is a unique example (I-8).

Those unfinished childhood projects, which could be easily carried, serve as visual records of early learning experiences. One especially significant piece as a visual record is the needlework of Hannah

Rawlinson (III-7), the woman who did not survive to reach Zion herself but her treasured handwork did and was preserved.

Traditionally, regional quilts reveal themes of the early development of community resources and the women's mutual concerns over social, political, and economic issues. The time they spent making quilts marked the beginning of women and their families moving from a pattern of home-centered to community-oriented activity. Pioneering in a new region required constant effort just to survive during the first years. As families became established, a wider allocation of tasks freed them for other responsibilities and concerns. Group quilts known to be made by identifiable groups of women can contribute much to the understanding of the socialization of the community. Many historical quilts exist, representing institutions such as churches and fraternal organizations, and exhibiting social concerns such as relief efforts and women's suffrage. These quilts confirm the economic and social contributions of women to the development of the community in settling an area. While these traditions are highly prized within the broader spectrum of quiltmaking, they also validate a major theme in Mormon social history.

TRADITIONS OF KINSHIP AND FRIENDSHIP

From its earliest beginnings and continuing to the present time, the Church has taken pride in its ability to reach out to others to build and support their programs and fellowship through the bonds of friendship and kinship.[9] For the women in this study, the Mormon sense of community and concern for one another often began at the time of their initial migration or when they joined the Church. Because they were often left alone with their children while their husbands and fathers were away, these women gathered together for survival and support. Their quilts serve as visual records of a life lived within a structure defined by their Church, regimented by environmental factors, and refined by their personal choices and decisions.

They also felt that contributing to their Church and their community enriched their lives. The evidence is found in the words they wrote about their daily activities; in the recorded testimonies of their lives; and in their stitched treasures. The plural wives of Henry Lunt cooperated to make utilitarian quilts (II-10). The three generations of Shepherd women created their heirloom treasure of 10,513 squares (III-15). Elizabeth Williams (III-12) and Anna Sewall Hawkins (II-17) collected fabrics for their woolen quilts from their friends and families. Another quiltmaker, Mary Priscilla Burriston, gathered her friends together to collect wool for their quilts from fences and bushes after herds of sheep passed by.[10]

Women participated in their church fellowship groups to create for their leaders the 20th Ward Relief Society Presentation quilt (I-4) and the Hawaiian Presentation quilt (IV-6). They created the Mormon Mothers quilt (I-20) and the Byron Relief Society quilt (IV-5) to commemorate special activities or events. The Pine Valley women shared the Sunrise in the Pines pattern, probably kept in "Sister Slade's Trunk" at the Relief Society (III-1a and 2).

MIGRATION

Comparing this study's quilts for themes of migration with those of the project on Oregon Trail quilts yields some significant, yet understandable differences.[11] Practically no quilts in this study were made just prior to the major migration, either across the ocean or the Plains, as was the case with quilts of the Oregon Trail. None of the typical migration patterns appear here, such as Wandering Foot, nor tulip, rose, or peony florals expressing love, concern, or well wishes for the journey. For the most part, the Mormon companies consisted of friends and families traveling together. Women were forced by circumstances to flee without time to prepare. They traveled with limited amounts of extra space over an extended period of time, often years. Although they were told to bring bedding, it was limited to what was needed for warmth and protection.

However, some quilts made after subsequent moves to pioneer other areas do contain themes of migration. There are two geese patterns, in which migrating birds represent movement and change of location (I-3 and III-9). There are also two pieced Irish Chain quilts presenting a sense of visual movement through the diagonal placement of pattern pieces (I-6 and I-19).

The Mormons had fewer possibilities for constructing a quilt while on a major migration, yet more significant finds surfaced than in the Oregon study. These are the Mormon Mothers' Rocky Mountain variation (I-20); the Cunningham quilt (IV-3); and the Slade Victory quilt (III-1). These reflect unique individual episodes within the broad range of Mormon migration experiences. Many women in the migrations before 1855 actively participated in the tasks and responsibilities of migrating. Later, the women traveled in structured trains, which had scheduled routines and used resources the Church had established along the way. Available time for stitching did not often occur either in long layovers or waits for river crossings.

Little recorded evidence exists of quiltmaking taking place during migrations, perhaps because few women's diaries and journals have surfaced thus far with entries of daily migration activities. In addition, a fair number of women were probably illiterate, and some were unable to read or write the English language. One key exception is Eliza R. Snow's writing of the unique outdoor quilting in an early temporary settlement in Iowa. Another is the reference to Dorinda Moody Slade's making a Rising Sun quilt for Melissa Meeks during her extended layover in the army barracks in the Cherokee Nation.

LOCATION

The overall theme presented by a large number of these quilts is the geographic and environmental impact of the Intermountain West on the lives of the people. The quilts, as a group, reflect the aridity and harshness of the climate, the disparity of resources, and the economic and social isolation from either coast. Such factors were expressed through the choice of patterns and fabrics, the embroidered images, the dye sources, and the style of quilts.

There are four Log Cabin quilts, compared to one in the Oregon Trail study (I-5, I-9, II-4, III-12). These may reflect the repeated pioneering in Utah and the lack of resources. Wood and logs for homes were much scarcer in the intermountain area than in the Pacific Northwest. Mormons in Utah tended to live for longer periods of time in tents, dugouts, and log cabins than people did in Oregon. In Utah, a log cabin could be a permanent residence, constructed with great sacrifice and labor. Logs had to be hauled a great distance from the mountains to the valley. In Oregon, a log cabin was a more temporary structure, often built fairly quickly and easily from trees on the land one had claimed.

The quiltmakers chose pieced block patterns that suggest themes of outdoor living. There are twelve Star quilts, one Noonday, and two Sunrises. These celestial elements symbolized the timing of the day's activities. The star also represented an appeal or wish for divine guidance in the midst of harrowing pioneering experiences. This belief and faith in God was the most common unifying theme among Mormons, as it was among other religiously motivated pioneers.

There are ten quilts with floral motifs, which suggest the discovery of natural resources, the determination to master the earth by raising flowers and crops, and the desire to beautify homes and gathering places. Of particular interest is that the flowers chosen were bulbs that bloom in the early spring, such as tulips, when enough water would be available for successful growth and flowering (II-2 and II-21). Another was the Sego lily, the state flower and an important native food source for these pioneers; it appears in the quilt made by Eliza Hall (II-13).

The appliquéd floral pattern Washington Plume surfaced four times in the study, but of these only the King quilt qualified to be included (II-9). The choice of this pattern by Utah-based quiltmakers deserves future consideration.

Surprisingly, other important historical symbols specific to the Church and Utah, such as the honeybee and beehive, appeared fewer times than expected. They were found only in the 20th Ward Relief Society quilt (I-4) and the Hawkins Crazy quilt (II-17).

The decorative images used to embellish the quilts reveal the challenges of living in the West. Several stitched flowers were worked with their bulb bases, creating the visual message that one's survival often depends on carrying one's own food (II-17 and IV-3). The inclusion of the embroidered laundress and the Old Dutch Cleanser motifs portray the constant struggle to deal with dirt and dust within their daily routines (IV-3 and I-10, respectively).

The use of sagebrush and cedar berries as natural dye sources was directly mentioned in the quiltmaking activities of Sarah Jane Rich (I-3), Mary Jane Butterfield (II-4), and Dorinda Moody Slade (III-1a).

No doubt other quiltmakers used these and other natural dyestuffs as well.

The camp quilt with its large-scale block and simplicity of design is reminiscent of quilts needed to provide warmth in western logging, mining, and ranching camps (III-16). The design could be made quickly when a large number of bed quilts were needed. The classification name even reflects western outdoor living.

The Utah-based, factory-produced textiles in these quilts reveal the broad dimension of that industry. The industry went beyond the expected production of woolen cloth to that of cotton and silk fabrics. The goal was to meet the declared need for self-sufficiency, a need reinforced by political conflicts. Several quilts made from cloth produced in local factories indicate the women's sense of pride as they attempted to alter its plainness by using natural dyes to produce the colors they desired. Sage Jones was one quiltmaker known to use the plain woolen cloth for dressmaking (II-15). Other quilts, such as the Carter quilt, may include small swatches of silk cloth produced during the period of that industry's activity between 1855 and 1900 (I-5).

As the discovery and sharing of more heirloom treasures occur and new research appears, additional quilts may further validate these findings and expand the interpretation of themes of women's life in the American West.

Quilt Maker and Quilt Identification Chart

Quiltmaker/Owner	Quilt Pattern	Number	Page
Ashworth	Pieced Baby Dress	II–14	86
Babcock	Butler Album	IV–4	166
Barkdull	Basket	II–8	74
Barton	Framed Center Medallion	III–13	138
Bjork	Crazy Patch I	IV–2	160
Bjork	Crazy Patch II	IV–2a	162
Bracken/Day	Sunrise in the Pines	III–2	117
Bryon Relief Society	Friendship Crazy Quilt	IV–5	168
Bullock	Peter and Paul or Pincushion	II–11	80
Burton	Triple Irish Chain	I–19	48
Butterfield	Log Cabin	II–4	66
Bybee	Bow Tie	II–7	72
Cain	Feathered Star	I–7	24
(Call) Loyd	Ocean Waves	II–1	60
Carter	Log Cabin	I–5	20
Chase	Whole Cloth	I–11	32
Coray	Grape with Flowers	IV–1	156
Coray	Peony	IV–1a	158
Cossitt/Chaffin	Star	II–12	82
Cowdery	Whig's Defeat	I–1	12
Cunningham	Crazy Quilt	IV–3	164
Dalton	Woolen Quilt Fragment	II–6	71
Davis	Strip Quilt	II–16	90
Evans	Nine Patch variation	II–19	96
Fairbanks	Framed Center Medallion	I–8	26
Fox	Tulip	II–21	100
Giles	Finger Quilt	III–5	122
Hall	Floral	II–13	84
Harris/Bankhead	Noonday or Sunburst	I–17	44
Hawaiian Saints/Noall	Hawaiian Presentation	IV–6	174
Hawkins	Crazy Quilt	II–17	92
Heward	Stenciled Quilt I	I–14	38
Heward	Stenciled Quilt II	I–14a	38
Jensen	Star	III–16	144
Johnson	Crazy Quilt	I–10	30
Jones, Rebecca	Tulip	II–2	62
Jones, Sage	Star	II–15	88
Kimball	One Patch	II–3	64
King	Washington Plume	II–9	76
Lathrom/Young, Zina	Woolen Whole Cloth	I–13	36
Lunt, Ellen	Star Quilt Fragment	II–10	78
Lunt, Ann			
MacKay	Crazy Quilt	II–18	94
McArthur	Album Block	I–15	40
Mormon Mothers	Rocky Mountain variation	I–20	50
Moses	Wild Geese	III–9	130
Parsons	Nine Patch	III–10	132
Rawlinson	Pieced Diamonds segment	III–7	126
Rich, Sarah Jane	Flying Geese	I–3	16
Rich, Sarah Pea	Star	I–2	14
Ricks	Rose of Sharon variation	III–14	140
Shepherd	Trip Around the World	III–15	142
Slade	Victory	III–1	112
Slade	Sunrise in the Pines	III–1a	115
Smith, Amanda	Framed Four–patch Center Medallion	II–5	68
Smith, Betsy	Star	III–3	118
Snow	Star	I–12	34
Staley	Star with Nine Patch	I–18	46
Stringham	Log Cabin	I–9	28
Treseder	Basket with Floral Stitchery	III–11	134
20th Ward/Relief Society/Smoot	Friendship	I–4	18
Unknown/Martin	Nine Patch Star	II–20	98
Weech	Oak Leaf and Reel	III–8	128
Whitmore	Nine Patch variation	III–6	124
Wilcox	Double Irish Chain	I–6	22
Williams	Log Cabin	III–12	136
Winters	Four Patch	I–16	42
Young, Eleanor	Feathered Star	III–4	120

APPENDIX B

PRESERVING THE TREASURES

MANY PEOPLE ARE NOW DISCOVERING THEIR family quilts. The revival of quilts as part of our American tradition has now reached all levels of culture as people realize their value and importance. Quilts can record passages of our lives and give us a sense of security and warmth. People also create quilts as a special gift for a loved one and even use them as metaphors for life's experiences. Thus, as more people become aware of quilts in today's world, they are seeking out those from their past and wondering how to appropriately enjoy and enhance their appreciation of these quilts without destroying them by regular use. These Mormon quilts serve as examples of the appropriate and inappropriate methods to follow.

The first step is to learn all the information possible about the quilt and its maker. Check for accuracy in order to avoid errors, incorrect interpretations, and the perpetuation of myths. Study the quilt carefully and record any writing that appears on it. Make notes about the quilt's condition and its history. Learn if other quilts exist that were made by the same maker. Since quilts were generally made within a defined time and place, do not view the quilt as presenting clues to the maker's entire life. Instead, consider the existing facts as leads to other information.

Concerning the maker, ask the basic research questions of who, what, when, where, why, and how. It also helps to gather certain artifacts: photographs of the maker, her family, her home, her community; written documents such as diaries and letters; tools she used in her needlework; and anything else significant that relates to her life's experience. In the case of quilts or other textile treasures, gather samples of fabrics, patterns, sewing items, and related materials. Thinking about this information will lead to questions about the maker's life within the time and place she lived. Answers to these questions can be discovered through local and state histories, church and county records, and historical books related to specific activities or events.

From studying the quilts and diary of their great-great-grandmother Elizabeth Terry Heward (I-14), Christine Reynolds and Patrice Cunningham have gained strength for their personal lives. Christine thinks of her Grandmother Heward as a role model as she contemplates her life's challenges and opportunities as a mother and writer.

Second, it is important to photograph the quilt to the highest level of quality possible within your budget. Try to shoot the overall image as well as significant details. Photographs of quilts are helpful to share with others when seeking additional information instead of having to carry along the quilt itself.

Once all the material is gathered, there are several important decisions about what to do with the quilt.

The first is the organization of the information. Write down the basic facts on archival paper and expand on the story. This could be as simple as writing one page or as complex as writing an entire book. Make multiple copies of all written and photographic materials. One copy should be placed directly with the quilt where it always will be accessible. Distribute other copies to family members.

A second decision concerns the quilt's future. Consider personal factors that may affect your decision, such as your preferences, financial resources, family relationships, and interest in the quilt. List possible owners, first from among family and friends and then others such as a museum, textile collection, or historical society. It is important to consider the quilt's valuable history as a visual record of the maker's experience and as a source of clues to other information. Be sure, therefore, to consider possible sites near the location where the maker lived at the time the quilt was made or where she lived out her life. Inquire if the institutions are interested in having the quilt in their collection. Possible questions to ask are how the piece would compliment their existing collection, how it would be stored, and how the institution would anticipate using it. Also ask to be notified when the quilt is to be exhibited.

Ask for copies of each institution's mission statement, program descriptions, and promotional materials. This will help to narrow the possible choices. Then ask what additional information they would like that will enhance their ownership of the quilt. Such information will help the museum to use the piece in carrying out their goal of educational outreach.

In addition to the above, it is helpful to include a bibliography of sources with information about the family, a list of descendants who might be contacted for additional information, and any other relevant notations. These items help tremendously in research projects such as this one in which questions arose that were not anticipated at the time of the donation.

An appropriate example of preserving quilt treasures is the return of the Relief Society Quilt to the Byron Museum in Wyoming (IV-5), where it has generated new interest in family history. The quilt was a central focus of their museum's dedication on July 2, 1994. It is displayed behind a protective covering where it can be enjoyed by all the visitors.

The decision on a quilt's future home is particularly important as people move into smaller residences and families become more dispersed.

Donors David and Ruth Moses faced that situation and decided to send the quilt from California to the Salt Lake City ISDUP Pioneer Memorial Museum where "it could be seen and enjoyed by all" (III-9).[1]

Several quilts in this study illustrate an inappropriate way to share family heirlooms. When a quilt is cut up into fragments, there is no way to know what the original complete quilt was like. This is demonstrated in the Davis and Lunt quilt fragments. Someone probably had good intentions but did not know the future value of and interest in the quilt.

By contrast, the Fairbanks quilt (I-8) shows a more appropriate method of preservation. The center, made from an historic textile that had originally been bed curtains, is large enough to see the repeat of the print. Placing the fabric in the center and surrounding it by borders protect it against physical handling. Note that the quilt was probably made before 1850 and is still available to be appreciated. This was the technique used not only to recycle fabrics but to preserve them as significant family heirlooms.

If the condition of the quilt appears to need attention, the most appropriate solution is to contact a textile conservator. These people are trained to recognize and recommend the best possible ways of handling heirloom treasures. The fabrics in the Cunningham quilt (IV-3) were recently evaluated by professional textile conservator Terri Schindel. Her recommendations were to photograph and record the condition, clean with a low-vacuum suction through a teflon screen, stabilize damaged areas using an appropriate conservation treatment, support the quilt, and exhibit the quilt for no more than three months at a time.[2]

To identify a trained professional in an area, contact the Foundation of the American Institute for Conservation of Historic and Artistic Works (FAIC) Conservation Services Referral System in Washington, D.C. at (202) 452-9545.[3]

If you want to use the quilt or complete an unfinished quilt top, the better alternative is to make a reproduction and use that quilt instead. This preserves the historic value of the original while allowing the owner to have a visual reproduction to enjoy. The main reason for not using an original is that a fabric's life has a definite time limitation, and regular usage has a cumulative effect on the deterioration of the fibers.

In recent years, many fabric companies have been printing authentic reproductions of historic fabrics for interior decoration and fashion design. For example, the Scalamandre Company has reproduced the center panel fabric from the Fairbanks quilt (I-8), as indicated in Jane Nylander's *Fabrics for Historic Buildings*.[4] The search for patterned fabrics similar to those in the historic quilt can add to the joy of making the reproduction. Visit a local independent quilt or decorator shop and ask the owner if something is available. Take along a high-quality color copy or photograph of the fabric to leave with the owner so that she can show it to the company sales representatives as they make their calls or carry it with her as she shops the wholesale market. Sometimes it is possible to contact the wholesale company directly but

Gayle Franszen, Great-great-granddaughter of Matilda Robison King (Quilt II-9)

Joyce Weeks, great-granddaughter of Mary Alice Klingensmith Benson

only with the backing of a retailer. This search is the type of service that locally owned stores are able to provide. It is a rewarding experience for them as well.[5]

Reproducing a family heirloom quilt has an added advantage. By repeating the production process, the current quiltmaker is able to make a special connection with the original quilter. From the thought process associated with design to the physical activity of making the same stitches and hand motions, there is a special feeling of bonding with the older quiltmaker.

This has been the experience of several Utah families and quiltmakers as they have worked to reproduce their grandmothers' quilts. A tulip quilt has been reproduced and shared multiple times through six generations of the Joseph and Mary Leight Oxborrow family. The story is that Mary originally brought a wool tulip quilt with her from England before her 1870 marriage in Salt Lake City. Her daughter Elizabeth traced the pattern and made the quilt many times for family members, teaching her daughters to quilt and continue the tradition. One of the quilts made by Elizabeth and her daughter Clio was given to Camellia Carter Sullivan at the time of her marriage to Robert Sullivan in 1958.[6]

Gayle Franszen and Joyce Weeks are individually reproducing the Washington Plume pattern, one of the few quilt patterns seen multiple times in this project. Both have spent time carefully studying the heirlooms for the appliqué dimensions and quilting patterns. They have studied their families' histories and personal stories. Gayle Franszen's great-grandmother was Matilda Robison King (II-9). Joyce Weeks's great-grandmother Mary Alice Klingensmith Benson was a native pioneer, born in 1857, who did not participate in a migration. She was left an orphan with her two sisters to survive on their own after their mother died and their polygamous father deserted them. She soon joined the community spinning club organized by the Relief Society to produce cloth for needy families. Here, she may have met member Phoebe Forrester Benson, who would later become her aunt by marriage. Each woman served as Relief Society president and produced a quilt of the Washington Plume pattern. Now Joyce Weeks is carrying on the family tradition of serving as an organization president and making a quilt. She wrote:

> I am currently reproducing this quilt for my own collection. The quilt my great-grandmother made belongs to my aunt LaBerta Benson Whitlock. The quilt will go to LaBerta's granddaughter. This is why I decided to reproduce this quilt. I am currently president of the Utah Quilt Guild, so the reproduction of the quilt will be in the making for quite sometime.[7]

Lightning Storm *by William Henry Jackson*

CHRONOLOGY OF RELATED MORMON HISTORY, 1830–1900

1830 The first edition of the Book of Mormon was published in March.

On April 6 the Church of Christ was organized.

1831 By May the majority of the Saints moved to the Kirtland, Ohio, area.

The Prophet Joseph Smith began moving members to Jackson County, Missouri, the New Jerusalem.

In both Kirtland and Jackson County, the Saints were heavily persecuted.

1832 Missionaries went into Canada, the first missionary effort outside the United States.

1833 In Kirtland, Joseph Smith received the revelation known as the Word of Wisdom.

The First Presidency was organized; Sidney Rigdon and Frederick G. Williams were called to be counselors to Joseph Smith.

Because of mob persecution, the Saints left Jackson County, Missouri.

1834 The first high council was organized.

At a conference in Kirtland, the Church was named "The Church of the Latter-day Saints."

"Zion's Camp" marched from Ohio to Missouri to assist persecuted Missouri Saints.

1835 Twelve apostles were chosen by the Three Witnesses to the Book of Mormon.

The First Quorum of Seventy was organized.

1836 The Kirtland Temple, the first temple of this dispensation, was dedicated in March.

1837 First missionaries were sent to Great Britain in June.

In July nine persons were baptized in the River Ribble, Preston, England.

1838 Exodus from Kirtland, Ohio.

The name of the Church was changed to "The Church of Jesus Christ of Latter-day Saints."

In July the law of tithing was given at Far West, Missouri.

In October Missouri governor Lilburn Boggs issued an "exterminate or expel order against the Saints; the Haun's Mill Massacre occurred; Joseph Smith and others were arrested by militia.

In December Joseph Smith and others began a six-month imprisonment in Liberty Jail.

1839 Brigham Young removed the Saints to Illinois.

Joseph Smith and others were released from Liberty Jail in April.

Commerce, Illinois, was selected as the next gathering place for the Saints. Its name was changed to Nauvoo.

1840 Converts from Europe began immigrating to the United States.

The "Nauvoo Charter" bill was signed into law by Illinois governor Thomas Carlin.

1842 The Female Relief Society was organized in Nauvoo. The Articles of Faith were published for the first time in the *Times and Seasons*.

1844 On June 27 the Prophet Joseph Smith and his brother Hyrum were murdered at Carthage Jail.

In August Brigham Young and the Twelve were sustained by vote to lead the Church.

1846 The westward migration of the Saints began in February.

Temporary settlements were established at Mt. Pisgah, Iowa; Council Bluffs, Iowa; and Winter Quarters, Nebraska.

In July the Mormon Battalion was organized and left for Fort Leavenworth.

1847 The first pioneer wagon companies arrived in the Salt Lake Valley on July 24.

In December Brigham Young was sustained as president of the Church.

1848 Mormon Battalion members were at Sutter's Mill, California, when gold was discovered.

Seagulls devoured the millions of crickets that were ruining the pioneers' crops.

1849 The Perpetual Emigrating Fund was established to help the poor come to Utah.

1850 Utah was made a territory with Brigham Young as governor.

1852 The doctrine of polygamy was publicly announced.

1853 The Salt Lake Temple site was dedicated in February, and the cornerstone laid in April.

1856 The first handcart companies left Iowa City, Iowa. The Willie and Martin handcart disasters occurred.

1857 The Mountain Meadows Massacre tragedy took place in September.

Johnston's Army (federal troops) tried and failed to enter Salt Lake City.

1858 In June federal troops peacefully entered Salt Lake City.

1860 The last companies to use handcarts arrived in Salt Lake City in September.

1861 The transcontinental telegraph was joined in Salt Lake City.

1862 The U.S. Congress declared polygamy a crime.

1867 Brigham Young requested bishops to reorganize ward Relief Societies, which had been disbanded during the Utah War.

1869 In May the transcontinental railroads were joined at Promontory, Utah.

ZCMI opened its doors for business.

The Young Ladies' Retrenchment Association was formed, later renamed the Young Women's Mutual Improvement Association.

Brigham Young University was founded.

1877 On April 6 the St. George Temple was dedicated.

On August 29 Brigham Young died.

The Quorum of the Twelve, with John Taylor at the head, assumed leadership of the Church.

1878 The first Mormon settlement in Colorado was founded in Conejos County.

1880 In October John Taylor was sustained as president of the Church.

1882 The Edmunds antipolygamy bill became law. Many men were imprisoned because of it.

1883 The first Maori branch was organized in New Zealand.

1884 The Logan Temple was dedicated on May 17.

1885 President John Taylor and others went into hiding to avoid antipolygamy harassment.

1886 The first LDS meetinghouse was built and used in Colonia Juarez.

1887 The Edmunds-Tucker Act became law, toughening the 1882 antipolygamy bill.

Cardston, Alberta, Canada, was established by the Latter-day Saints.

President John Taylor died on July 25. The Council of the Twelve assumed leadership of the Church.

1888 The Manti Temple was dedicated.

The first authorized missionary was sent to Samoa.

1889 In April Wilford Woodruff was sustained as president of the Church.

1890 President Wilford Woodruff issued the "Manifesto," which officially ended the practice of polygamy by the Church.

1893 U.S. President Benjamin Harrison issued a proclamation of amnesty to all polygamists who entered marriage before November 1, 1890.

On April 6 the Salt Lake Temple was dedicated.

1894 The Genealogical Society of Utah was organized.

1896 Utah was granted statehood.

1897 The *Improvement Era* began publication, continuing until 1970.

1898 President Wilford Woodruff died on September 2.

On September 13 Lorenzo Snow became the fifth president of the Church.

1900 Eight companies of pioneers leave for the Big Horn Basin of northern Wyoming to build the Sidon Irrigation Canal and lay the Burlington railroad tracks in one of the last settlement efforts.

Source for chronology: William W. Slaughter, *Life in Zion: An Intimate Look at the Latter-day Saints 1820–1995*, (Salt Lake City, UT: Deseret Book Company, 1995), 190–192.

PIONEER EMIGRATION AND MIGRATION COMPANY LISTS

THE FOLLOWING SHIP LISTS, HAND-CART AND WAGON train company lists are included to give an indication of the general scope of the Mormon migrations. The publicly-held notion traditionally has been that the migrations were overland journeys of families pulling handcarts. More actually, these lists reveal the extensive recordkeeping done by the Saints of their tightly-structured, constantly-changing migration organization. A quick review of passage days shows the declining number as the transportation power source changed from unpredictable wind to water-generated steam.

In addition, the maps throughout the text are helpful in tracing the water and land routes to Zion. The key and notes below are provided to clarify the terms and places mentioned in the first section, Emigrant Companies That Crossed the Ocean 1840–1890:

RIG

Ship	- a sailing vessel wih at least three masts and square-rigged across all masts
Bark	- a sailing vessel with three or more masts and square-rigged only on the first two masts
Bkt. or Barkentine	- a sailing vessel with three or more masts and only square-rigged on the first mast
Brig	- a sailing vessel with two masts and square-rigged on both masts
Stmr	- steamer powered by steam engines

DEPARTURE PORT

Liv.	- Liverpool, England
Amst.	- Amsterdam, Holland
Sydney	- Sydney, Australia
Auck.	- Auckland, New Zealand
London	- London, England
Hamb.	- Hamburg, Germany
Calcutta	- Calcutta, India
Melb.	- Melbourne, Australia
P. Eliz., Pt. Eliz.	- Port Elizabeth, South Africa
Newcastle	- Newcastle, England
LeHavre	- LeHavre, France
Tahiti	- An island in the Pacific Ocean
Bristol	- Bristol, England
N.Y.	- New York

ARRIVAL PORT

N.Y.	- New York
N.O.	- New Orleans
Quebec	- Quebec, Canada
S.F.	- San Francisco, California
Boston	- Boston, Massachusetts
S. Pedro	- San Pedro, California
Phil.	- Philadelphia, Pennsylvania
Hono.	- Honolulu, Hawaii

*Asterisked items are estimates.
[a]Voyage incomplete.
[b]About this time the *Cynosure* was sold to British owners.
[c]The *Nevada* was a side-wheel steamship that traded in the Pacific.

[d]Registered tonnage revised.
[e]Possibly the Dutch ship *Edam*, which arrived in New York from Amsterdam on May 13, 1889; passenger list is almost illegible.

Source: Sonne, Conway B. *Saints on the Seas: A Maritime History of Mormon Migration 1830–1980.* Salt Lake City: University of Utah Press, 1983. Appendix One.

Emigrant Companies That Crossed the Ocean 1840–1890

Vessel	Rig	Registry	Tons	Master	No. LDS Pass.	Departure Port	Departure Date	Arrival Port	Arrival Date	Passage Days	Company Leader
Britannia	Ship	U.S.	630	E. Cook	41	Liv.	6-6-40	N.Y.	7-20-40	44	J. Moon
North America	Ship	U.S.	611	A. Lowber	201	Liv.	9-8-40	N.Y.	10-12-40	34	T. Turley
Isaac Newton	Ship	U.S.	600	L. Spaulding	50*	Liv.	10-15-40	N.O.	12-2-40	48	S. Mulliner
Sheffield	Ship	U.S.	590	R. Porter	235	Liv.	2-7-41	N.O.	3-30-41	51	H. Clark
Caroline	Bark	Br.	330	R. Turner	?	—	- -41	—	- -41		T. Clark
Echo	Ship	U.S.	668	A. Wood	109	Liv.	2-16-41	N.O.	4-16-41	59	D. Browett
Alesto	Ship	U.S.	420	H. Whiting	54	Liv.	3-17-41	N.O.	5-16-41	60	T. Smith
Rochester	Ship	U.S.	714	P. Woodhouse	130	Liv.	4-21-41	N.Y.	5-20-41	29	B. Young
Harmony	Ship	Br.	832	J. Jamison	50	Bristol	5-10-41	Quebec	7-12-41	63	T. Kingston
Caroline	Bark	Br.	330	R. Turner	100*	Bristol	8-8-41	Quebec	10-22-41	75	T. Richardson
Tyrian	Ship	U.S.	511	D. Jackson	207	Liv.	9-21-41	N.O.	11-9-41	49	J. Fielding
Chaos	Ship	U.S.	771	L. Pratt	170	Liv.	11-8-41	N.O.	1-14-42	67	P. Melling
Tremont	Ship	U.S.	368	J. Gillespie	143	Liv.	1-12-42	N.O.	3-10-42	57	—
Hope	Ship	U.S.	881	F. Soule	270	Liv.	2-5-42	N.O.	4-1-42	55	J. Burnham
John Cumming	Ship	U.S.	721	G. Thayer	200*	Liv.	2-20-42	N.O.	4-26-42	65	—
Hanover	Ship	U.S.	577	J. Drummond	200*	Liv.	3-12-42	N.O.	5-2-42	51	A. Fielding
Sidney	Ship	U.S.	450	R. Cowen	180	Liv.	9-17-42	N.O.	11-11-42	55	L. Richards
Medford	Ship	U.S.	545	U. Wilber	214	Liv.	9-25-42	N.O.	11-13-42	49	O. Hyde
Henry	Ship	U.S.	395	B. Pierce	157	Liv.	9-29-42	N.O.	11-10-42*	42	J. Snyder
Emerald	Ship	Br.	642	W. Leighton	250	Liv.	10-29-42	N.O.	1-5-43*	68	P. Pratt
Swanton	Ship	U.S.	677	S. Davenport	212	Liv.	1-16-43	N.O.	3-16-43	59	L. Snow
Yorkshire	Bark	Br.	658	W. Bache	83	Liv.	3-8-43	N.O.	5-10-43	63	T. Bullock
Claiborne	Ship	U.S.	663	J. Burgess	106	Liv.	3-21-43	N.O.	5-13-43	53	—
Metoka	Ship	U.S.	775	J. McLaren	280	Liv.	9-5-43	N.O.	10-27-43	52	—
Champion	Bark	Br.	795	J. Cochrane	91	Liv.	10-21-43	N.O.	12-6-43	46	—
Fanny	Bark	U.S.	529	T. Patterson	210	Liv.	1-23-44	N.O.	3-7-44	44	W. Kay
Isaac Allerton	Ship	U.S.	595	T. Torrey	60	Liv.	2-6-44	N.O.	3-22-44*	45	—
Swanton	Ship	U.S.	677	S. Davenport	81	Liv.	2-11-44	N.O.	4-5-44	54	—
Glasgow	Ship	U.S.	594	J. Lambert	150	Liv.	3-5-44	N.O.	4-13-44	39	H. Clark
Norfolk	Ship	U.S.	548	D. Elliot	143	Liv.	9-19-44	N.O.	11-11-44	53	—
Palmyra	Ship	U.S.	612	Barstow	200*	Liv.	1-17-45	N.O.	3-11-45	53	A. Fielding
Parthenon	Ship	U.S.	536	S. Woodbury	10*	Liv.	3-30-45	N.O.	5-12-45	43	—
Oregon	Ship	U.S.	649	J. Borland	125*	Liv.	9-1-45	N.O.	10-28-45	57	—
Liverpool	Ship	U.S.	623	S. Davenport	45	Liv.	1-16-46	N.O.	3-25-46	68	H. Clark
Brooklyn	Ship	U.S.	445	A. Richardson	235	N.Y.	2-4-46	S.F.	7-31-46	177	S. Brannan
Montezuma	Ship	U.S.	924	A. Lowber	10*	Liv.	8-15-46	N.Y.	9-17-46	33	—
America	Ship	U.S.	1137	Trussell	50*	Liv.	2-1-47	N.O.	3-10-47	37	J. Taylor
Empire	Ship	U.S.	1049	J. Russell	24	Liv.	7-6-47	N.Y.	8-10-47	35	L. Scovil
Carnatic	Bark	Br.	654	W. McKenzie	120	Liv.	2-20-48	N.O.	4-19-48	59	F. Richards
Sailor Prince	Ship	Br.	950	A. McKechnie	80	Liv.	3-9-48	N.O.	4-28-48	50	M. Martin
Erin's Queen	Ship	Br.	821	H. Campbell	232	Liv.	9-7-48	N.O.	10-28-48	51	S. Carter
Sailor Prince	Ship	Br.	950	A. McKechnie	311	Liv.	9-24-48	N.O.	11-20-48	57	L. Butler
Lord Sandon	Bark	Br.	678	G. Welsh	11	Liv.	12-30-48*	N.O.	2-17-49	49	—
Zetland	Ship	Br.	1283	H. Brown	358	Liv.	1-29-49	N.O.	4-2-49	63	O. Spencer
Ashland	Ship	U.S.	422	W. Harding	187	Liv.	2-6-49	N.O.	4-18-49	71	J. Johnson
Henry Ware	Ship	U.S.	540	E. Nason	225	Liv.	2-7-49	N.O.	4-8-49	60	R. Martin
Buena Vista	Ship	U.S.	547	E. Linnell	249	Liv.	2-25-49	N.O.	4-19-49	53	D. Jones
Hartley	Ship	U.S.	469	S. Cammett	220	Liv.	3-5-49	N.O.	4-28-49	54	W. Hulme
Emblem	Ship	U.S.	610	W. Cammett	100*	Liv.	3-12-49	N.O.	5-4-49	53	R. Deans
James Pennell	Ship	U.S.	571	J. Fullerton	236	Liv.	9-2-49	N.O.	10-22-49	50	T. Clark
Berlin	Ship	U.S.	613	A. Smith	253	Liv.	9-5-49	N.O.	10-22-49	47	J. Brown
Zetland	Ship	Br.	1283	H. Brown	250*	Liv.	11-10-49	N.O.	12-24-49	44	S. Hawkins
Argo	Ship	Br.	999	C. Mills	402	Liv.	1-10-50	N.O.	3-8-50	57	J. Clinton
Josiah Bradlee	Ship	U.S.	648	C. Mansfield	263	Liv.	2-18-50	N.O.	4-18-50	59	T. Day
Hartley	Ship	U.S.	469	C. Morrill	109	Liv.	3-2-50	N.O.	5-2-50	61	D. Cook
North Atlantic	Ship	U.S.	799	H. Cook	357	Liv.	9-4-50	N.O.	11-1-50	58	D. Sudworth
James Pennell	Ship	U.S.	571	J. Fullerton	254	Liv.	10-2-50	N.O.	11-22-50	51	C. Layton
Joseph Badger	Ship	U.S.	891	T. Skolfield	227	Liv.	10-17-50	N.O.	11-22-50	36	J. Morris

Emigrant Companies That Crossed the Ocean 1840–1890 *(continued)*

Vessel	Rig	Registry	Tons	Master	No. LDS Pass.	Departure Port	Arrival Date	Passage Port	Company Date	Days	Leader
Ellen	Ship	Br.	893	A. Phillips	466	Liv.	1-8-51	N.O.	3-14-51	65	J. Cummings
George W. Bourne	Ship	U.S.	663	W. Williams	281	Liv.	1-22-51	N.O.	3-20-51	57	W. Gibson
Ellen Maria	Ship	U.S.	768	A. Whitmore	378	Liv.	2-2-51	N.O.	4-6-51	63	G. Watt
Olympus	Ship	U.S.	744	H. Wilson	245	Liv.	3-4-51	N.O.	4-27-51	54	W. Howell
Kennebec	Ship	U.S.	926	J. Smith	333	Liv.	1-10-52	N.O.	3-14-52	64	J. Higbee
Ellen Maria	Ship	U.S.	768	A. Whitmore	369	Liv.	2-10-52	N.O.	4-5-52	55	I. Haight
Niagara	Stmr.	Br.	1825	J. Stone	20*	Liv.	3-6-52	Boston	3-19-52	13	J. Taylor
Rockaway	Ship	U.S.	815	G. Preble	30	Liv.	3-6-52	N.O.	4-25-52	50	E. Morris
Italy	Ship	U.S.	749	J. Reed	28	Liv.	3-11-52	N.O.	5-10-52	60	O. Monster
Forest Monarch	Ship	Br.	977	E. Brewer	297	Liv.	1-16-53	N.O.	3-16-53	59	J. Forsgren
Ellen Maria	Ship	U.S.	768	A. Whitmore	332	Liv.	1-17-53	N.O.	3-6-53	48	M. Clawson
Golconda	Ship	Br.	1124	G. Kerr	321	Liv.	1-23-53	N.O.	3-26-53	62	J. Gates
Jersey	Ship	U.S.	849	J. Day	314	Liv.	2-5-53	N.O.	3-21-53	44	G. Halliday
Elvira Owen	Ship	U.S.	874	C. Owen	345	Liv.	2-15-53	N.O.	3-31-53	44	J. Young
International	Ship	U.S.	1003	D. Brown	425	Liv.	2-28-53	N.O.	4-23-53	54	C. Arthur
Falcon	Ship	U.S.	813	Wade	324	Liv.	3-26-53	N.O.	5-18-53	53	C. Bagnall
Camillus	Ship	U.S.	717	C. Day	228	Liv.	4-6-53	N.O.	6-7-53	62	C. Bolton
Envelope	Bark	Br.	402	Smith	30*	Sydney	4-6-53	S.F.	7-8-53	94	C. Wandell
R. K. Page	Ship	U.S.	995	W. Strickland	17	Liv.	9-1-53	N.O.	10-28-53	57	Bender
Jessie Munn	Ship	Br.	875	J. Duckitt	335	Liv.	1-3-54	N.O.	2-20-54	48	C. Larsen
Benjamin Adams	Ship	U.S.	1170	J. Drummond	384	Liv.	1-28-54	N.O.	3-22-54	53	H. Olsen
Golconda	Ship	Br.	1124	G. Kerr	464	Liv.	2-4-54	N.O.	3-18-54	42	D. Curtis
Windermere	Ship	U.S.	1108	J. Fairfield	477	Liv.	2-22-54	N.O.	4-24-54	61	D. Garn
Old England	Ship	U.S.	917	J. Barstow	45	Liv.	3-5-54	N.O.	4-26-54	52	J. Angus
John M. Wood	Ship	U.S.	1146	R. Hartley	397	Liv.	3-12-54	N.O.	5-2-54	51	R. Campbell
Julia Ann	Bark	U.S.	372	C. Davis	63	Newcastle	3-22-54	S. Pedro	6-12-54	83	W. Hyde
Germanicus	Ship	U.S.	1167	A. Fales	220	Liv.	4-4-54	N.O.	6-12-54	69	R. Cook
Marshfield	Ship	U.S.	999	J. Torrey	366	Liv.	4-8-54	N.O.	5-29-54	51	W. Taylor
Martha Whitmore	Ship	U.S.	649	P. Whitmore	10*	Liv.*	-54	N.O.*	-54	—	—
Clara Wheeler	Ship	U.S.	996	J. Nelson	29	Liv.	4-24-54	N.O.	7-3-54	70	—
Clara Wheeler	Ship	U.S.	996	J. Nelson	422	Liv.	11-24-54	N.O.	1-11-55	48	H. Phelps
Rockaway	Ship	U.S.	815	S. Goodwin	24	Liv.	1-6-55	N.O.	2-26-55	51	S. Glasgow
James Nesmith	Ship	U.S.	991	H. Mills	440	Liv.	1-7-55	N.O.	2-23-55	47	P. Hansen
Neva	Ship	U.S.	849	T. Brown	13	Liv.	1-9-55	N.O.	2-22-55	44	T. Jackson
Charles Buck	Ship	U.S.	1424	W. Smalley	403	Liv.	1-17-55	N.O.	3-14-55	56	R. Ballantyne
Isaac Jeanes	Ship	U.S.	843	W. Chipman	16	Liv.	2-3-55	Phil.	3-5-55	30	G. Riser
Siddons	Ship	U.S.	895	J. Taylor	430	Liv.	2-27-55	Phil.	4-20-55	52	J. Fullmer
Juventa	Ship	U.S.	1187	A. Watts	573	Liv.	3-31-55	Phil.	5-5-55	35	W. Glover
Chimborazo	Ship	U.S.	916	P. Vesper	431	Liv.	4-17-55	Phil.	5-22-55	35	E. Stevenson
S. Curling	Ship	U.S.	1468	S. Curling	581	Liv.	4-22-55	N.Y.	5-22-55	30	I. Barlow
Tarquinia	Brig	U.S.	210	E. Meyers	72	Melb.	4-27-55	Hono.	7-5-55*	69	B. Frost
William Stetson	Ship	U.S.	1147	J. Jordan	293	Liv.	4-26-55	N.Y.	5-27-55	31	A. Smethurst
Frank Johnson	Ship	U.S.	529	A. Lothrop	10*	Calcutta	5-29-55	S.F.	9-18-55	112	—
Cynosure	Ship	U.S.	1258	J. Pray	159	Liv.	7-29-55	N.Y.	9-5-55	38	G. Seager
Julia Ann	Bark	U.S.	372	B. Pond	28	Sydney	9-7-55	Wrecked, Scilly Is.	10-3-55		J. Penfield
Emerald Isle	Ship	U.S.	1736	G. Cornish	350	Liv.	11-30-55	N.Y.	12-29-55	29	P. Merrill
John J. Boyd	Ship	U.S.	1311	T. Austin	512	Liv.	12-12-55	N.Y.	2-16-56	66	K. Peterson
Caravan	Ship	U.S.	1363	W. Sands	457	Liv.	2-14-56	N.Y.	3-27-56	41	D. Tyler
Enoch Train	Ship	U.S.	1618	H. Rich	534	Liv.	3-23-56	Boston	5-1-56	39	J. Ferguson
S. Curling	Ship	U.S.	1468	S. Curling	707	Liv.	4-19-56	Boston	5-23-56	34	D. Jones
Thornton	Ship	U.S.	1422	C. Collins	764	Liv.	5-4-56	N.Y.	6-14-56	41	J. Willie
G. W. Kendall	Brig	U.S.	183	H. Wilson	9	Tahiti	5-5-56	S.F.	6-27-56	52	Anderson
Horizon	Ship	U.S.	1775	W. Reed	856	Liv.	5-25-56	Boston	6-20-56	26	E. Martin
Jenny Ford	Bark	U.S.	397	S. Sargent	20*	Sydney	5-28-56	S. Pedro	8-15-56	80	A. Farnham
Wellfleet	Ship	U.S.	1353	I. Westcott	146	Liv.	5-31-56	Boston	7-13-56	43	J. Aubrey
Lucy Thompson	Ship	U.S.	1500	C. Pendleton	14	Liv.	7-5-56	N.Y.	8-8-56	34	J. Thompson
Columbia	Ship	U.S.	1051	C. Hutchinsen	223	Liv.	11-18-56	N.Y.	1-1-57	44	J. Williams
Escort	Ship	U.S.	1454	E. A. Hussey	10*	Calcutta	12-10-56	N.Y.	3-3-57	83	M. McCune
George Washington	Ship	U.S.	1534	J. Comings	817	Liv.	3-28-57	Boston	4-20-57	23	J. Park
Westmoreland	Ship	U.S.	999	R. Decan	544	Liv.	4-25-57	Phil.	5-31-57	36	M. Cowley
Tuscarora	Ship	U.S.	1232	R. Dunlevy	547	Liv.	5-30-57	Phil.	7-3-57	34	R. Harper

Emigrant Companies That Crossed the Ocean 1840–1890 *(continued)*

Vessel	Rig	Registry	Tons	Master	No. LDS Pass.	Departure Port	Arrival Date	Passage Port	Company Date	Days	Leader
Lucas	Ship	U.S.	350	J. Daggett	69	Sydney	6-27-57	S. Pedro	10-8-57*	103	W. Wall
Wyoming	Ship	U.S.	891	E. Brooks	36	Liv.	7-18-57	Phil.	9-3-57	47	C. Harmon
Underwriter	Ship	U.S.	1168	J. Roberts	25	Liv.	1-21-58	N.Y.	3-11-58	49	H. Harriman
Empire (II)	Ship	U.S.	1273	E. Coombs	64	Liv.	2-19-58	N.Y.	3-19-58	28	J. Hobson
John Bright	Ship	U.S.	1444	R. Cutting	89	Liv.	3-22-58	N.Y.	4-23-58	32	I. Iversen
Milwaukie	Ship	U.S.	738	C. Rhoades	10*	Melb.	12-28-58	S.F.	3-18-59	81	—
Gemsbok	Bark	U.S.	622	S. Mayo	5	P. Eliz.	1-22-59	Boston	3-18-59	55	—
Alacrity	Bark	Br.	317	J. Cooper	28	P. Eliz.	3-9-59	Boston	5-19-59	71	J. Humphreys
William Tapscott	Ship	U.S.	1525	J. Bell	725	Liv.	4-11-59	N.Y.	5-14-59	33	R. Neslen
Antarctic	Ship	U.S.	1116	G. Stouffer	30	Liv.	7-10-59	N.Y.	8-21-59	42	J. Chaplow
Emerald Isle	Ship	U.S.	1736	G. Cornish	54	Liv.	8-20-59	N.Y.	10-1-59	42	H. Hug
Underwriter	Ship	U.S.	1168	J. Roberts	594	Liv.	3-30-60	N.Y.	5-1-60	32	J. Ross
William Tapscott	Ship	U.S.	1525	J. Bell	730	Liv.	5-11-60	N.Y.	6-15-60	35	A. Calkin
Manchester	Ship	U.S.	1067	G. Trask	379	Liv.	4-16-61	N.Y.	5-14-61	28	C. Spencer
Underwriter	Ship	U.S.	1168	J. Roberts	624	Liv.	4-23-61	N.Y.	5-22-61	29	M. Andrus
Monarch of the Sea	Ship	U.S.	1979	W. Gardner	955	Liv.	5-16-61	N.Y.	6-19-61	34	J. Woodward
Humboldt	Ship	Ger.	789	H. Boysen	323	Hamb.	4-9-62	N.Y.	5-20-62	41	H. Hansen
Franklin	Ship	Ger.	708	R. Murray	413	Hamb.	4-15-62	N.Y.	5-29-62	44	C. Madsen
Electric	Ship	Ger.	1274	H. Johansen	336	Hamb.	4-18-62	N.Y.	6-5-62	48	S. Christoffersen
Athena	Ship	Ger.	1058	D. Schilling	484	Hamb.	4-21-62	N.Y.	6-7-62	47	O. Liljenquist
John J. Boyd	Ship	U.S.	1311	J. Thomas	702	Liv.	4-23-62	N.Y.	6-1-62	39	J. Brown
Manchester	Ship	U.S.	1067	G. Trask	376	Liv.	5-6-62	N.Y.	6-12-62	37	J. McAllister
William Tapscott	Ship	U.S.	1525	J. Bell	807	Liv.	5-14-62	N.Y.	6-25-62	42	W. Gibson
Windermere	Ship	U.S.	1108	D. Harding	110	Le Havre	5-15-62	N.Y.	7-8-62	54	S. Ballif
Antarctic	Ship	U.S.	1116	G. Stouffer	38	Liv.	5-18-62	N.Y.	6-27-62	40	W. Moody
Rowena	Bark	Br.	319	L. Stapleton	15	Pt. Eliz.	3-14-63	N.Y.	5-22-63	69	R. Grant
Henry Ellis	Ship	Br.	401	J. Phillips	32	Pt. Eliz.	3-31-63	N.Y.	5-28-63	58	Stock & Zyderlaam
John J. Boyd	Ship	U.S.	1311	J. Thomas	767	Liv.	4-30-63	N.Y.	5-29-63	29	W. Cluff
B. S. Kimball	Ship	U.S.	1192	H. Dearborn	657	Liv.	5-8-63	N.Y.	6-15-63	38	H. Lund
Consignment	Ship	U.S.	1132	Tukey	38	Liv.	5-8-63	N.Y.	6-20-63	43	A. Christensen
Antarctic	Ship	U.S.	1116	G. Stouffer	486	Liv.	5-23-63	N.Y.	7-10-63	48	J. Needham
Cynosure	Ship	U.S.b	1258	Drum or Wms.	775	Liv.	5-30-63	N.Y.	7-19-63	50	D. Stuart
Amazon	Ship	U.S.	1771	H. Hovey	895	London	6-4-63	N.Y.	7-18-63	44	W. Bramall
Echo	Bark	Br.	256	E. Dent	9	Pt. Eliz.	4-5-64	Boston	6-12-64	68	J. Talbot
Susan Pardew	Bark	Br.	378	J. Davis	18	Pt. Eliz.	4-10-64	Boston	6-11-64	62	W. Fotheringham
Monarch of the Sea	Ship	U.S.	1979	R. Kirkaldy	974	Liv.	4-28-64	N.Y.	6-3-64	36	J. Smith
General McClellan	Ship	U.S.	1518	G. Trask	802	Liv.	5-21-64	N.Y.	6-23-64	33	T. Jeremy
Hudson	Ship	U.S.	1618	I. Pratt	863	London	6-3-64	N.Y.	7-19-64	46	J. Kay
Mexicana	Brig	Br.	276	W. Sanderson	47	Pt. Eliz.	4-12-65	N.Y.	6-18-65	67	M. Atwood
Belle Wood	Ship	Br.	1399	T. W. Freeman	636	Liv.	4-29-65	N.Y.	5-31-65	32	W. Shearman
B. S. Kimball	Ship	U.S.	1192	H. Dearborn	558	Hamburg	5-8-65	N.Y.	6-14-65	37	A. Winberg
David Hoadley	Ship	U.S.	981	I. Hayden	24	Liv.	5-10-65	N.Y.	6-19-65	40	W. Underwood
Bridgewater	Ship	U.S.	1479	C. Sisson	7	Liv.	6-7-65	N.Y.	7-14-65	37	—
Albert	Bark	Br.	319	P. Holkins	15*	Melb.	10-17-65	S.F.	1-26-66	100	J. Spencer
John Bright	Ship	U.S.	1444	W. Dawson	747	Liv.	4-30-66	N.Y.	6-6-66	37	C. Gillet
Caroline	Ship	Br.	1133	S. Adey	389	London	5-5-66	N.Y.	6-11-66	37	S. Hill
American Congress	Ship	U.S.	863	Woodman	350	London	5-23-66	N.Y.	7-4-66	42	J. Nicholson
Kenilworth	Ship	Br.	987	J. Brown	684	Hamburg	5-25-66	N.Y.	7-16-66	52	S. Sprague
Arkwright	Ship	U.S.	1266	D. Caulkins	450	Liv.	5-30-66	N.Y.	7-6-66	37	J. Wixom
Cornelius Grinnell	Ship	U.S.	1118	A. Spencer	26	London	5-30-66	N.Y.	7-11-66	42	R. Harrison
Cavour	Bark	Nor.	369	A. Foyen	201	Hamburg	6-1-66	N.Y.	7-31-66	60	N. Nielsen
Humboldt	Ship	Ger.	789	H. Boysen	328	Hamburg	6-2-66	N.Y.	7-18-66	46	G. Brown
St. Mark	Ship	U.S.	1448	W. Howard	104	Liv.	6-6-66	N.Y.	7-24-66	48	A. Stevens
Hudson	Ship	U.S.	1618	I. Pratt	20	London	6-1-67	N.Y.	7-19-67	48	—
Manhattan	Stmr.	Br.	2869	J. Williams	482	Liv.	6-21-67	N.Y.	7-4-67	13	A. Hill
John Bright	Ship	U.S.	1444	J. Howart	720	Liv.	6-4-68	N.Y.	7-13-68	39	J. McGaw
Emerald Isle	Ship	U.S.	1736	Gillespie	876	Liv.	6-20-68	N.Y.	8-14-68	55	H. Hals

Emigrant Companies That Crossed the Ocean 1840–1890 (continued)

Vessel	Rig	Registry	Tons	Master	No. LDS Pass.	Departure Port	Arrival Date	Passage Port	Company Date	Days	Leader
Constitution	Ship	Br.	1327	W. Hatten	457	Liv.	6-24-68	N.Y.	8-5-68	42	H. Cluff
Minnesota	Stmr.	Br.	2869	J. Price	534	Liv.	6-30-68	N.Y.	7-12-68	12	J. Parry
Colorado	Stmr.	Br.	2927	R. Cutting	600	Liv.	7-14-68	N.Y.	7-28-68	14	W. Preston
Minnesota	Stmr.	Br.	2869	J. Price	338	Liv.	6-2-69	N.Y.	6-14-69	12	E. Morris
Minnesota	Stmr.	Br.	2869	J. Price	598	Liv.	7-15-69	N.Y.	7-28-69	13	O. Olsen
Colorado	Stmr.	Br.	2927	J. Williams	365	Liv.	7-28-69	N.Y.	8-10-69	13	J. Pace
Minnesota	Stmr.	Br.	2869	J. Price	443	Liv.	8-25-69	N.Y.	9-6-69	12	M. Ensign
Manhattan	Stmr.	Br.	2869	W. Forsyth	242	Liv.	9-22-69	N.Y.	10-7-69	15	J. Lawson
Minnesota	Stmr.	Br.	2869	J. Price	294	Liv.	10-6-69	N.Y.	10-17-69	11	J. Needham
Colorado	Stmr.	Br.	2927	J. Williams	16	Liv.	10-20-69	N.Y.	11-1-69	12	C. Wilden
Colorado	Stmr.	Br.	2927	T. F. Freeman	20	Liv.	6-28-70	N.Y.	7-12-70	14	—
Manhattan	Stmr.	Br.	2869	W. Forsyth	269	Liv.	7-13-70	N.Y.	7-26-70	13	K. Maeser
Minnesota	Stmr.	Br.	2869	E. Whineray	357	Liv.	7-20-70	N.Y.	8-1-70	12	J. Smith
Idaho	Stmr.	Br.	3132	J. Price	186	Liv.	9-7-70	N.Y.	9-21-70	14	F. Hyde
Nevada	Stmr.	Br.	3125	W. Green	26	Liv.	9-14-70	N.Y.	9-26-70	12	B. Walter (?)
Manhattan	Stmr.	Br.	2869	W. Forsyth	59	Liv.	11-16-70	N.Y.	12-2-70	16	R. Thompson
Wyoming	Stmr.	Br.	3238	E. Whineray	10	Liv.	5-10-71	N.Y.	5-22-71	12	J. Parry
Wonga Wonga	Stmr.	Br.	1002	Stewart	20*	Sydney	6-4-71	S.F.	7-8-71	33	E. Kearsley
Wyoming	Stmr.	Br.	3238	E. Whineray	248	Liv.	6-21-71	N.Y.	7-3-71	12	G. Lake
Minnesota	Stmr.	Br.	2869	T. W. Freeman	397	Liv.	6-28-71	N.Y.	7-13-71	15	W. Cluff
Colorado	Stmr.	Br.	2927	T. F. Freeman	146	Liv.	7-12-71	N.Y.	7-25-71	13	H. Park
Nevada	Stmr.	Br.	3125	W. Forsyth	93	Liv.	7-26-71	N.Y.	8-7-71	12	L. Smith
Minnesota	Stmr.	Br.	2869	T. W. Freeman	60	Liv.	8-9-71	N.Y.	8-21-71	12	W. Douglass
Nevada	Stmr.	Br.	3125	W. Forsyth	263	Liv.	9-6-71	N.Y.	9-18-71	12	J. Hart
Nevada	Stmr.	Br.	3125	W. Forsyth	300	Liv.	10-18-71	N.Y.	11-1-71	14	G. Peterson
Nevada[c]	Stmr.	U.S.	2143	J. Blethen	11	Auck.	12-30-71	S.F.*	1-30-72*	30*	—
Manhattan	Stmr.	Br.	2869	J. Price	221	Liv.	6-12-72	N.Y.	6-26-72	14	D. Brinton
Nevada	Stmr.	Br.	3125	W. Forsyth	426	Liv.	6-26-72	N.Y.	7-8-72	12	E. Peterson
Wisconsin	Stmr.	Br.	3238	T. W. Freeman	179	Liv.	7-31-72	N.Y.	8-12-72	12	G. Ward
Minnesota	Stmr.	Br.	2869	J. Morgan	602	Liv.	9-4-72	N.Y.	9-17-72	13	G. Wilkins
Minnesota	Stmr.	Br.	2869	J. Morgan	203	Liv.	10-16-72	N.Y.	10-29-72	13	T. Dobson
Manhattan	Stmr.	Br.	2869	J. Price	35	Liv.	12-4-72	N.Y.	12-21-72	17	D. Kennedy
Nevada	Stmr.	Br.	3125	W. Forsyth	246	Liv.	6-4-73	N.Y.	6-16-73	12	C. Wilcken
Wisconsin	Stmr.	Br.	3238	T. W. Freeman	976	Liv.	7-2-73	N.Y.	7-15-73	13	D. Calder
Nevada	Stmr.	Br.	3125	W. Forsyth	283	Liv.	7-10-73	N.Y.	7-23-73	13	E. Box
Wyoming	Stmr.	Br.	3238	J. Morgan	510	Liv.	9-3-73	N.Y.	9-20-73	17	J. Fairbanks
Idaho	Stmr.	Br.	3132	J. Moore	522	Liv.	10-22-73	N.Y.	11-4-73	13	J. Hart
Nevada	Stmr.	Br.	3125	J. Price	155	Liv.	5-6-74	N.Y.	5-21-74	15	L. Herrick
Nevada	Stmr.	Br.	3125	J. Price	243	Liv.	6-11-74	N.Y.	6-23-74	12	J. Birch
Idaho	Stmr.	Br.	3132	W. Forsyth	806	Liv.	6-24-74	N.Y.	7-6-74	12	P. Carstensen
Minnesota	Stmr.	Br.	2869	T. Jones	81	Liv.	7-8-74	N.Y.	7-21-74	13	J. Keller
Wyoming	Stmr.	Br.	3238	C. Beddoe	558	Liv.	9-2-74	N.Y.	9-14-74	12	J. Graham
Wyoming	Stmr.	Br.	3238	C. Beddoe	155	Liv.	10-14-74	N.Y.	10-26-74	12	W. Fife
Wyoming	Stmr.	Br.	3238	J. Guard	176	Liv.	5-12-75	N.Y.	5-24-75	12	H. Gowans
Wisconsin	Stmr.	Br.	3238	W. Forsyth	167	Liv.	6-16-75	N.Y.	6-27-75	11	R. Burton
Idaho	Stmr.	Br.	3132	C. Beddoe	765	Liv.	6-30-75	N.Y.	7-14-75	14	C. Larsen
Wyoming	Stmr.	Br.	3238	J. Price	300	Liv.	9-15-75	N.Y.	9-27-75	12	R. Morris
Dakota	Stmr.	Br.	4332	W. Forsyth	120	Liv.	10-14-75	N.Y.	10-24-75	10	B. Eardley
Montana	Stmr.	Br.	4321	C. Beddoe	20	Liv.	1-19-76	N.Y.	1-31-76	12	I. Coombs
Nevada	Stmr.	Br.	3125	T. W. Freeman	131	Liv.	5-24-76	N.Y.	6-5-76	12	J. Woodhouse
Idaho	Stmr.	Br.	3132	C. Beddoe	628	Liv.	6-28-76	N.Y.	7-10-76	12	N. Flygare
Nevada	Stmr.	Br.	3125	J. Guard	5	Liv.	8-23-76	N.Y.	9-5-76	13	—
Wyoming	Stmr.	Br.	3238	T. Jones	322	Liv.	9-13-76	N.Y.	9-23-76	10	W. Binder
Wyoming	Stmr.	Br.	3238	T. Jones	118	Liv.	10-25-76	N.Y.	11-4-76	10	P. Barton
Wyoming	Stmr.	Br.	3238	T. Jones	186	Liv.	6-13-77	N.Y.	6-23-77	10	D. Udall
Wisconsin	Stmr.	Br.	3238	W. Forsyth	714	Liv.	6-27-77	N.Y.	7-7-77	10	J. Rowberry
Wisconsin	Stmr.	Br.	3238	W. Forsyth	482	Liv.	9-19-77	N.Y.	9-30-77	11	H. Park
Idaho	Stmr.	Br.	3132	W. Holmes	150	Liv.	10-17-77	N.Y.	10-29-77	12	W. Paxman

Emigrant Companies That Crossed the Ocean 1840–1890 *(continued)*

Vessel	Rig	Registry	Tons	Master	No. LDS Pass.	Departure Port	Arrival Date	Passage Port	Company Date	Days	Leader
Nevada	Stmr.	Br.	3125	W. Gadd	354	Liv.	5-25-78	N.Y.	6-5-78	11	T. Judd
Montana	Stmr.	Br.	4321	C. Beddoe	221	Liv.	6-15-78	N.Y.	6-25-78	10	T. Brandley
Nevada	Stmr.	Br.	3125	T. Owen	569	Liv.	6-29-78	N.Y.	7-10-78	11	J. Cook
Wyoming	Stmr.	Br.	3238	H. Gadd	609	Liv.	9-14-78	N.Y.	9-25-78	11	H. Naisbitt
Nevada	Stmr.	Br.	3125	C. Rigby	20*	Liv.	9-21-78	N.Y.	10-3-78	12	J. Christensen
Wyoming	Stmr.	Br.	3238	H. Gadd	145	Liv.	10-19-78	N.Y.	10-29-78	10	A. Miner
Malay	Bkt.	U.S.	812	Love	10*	Sydney	2-21-79	S.F.	5-10-79*	77	—
Wyoming	Stmr.	Br.	3238	H. Gadd	170	Liv.	4-19-79	N.Y.	4-30-79	11	C. Nibley
Wyoming	Stmr.	Br.	3238	T. Jones	162	Liv.	5-24-79	N.Y.	6-3-79	10	A. McDonald
Wyoming	Stmr.	Br.	3238	G. Murray	622	Liv.	6-28-79	N.Y.	7-8-79	10	W. Williams
Wyoming	Stmr.	Br.	3238	G. Murray	336	Liv.	9-6-79	N.Y.	9-16-79	10	N. Flygare
Arizona	Stmr.	Br.	5147	T. Jones	224	Liv.	10-18-79	N.Y.	10-27-79	9	W. Bramall
Wyoming	Stmr.	Br.	3238	C. Rigby	120	Liv.	4-10-80	N.Y.	4-21-80	11	J. Bunting
Wisconsin	Stmr.	Br.	3238	E. Bentley	332	Liv.	6-5-80	N.Y.	6-15-80	10	J. Jones
Australia	Stmr.	Br.	1938	Cargill	25*	Sydney	6-17-80	S.F.	7-15-80	27	F. May
Wisconsin	Stmr.	Br.	3238	E. Bentley	727	Liv.	7-10-80	N.Y.	7-21-80	11	N. Rasmussen
Nevada	Stmr.	Br.	3125	T. Jones	338	Liv.	9-4-80	N.Y.	9-14-80	10	J. Rider
Wisconsin	Stmr.	Br.	3238	E. Bentley	258	Liv.	10-23-80	N.Y.	11-2-80	10	J. Nicholson
Wyoming	Stmr.	Br.	3238	C. Rigby	186	Liv.	4-16-81	N.Y.	4-26-81	10	D. Dunbar
City of Sydney	Stmr.	U.S.	3016	Dearborn	27	Auck.	4-26-81	S.F.	5-17-81	20	G. Batt
Wyoming	Stmr.	Br.	3238	C. Rigby	297	Liv.	5-21-81	N.Y.	6-1-81	11	J. Matthews
Nevada	Stmr.	Br.	3125	T. Jones	11	Liv.	6-11-81	N.Y.	6-23-81	12	R. Runolfsen
Wyoming	Stmr.	Br.	3238	C. Rigby	775	Liv.	6-25-81	N.Y.	7-7-81	12	S. Roskelly
Nevada	Stmr.	Br.	3125	T. Jones	22	Liv.	7-16-81	N.Y.	7-27-81	11	J. Eyvindson
Wyoming	Stmr.	Br.	3238	C. Rigby	644	Liv.	9-3-81	N.Y.	9-13-81	10	J. Finlayson
Wisconsin	Stmr.	Br.	3238	E. Bentley	396	Liv.	10-22-81	N.Y.	11-2-81	11	L. Martineau
Nevada	Stmr.	Br.	3617[d]	T. Jones	342	Liv.	4-12-82	N.Y.	4-24-82	12	J. Donaldson
Nevada	Stmr.	Br.	3617	T. Jones	392	Liv.	5-17-82	N.Y.	5-27-82	10	W. Webb
Nevada	Stmr.	Br.	3617	A. Bremmer	933	Liv.	6-21-82	N.Y.	7-2-82	11	R. Irvine
Arizona	Stmr.	Br.	5147	S. Brooks	18	Liv.	7-22-82	N.Y.	8-1-82	10	—
Wyoming	Stmr.	Br.	3238	J. Douglas	662	Liv.	9-2-82	N.Y.	9-12-82	10	W. Cooper
Abyssinia	Stmr.	Br.	3253	E. Bentley	416	Liv.	10-21-82	N.Y.	11-3-82	13	G. Stringfellow
Nevada	Stmr.	Br.	3617	A. Bremmer	352	Liv.	4-11-83	N.Y.	4-22-83	11	D. McKay
Nevada	Stmr.	Br.	3617	A. Bremmer	427	Liv.	5-16-83	N.Y.	5-27-83	11	B. Rich
Nevada	Stmr.	Br.	3617	A. Bremmer	697	Liv.	6-20-83	N.Y.	7-1-83	11	H. Magleby
Wisconsin	Stmr.	Br.	3238	C. Rigby	18	Liv.	7-14-83	N.Y.	7-25-83	11	J. Sutton
Nevada	Stmr.	Br.	3617	A. Bremmer	682	Liv.	8-29-83	N.Y.	9-10-83	12	P. Goss
Wisconsin	Stmr.	Br.	3238	C. Rigby	369	Liv.	10-27-83	N.Y.	11-7-83	11	J. Pickett
Nevada	Stmr.	Br.	3617	A. Bremmer	319	Liv.	4-9-84	N.Y.	4-19-84	10	C. Fjeldsted
Arizona	Stmr.	Br.	5147	S. Brooks	287	Liv.	5-17-84	N.Y.	5-26-84	9	E. Williams
Arizona	Stmr.	Br.	5147	S. Brooks	531	Liv.	6-14-84	N.Y.	6-23-84	9	E. Nye
Nevada	Stmr.	Br.	3617	A. Bremmer	14	Liv.	8-2-84	N.Y.	8-13-84	11	H. Attley
Wyoming	Stmr.	Br.	3238	J. Douglas	496	Liv.	8-30-84	N.Y.	9-9-84	10	B. Bennett
City of Berlin	Stmr.	Br.	5491	S. Kennedy	93	Liv.	10-23-84	N.Y.	11-2-84	10	C. Ek
Arizona	Stmr.	Br.	5147	S. Brooks	163	Liv.	11-1-84	N.Y.	11-11-84	10	J. Smith
Wisconsin	Stmr.	Br.	3238	E. Bentley	187	Liv.	4-11-85	N.Y.	4-22-85	11	L. Lund
Wisconsin	Stmr.	Br.	3238	E. Bentley	274	Liv.	5-16-85	N.Y.	5-27-85	11	N. Hodges
Wisconsin	Stmr.	Br.	3238	E. Bentley	541	Liv.	6-20-85	N.Y.	7-1-85	11	J. Hansen
Wisconsin	Stmr.	Br.	3238	E. Bentley	329	Liv.	8-29-85	N.Y.	9-8-85	10	J. Thornley
Nevada	Stmr.	Br.	3617	J. Douglas	313	Liv.	10-24-85	N.Y.	11-4-85	11	A. Lund
Nevada	Stmr.	Br.	3617	J. Douglas	179	Liv.	4-17-86	N.Y.	4-27-86	10	E. Woolley
Arizona	Stmr.	Br.	5147	S. Brooks	15	Liv.	5-15-86	N.Y.	5-24-86	9	I. Gadd
Nevada	Stmr.	Br.	3617	J. Douglas	279	Liv.	5-22-86	N.Y.	6-1-86	10	M. Pratt
Nevada	Stmr.	Br.	3617	J. Douglas	426	Liv.	6-26-86	N.Y.	7-7-86	11	C. Olsen
Alaska	Stmr.	Br.	6392	G. Murray	23	Liv.	7-10-86	N.Y.	7-18-86	8	—
Wyoming	Stmr.	Br.	3238	C. Rigby	301	Liv.	8-21-86	N.Y.	8-31-86	10	D. Kunz
British King	Stmr.	Br.	3412	J. Kelly	307	Liv.	10-13-86	Phil.	10-27-86	14	J. Greenwood
Nevada	Stmr.	Br.	3617	J. Cushing	194	Liv.	4-16-87	N.Y.	4-28-87	12	D. Callister
Nevada	Stmr.	Br.	3617	J. Cushing	187	Liv.	5-21-87	N.Y.	6-1-87	11	E. Davis

Emigrant Companies That Crossed the Ocean 1840–1890 *(continued)*

Vessel	Rig	Registry	Tons	Master	No. LDS Pass.	Departure Port	Arrival Date	Passage Port	Company Date	Days	Leader
Wyoming	Stmr.	Br.	3238	C. Rigby	159	Liv.	6-4-87	N.Y.	6-15-87	11	J. Nielsen
Wisconsin	Stmr.	Br.	3238	E. Bentley	646	Liv.	6-18-87	N.Y.	6-28-87	10	Q. Nichols
Wisconsin	Stmr.	Br.	3238	E. Bentley	406	Liv.	8-27-87	N.Y.	9-8-87	12	J. Hart
Nevada	Stmr.	Br.	3617	J. Douglas	278	Liv.	10-8-87	N.Y.	10-18-87	10	J. Wells
Alameda	Stmr.	U.S.	3158	Morse	25*	Sydney	4-18-88*	S.F.	5-13-88	24	J. Blythe
Wisconsin	Stmr.	Br.	3238	E. Bentley	74	Liv.	4-28-88	N.Y.	5-10-88	12	F. Bramwell
Wyoming	Stmr.	Br.	3238	C. Rigby	137	Liv.	5-19-88	N.Y.	5-29-88	10	W. Wood
Arizona	Stmr.	Br.	5147	S. Brooks	11	Liv.	5-26-88	N.Y.	6-4-88	9	—
Wisconsin	Stmr.	Br.	3238	E. Bentley	210	Liv.	6-2-88	N.Y.	6-13-88	11	C. Dorius
Nevada	Stmr.	Br.	3617	J. Cushing	70	Liv.	6-9-88	N.Y.	6-20-88	11	J. Stucki
Wyoming	Stmr.	Br.	3238	C. Rigby	118	Liv.	6-23-88	N.Y.	7-2-88	9	H. Bowring
Wisconsin	Stmr.	Br.	3238	E. Bentley	7	Liv.	7-7-88	N.Y.	7-18-88	11	R. Lindsay
Wyoming	Stmr.	Br.	3238	C. Rigby	136	Liv.	7-28-88	N.Y.	8-8-88	11	H. Christiansen
Wisconsin	Stmr.	Br.	3238	E. Bentley	155	Liv.	8-11-88	N.Y.	8-24-88	13	L. Naylor
Wyoming	Stmr.	Br.	3238	C. Rigby	83	Liv.	9-1-88	N.Y.	9-11-88	10	A. Johnson
Wisconsin	Stmr.	Br.	3238	T. Dunn	145	Liv.	9-15-88	N.Y.	9-25-88	10	W. Phillips
Wyoming	Stmr.	Br.	3238	C. Rigby	123	Liv.	10-6-88	N.Y.	10-15-88	9	N. Lindelof
Wisconsin	Stmr.	Br.	3238	J. Morrall	125	Liv.	10-20-88	N.Y.	10-30-88	10	J. Quigley
Arizona	Stmr.	Br.	5147	S. Brooks	7	Liv.	11-17-88	N.Y.	11-27-88	10	L. Moench
?*			—		26	Amst.	4-27-89	N.Y.	—		M. Krumperman
Arizona	Stmr.	Br.	5147	S. Brooks	—	Liv.	5-11-89	N.Y.	5-20-89	9	H. Barrell
Wisconsin	Stmr.	Br.	3238	J. Morrall	142	Liv.	5-18-89	N.Y.	5-29-89	11	M. Dailey
Wyoming	Stmr.	Br.	3238	C. Rigby	359	Liv.	6-8-89	N.Y.	6-19-89	11	L. Anderson
Wisconsin	Stmr.	Br.	3238	J. Morrall	172	Liv.	6-22-89	N.Y.	7-3-89	11	J. Volker
Wyoming	Stmr.	Br.	3238	C. Rigby	191	Liv.	8-17-89	N.Y.	8-27-89	10	J. Weibye
Wisconsin	Stmr.	Br.	3238	J. Morrall	172	Liv.	8-31-89	N.Y.	9-11-89	11	W. Payne
Wyoming	Stmr.	Br.	3238	C. Rigby	113	Liv.	9-21-89	N.Y.	10-1-89	10	R. Larsen
Wisconsin	Stmr.	Br.	3238	J. Morrall	142	Liv.	10-5-89	N.Y.	10-17-89	12	E. Bennett
Wyoming	Stmr.	Br.	3238	C. Rigby	161	Liv.	10-26-89	N.Y.	11-6-89	11	A. Skanchy
Nevada	Stmr.	Br.	3617	J. Cushing	11	Liv.	11-16-89	N.Y.	11-27-89	11	R. Morse
Wisconsin	Stmr.	Br.	3238	J. Morrall	52	Liv.	4-19-90	N.Y.	4-29-90	10	O. Worthington
Wyoming	Stmr.	Br.	3238	C. Rigby	156	Liv.	5-3-90	N.Y.	5-13-90	10	A. Anderson
Wisconsin	Stmr.	Br.	3238	J. Morrall	122	Liv.	5-24-90	N.Y.	6-4-90	11	J. Hayes
Wyoming	Stmr.	Br.	3238	C. Rigby	304	Liv.	6-7-90	N.Y.	6-19-90	12	E. Willardson
Wisconsin	Stmr.	Br.	3238	J. Morrall	113	Liv.	6-28-90	N.Y.	7-10-90	12	A. Maw
Wisconsin	Stmr.	Br.	3238	J. Morrall	86	Liv.	8-2-90	N.Y.	8-13-90	11	L. Jordan
Wyoming	Stmr.	Br.	3238	C. Rigby	128	Liv.	8-16-90	N.Y.	8-26-90	10	J. Ostlund
Wisconsin	Stmr.	Br.	3238	J. Morrall	116	Liv.	9-6-90	N.Y.	9-17-90	11	J. Stucki
Wyoming	Stmr.	Br.	3238	C. Rigby	197	Liv.	9-20-90	N.Y.	10-1-90	11	J. Jensen
Wisconsin	Stmr.	Br.	3238	J. Morrall	—	Liv.	10-11-90	N.Y.	10-23-90	12	J. Golightly

Pioneer Companies That Crossed the Plains 1847–1868

Source: *Deseret News* 1976 Church Almanac

Outfitting Post	Date of Departure	Captain of Company and Company No.	Number Leaving Outfitting Post People/Wagons		Date Arrived	Roster (J.H. = Journal History of the Church) *Partial Roster
Winter Quarters, Nebraska (Omaha)	**1847** 14 Apr (last date in 1847 that Brigham Young left Winter Quarters	Brigham Young (Original)	148	72	21–24 July 1847 (Brigham Young entered 24th)	Church Emigration Book, (CEB) D.U.P. lesson for Apr. 1959; and Andrew Jenson's *Biographical Encyclopedia*, vol. 4, p. 693–725.
Winter Quarters, Neb (Left camp on Elkhorn River— abt. 27 mi. west of Winter Quarters	17 Jun 18 Jun	*Daniel Spencer* Capt. 1st Hundred Peregrine Sessions Capt. 1st Fifty (1)	185	75	24–25 Sep 1847	J.H. 21 Jun 1847, p. 6–11.
Elkhorn River)	17 Jun	Ira Eldredge Capt. 2nd Fifty (2) [Also known as Parley P. Pratt Co.]	177 (or 174)	76	19–22 Sep 1847	J.H. 21 Jun 1847, p. 11–16.

Pioneer Companies That Crossed the Plains 1847–1868 (*continued*)

Outfitting Post	Date of Departure	Captain of Company and Company No.	Number Leaving Outfitting Post People/Wagons		Date Arrived	Roster (J.H. = Journal History of the Church) *Partial Roster
Winter Quarters, Neb	abt. 17 Jun	*Edward Hunter* Capt. 2nd Hundred				
Elkhorn River	17 Jun	Joseph Horne Capt. 1st Fifty (3) [also known as John Taylor Co.]	197	72	29 Sep 1847	J.H. 21 Jun 1847, p. 17–22.
Elkhorn River	19 Jun	Jacob Foutz (4) Capt. 2nd Fifty	155	59	abt. 1 Oct 1847	J.H. 21 Jun 1847, p. 23–27.
Winter Quarters, Neb	abt. 17 Jun	*Jedediah M. Grant* Capt. 3rd Hundred			29 Sep 1847	
Elkhorn River	17 Jun	Joseph B. Noble Capt. 1st Fifty (5)	171		abt. 2 Oct 1847 (and during week)	J.H. 21 Jun 1847, p. 28–32.
Elkhorn River	19 Jun	Willard Snow Capt. 2nd Fifty (6)	160		abt. 4 Oct 1847 (and during week)	J.H. 21 Jun 1847, p. 33–37.
Winter Quarters, Neb	abt. 17 Jun	*Abraham O. Smoot* Capt. 4th Hundred				
Elkhorn River	18 Jun	George B. Wallace Capt. 1st Fifty (7)	223		25, 26, 29 Sep 1847	J.H. 21 Jun 1847, p. 38–44.
Elkhorn River	17 Jun?	Samuel Russell Capt. 2nd Fifty (8)	95		25 Sep 1847	J.H. 21 Jun 1847, p. 44–47.
Winter Quarters, Neb Elkhorn River	21 Jun	Charles C. Rich (9) 1847, p. 48–51	126		2 Oct 1847	J.H. 21 Jun.
	1848					
Winter Quarters, Neb	abt. 6 Jun	Brigham Young Capt. 1st Division	1220		20–24 Sep 1848	J.H. Supp. after 31 Dec 1848, p. 1–10.
Winter Quarters, Neb	29 May	Heber C. Kimball Capt. 2nd Division	662		24 Sep and later	J.H. Supp. after 31 Dec 1848, p. 11–16.
Winter Quarters, Neb	3 Jul Richard's Section; 30 or 31 Jun Lyman Section	Willard Richards Capt. 3rd Division (Amasa Lyman part of Co.)	526		Richard's 12, 17, 19 Oct, Lyman 10 Oct	J.H. Supp. after 31 Dec 1848, p. 17–20.
	1849					
Kanesville, Iowa (present day Council Bluffs)	Abt. 6 Jun	Orson Spencer and Samuel Gully (1)		100	22 Sep 1849	J.H. Supp. after 31 Dec 1849, p. 1–2.*
Source: *Deseret News* 1976 Church Almanac.						
Kanesville, Iowa	abt. 12 Jul	Allen Taylor (2)	abt. 500	100	abt. 10 Oct 1849	J.H. Supp after 31 Dec 1849, p. 3–4.*
Kanesville, Iowa Elkhorn River	10 Jul	Silas Richards (3)		abt. 100	abt. 27 Oct 1849	J.H. Supp. after 31 Dec 1849, p. 5A–5I.*
Kanesville, Iowa	4 Jul	George A. Smith (4) [Included Capt. Dan Jones' Welsh Company]	370 or 447 [Smith and Benson combined] as their companies traveled close together	120	27 and 28 Oct 1849	J.H. Supp. after 31 Dec 1849, p. 6–8G.
Kanesville, Iowa	4 Jul	Ezra T. Benson (5)			abt. 28 Oct	J.H. Supp. after 31 Dec 1849, p. 9–12H.*
Pottawattamie Co., Iowa	18 Apr	Howard Egan (Independent Company)	57	22	7 Aug	J.H. Supp. after 31 Dec 1849, p. 13–14 (also CEB, 1849).
	1850					
Kanesville, Iowa	3 Jun	Milo Andrus (1)	20 206	51	30 Aug	J.H. Supp. after 31 Dec 1850, p. 1.*

Pioneer Companies That Crossed the Plains 1847–1868 *(continued)*

Outfitting Post	Date of Departure	Captain of Company and Company No.	Number Leaving Outfitting Post People/Wagons		Date Arrived	Roster (J.H. = Journal History of the Church) *Partial Roster
Kanesville, Iowa	Before 7 Jun	Benjamin Hawkins (2)	150		9 Sep 1850	J.H. Supp. after 31 Dec 1850, p. 2–3.*
Kanesville, Iowa	Before 12 Jun	Aaron Johnson (3)	100		12 Sep 1850	J.H. Supp. after 31 Dec 1850, p. 3–5.*
Kanesville, Iowa	Before 7 Jun	James Pace (4)	100		abt. 20 Sep 1850	J.H. Supp after 31 Dec 1850, p. 5–6.*
Kanesville, Iowa (organized at 12-mile Creek near Missouri River)	4 Jul	Edward Hunter (5) [1st Perpetual Emigrating Fund Company]	261	67	13 Oct 1850	J.H. Supp. after 31 Dec 1850, p. 7–12.*
Kanesville, Iowa (organized near Missouri River)	15 Jun	Joseph Young (6)		42	1 Oct 1850	J.H. Supp. after 31 Dec 1850, p. 13–14.*
Kanesville, Iowa	15 Jun (organized 12 Jun)	Warren Foote (7)	abt. 540	104	17 Sep 1850	J.H. Supp. after 31 Dec 1850, p. 15–16 [heads of families in Church Emigration Book, CEB 540 1850].
Kanesville, Iowa	organized camp 20 Jun	Wilford Woodruff (8)	abt. 209	abt. 44	14 Oct 1850	J.H. Supp. after 31 Dec 1850, p. 17–18.*
Kanesville, Iowa	abt. 20 Jun	Stephen Markham (9)	50		1 Oct 1850	J.H. Supp. after 31 Dec 1850, p. 19.*
Kanesville, Iowa	abt. middle Jun, 1850	David Evans (10)	54		15 Sep 1850	J.H. Supp. after 31 Dec 1850, p. 20, also J.H. Supp. after 31 Dec 1850, p. 21–25, for emigrants not in above 10 companies.*
Kanesville, Iowa	**1851** abt. 1 May	John G. Smith (1)	150		some 23 Sep 1851	J.H. Supp. after 31 Dec 1851, p. 1.*
Kanesville, Iowa	abt. 10 Jun; turned back due to Indian trouble, left again 29 Jun	Easton Kelsey, Luman A. Shurtleff, Capt. 1st Fifty; Isaac Allred, Capt. 2nd Fifty (3)	100		Shurtlett's group, 23 Sep; after 31 Dec Allred's group, 2 Oct 1851	J.H. Supp. after 31 Dec 1851, p. 4–5.*
Kanesville, Iowa	21 Jun	James W. Cummings (2)	abt. 150	100	some 5 Oct 1851	J.H. Supp. after 31 Dec 1851, p. 2–3.* See CEB 1851.
Kanesville, Iowa	7 Jul	John Brown [a P.E.F. Company] (4)	50		28 Sep 1851	J.H. Supp. after 31 Dec 1851, p. 6A–6G.*
Kanesville, Iowa	Left Garden Grove, Iowa, 17 May	Garden Grove Co. Harry Walton, Capt.	21 Families from Garden Grove plus others	60	24 Sep 1851	J.H. Supp. after 31 Dec 1851, p. 7–9, also CEB 1851 under Garden Grove Co.
Kanesville, Iowa		George W. Oman			1 Sep 1851	Some names in J.H. Supp. after 31 Dec 1851, p. 1C–12 may be from this company.
Kanesville, Iowa	before 7 Jul	Morris Phelps			abt. 28 Sep 1851	J.H. Supp. after 31 Dec 1851, p. 10–12.
Kanesville, Iowa ?	before 12 Aug	Wilkins Freight (Train includes Scottish emigrants)	10		abt. 28 Sep 1851	J.H. Supp. after 31 Dec. 1851, p. 10–12.
		Ben Holliday's Freight Train			10 Aug 1851	J.H. Supp. after 31 Dec 1851, p. 10–12.

Pioneer Companies That Crossed the Plains 1847–1868 *(continued)*

Outfitting Post	Date of Departure	Captain of Company and Company No.	Number Leaving Outfitting Post People/Wagons		Date Arrived	Roster (J.H. = Journal History of the Church) *Partial Roster
Kanesville, Iowa	3 Aug	Thomas A. Williams' Freight Train			25 Aug 1851	J.H. Supp. after 31 Dec 1851, p. 10–12.
		Livingston and Kincade's Freight Company				J.H. Supp. after 31 Dec 1851, p. 10–12.
Kanesville, Iowa	**1852** 30 May	James W. Bay (1)	abt. 190		abt. 13 Aug 1852	J.H. Supp.* after 31 Dec 1852, p. 1–6.
Kanesville, Iowa	abt. 29 May	James J. Jepson (2)	abt. 220	abt. 32	some arrived 10 Sep	J.H. Supp.* after 31 Dec 1852, p. 7–11.
Kanesville, Iowa	7 Jun	Thomas C. D. Howell (3)	293 plus 10 families	abt. 65	27 Sep 1852	J.H. Supp.* after 31 Dec 1852, p. 12–18.
Kanesville, Iowa	abt. 10 Jun	Joseph Outhouse	230	50	6 Sep 1852	J.H. Supp.* after 31 Dec 1852, p. 19–24.
Kanesville, Iowa	early June	John Tidwell (5)	abt. 340	abt. 54	15 Sep 1852	J.H. Supp.* after 31 Dec 1852, p. 25–33.
Kanesville, Iowa		David Wood (6)	abt. 288	abt. 58	1 Oct 1852	J.H. Supp.* after 31 Dec 1852, p. 34–40.
Kanesville, Iowa	early Jun	Henry Bryant manning Jolly (7)	abt. 340	abt. 64	15 Sep 1852	J.H. Supp.* after 31 Dec 1852, p. 41–49.
		(8th Company) No report				
Kanesville, Iowa	Jun	Isaac M. Stewart (9)	abt. 245	53	28 Aug 1852	J.H. supp.* after 31 Dec 1852, p. 55–61.
Kanesville, Iowa	May	Benjamin Gardner (10)	241	45	24 and 27 Sep 1852	J.H. Supp.* after 31 Dec 1852, p. 61B; J.H. Supp. 24 and 27 Sep 1852.
Kanesville, Iowa	Jun	James McGaw (11)	239	54	20 Sep 1852	J.H. Supp.* after 31 Dec 1852, p. 67–73.
Kanesville, Iowa	Jun	Harmon Cutler (12)	262	63	Sep	J.H. Supp.* after 31 Dec 1852, p. 79–84.
		(13th Company) No report				
Kanesville, Iowa	5 Jul	John B. Walker (14)	abt. 258		3 Oct 1852	J.H. Supp.* after 31 Dec 1852, p. 89–95.
Kanesville, Iowa	Beginning of Jul	Robert Weimer (15)	230	130?	15 Sep 1852	J.H. Supp.* after 31 Dec 1852, p. 96–100.
Kanesville, Iowa	shortly after 24 Jun	Uriah Curtis (16)	abt. 365	51	1 Oct 1852	J.H. Supp.* after 31 Dec 1852, p. 101–107.
Kanesville, Iowa		Isaac Bullock (17)	abt. 175		21 Sep 1852	J.H. Supp.* after 31 Dec 1852, p. 98–111.
Kanesville, Iowa	middle of June	James C. Snow (18)	250	abt. 55	9 Oct 1852	J.H. Supp.* after 31 Dec 1852, p. 112–117.
Kanesville, Iowa	early July	Eli B. Kelsey (19) [includes first 28 saints from Scandinavia].	abt. 100		16 Oct 1852	J.H. Supp.* after 31 Dec 1852, p. 120–122.

Pioneer Companies That Crossed the Plains 1847–1868 (continued)

Outfitting Post	Date of Departure	Captain of Company and Company No.	Number Leaving Outfitting Post People/Wagons		Date Arrived	Roster (J.H. = Journal History of the Church) *Partial Roster
Kanesville, Iowa		Henry W. Miller (20)	abt. 229	63	abt. 21 Sep 1852	J.H. Supp.* after 31 Dec 1852, p. 123–128.
Kanesville, Iowa	July	Allen Weeks (21)	abt. 226		12 Oct 1852	J.H. Supp.* after 31 Dec 1852, p. 129–136.
Organized in St. Louis	4 Jun (left Independence Mo)	Thomas Marsden (22nd Company)	10		2 Sep 1852	J.H. Supp.* after 31 Dec 1852, p. 144.
	1 Jun (left Kansas City Mo)	Abraham O. Smoot [first company to cross by P.E.F.]	abt. 250	33	3 Sep 1852	J.H. Supp.* after 31 Dec 1852, p. 137–143.
1853						
Six-Mile Grove, Iowa or Neb (6 miles from Winter Quarters)	1 Jun	David Wilkin (1)	122	28	abt. 9 Sep 1853	J.H. 15 Jul 1853, p. 2–5.
Six-Mile Grove, Iowa or Neb	9 Jun	Daniel A. Miller and John W. Cooley (2)	282	70	some 9 Sep 1853	J.H. 9 Sep 1853, p. 2–24. See also J.H. 9 Aug 1853, p. 2–20.
Keokuk, Iowa	18 May (left Kanesville, Iowa, 1 Jul)	Jesse W. Crosby (3)	79	12	abt. 10 Sep 1853	J.H. 19 Aug 1853, p. 2.
Keokuk, Iowa (organized at Kanesville)	16 May (left Kanesville, 29 Jun)	Moses Clawson (4) [St. Louis Company]	295	56	abt. 15 Sep 1853	J.H. 19 Aug 1853, p. 3–7. See also J.H. 7 Aug 1853, p. 4–5.
Keokuk, Iowa	abt. 3 Jun	Jacob Gates (5) (5th Company)	262	33	28 Sep 1853	J.H. 9 Sep 1853, p. 25–28.
Keokuk, Iowa	21 May	John E. Forsgren (6)	294	34	30 Sep 1853	J.H. 30 Sep 1853, p. 3–7.*

See Andrew Jenson's *History of the Scandinavian Mission* and "Manuscript History of the Forsgren Company."

Outfitting Post	Date of Departure	Captain of Company and Company No.	Number Leaving Outfitting Post People/Wagons		Date Arrived	Roster
Keokuk, Iowa	1 Jul (left Missouri River)	Henry Ettleman (7)	40	11	abt. 1 Oct 1853	J.H. 19 Aug 1853, p. 1B.
Kanesville, Iowa	13 Jul (crossed Missouri River at Council Bluffs)	Vincent Shurtleff (8) [merchandise wagons and a few emigrants]			abt. 30 Sep 1853	no roster. See J.H. 17 Jul 1853, and 31 Aug 1853 for mention.
Keokuk, Iowa	3 Jun (crossed Missouri River 11 Jul)	Joseph W. Young (9)	402	abt. 54	10 Oct 1853	J.H. 22 Sep 1853, p. 1B–9.
Keokuk, Iowa	3 Jun (crossed Missouri River 11 Jul)	Cyrus H. Wheelock (10) [included a California company]	abt. 400	52	16 Oct 1853	J.H. 19 Sep 1853, p. 2–7.
Keokuk, Iowa or Kanesville, Iowa	3 Jun (crossed Missouri River)	Claudius V. Spencer (11)	abt. 250	40	abt. 24 Sep 1853	J.H. 17 Sep 1853, p. 1B–4.
Keokuk, Iowa or Kanesville, Iowa	14 Jul (crossed Missouri River)	Appleton M. Harmon (12)	abt. 200	abt. 22	16 Oct 1853	no roster.
Keokuk, Iowa	1 Jul	John Brown (13)	abt. 303		17 Oct 1853	no roster, see roster for ship Campillus in "Ms. History of British Mission" 6 Apr 1853.
1854						
Westport, Mo. (Kansas City area)	15 Jun	Hans Peter Olsen (1)	abt. 550	69	5 Oct 1854	no roster, see J.H. 5 Oct 1854, p. 1–6.

Pioneer Companies That Crossed the Plains 1847–1868 *(continued)*

Outfitting Post	Date of Departure	Captain of Company and Company No.	Number Leaving Outfitting Post People/Wagons		Date Arrived	Roster (J.H. = Journal History of the Church) *Partial Roster
Westport, Mo.	abt. 17 Jun	James Brown (2)	abt. 300	42	3 Oct 1854	no roster.
Westport, Mo.	abt. 17 Jun	Darwin Richardson (3)	abt. 300	40	30 Sep 1854	no roster.
Westport, Mo.	16 Jun	Job Smith (4) [independent company] (1C)	217	45	23 Sep 1854	no roster.
Westport, Mo.	2 Jul	Daniel Garn (5) [many members crossed ocean on ship Windermere]	477	abt. 40	1 Oct. 1854	no roster, see Ms. History of British Mission, 22 Feb 1854.
Westport, Mo.	14 Jul	Robert L. Campbell (6th Company)	397		28 Oct 1854	no roster, see J.H. 28 Oct 1854, p. 2–34.
	left Missouri River late in Jul	Initially, Orson Pratt and Horace S. Eldredge Subsequently, Ezra T. Benson and Ira Eldredge (7)			3 Oct 1854 [Pratt and Eldredge 27 Aug]	no roster, see J.H. 8 Aug 1854, p. 2–5.
Westport, Mo.	abt. 15 Jul	William Empey (8)		43	24 Oct 1854	no roster.
1855						
Mormon Grove, Kan. (Near Atchison)	7 Jun	John Hindley (1) (1C)	206	46	3 Sep 1855	J.H. 12 Sep 1855, and 3 Sep 1855, p. 2–12.
Mormon Grove, Kan	13 Jun	Jacob F. Secrist (died 2 Jul) subsequently, Noah T. Guyman (2)	368	58	7 Sep 1855	J.H. 12 Sep 1855, and 7 Sep 1855, p 1–11.
Mormon Grove, Kan.	15 Jun	Seth M. Blair (Blair became ill, succeeded on 22 Jun by Edward Stevenson) (3) (1C)	89	38	11 Sep 1855	no roster.
Mormon Grove, Kan.	1 Jul	Richard Ballantyne (4)	402	45	25 Sep 1855	J.H. 12 Sep 1855.
Mormon Grove, Kan.	4 Jul	Moses F. Thurston (5)	148	33	28 Sep 1855	J.H. 12 Sep 1855.
Mormon Grove, Kan.	24 Jul returned left again 28 Jul	Charles A. Harper (6) [P.E.F.]	305	39	29 Oct 1855	J.H. 12 Sep 1855.
Mormon Grove, Kan.	31 Jul	Isaac Allred (7) [merchandise train]	61	34–38	some 2 Nov others 13 Nov 1855	J.H. 12 Sep 1855.
Mormon Grove, Kan.	4 Aug	Milo Andrus (8) [P.E.F.]	461		24 Oct 1855	J.H. 24 Oct 1855, p. 1–13.
1856						
Iowa City, Iowa	9 Jun	Edmund Ellsworth (1st Handcart Co.)	275	52 handcarts; (hc) a few waggons	26 Sep 1856	J.H. 9 Jun 1856, p. 1; 26 Sep 1856, p. 23–30.

LeRoy Hafen's *Handcarts to Zion* (Glendale, Calif.: A. H. Clark, 1960) for rosters on all of the handcart companies.

Outfitting Post	Date of Departure	Captain of Company and Company No.	Number Leaving Outfitting Post People/Wagons		Date Arrived	Roster
Iowa City, Iowa	11 Jun	Daniel D. McArthur (2nd Handcart Co.)	222	48 (hc) 4 wagons	26 Sep 1856	J.H. 11 Jun 26 Sep 1856, p. 31–36.
Iowa City, Iowa	23 Jun (left Florence, Nebraska, 30 Jul)	Edward Bunker (3rd Handcart Co.)	abt. 300	60 (hc) 5 wagons	2 Oct 1856	J.H. 2 Oct 1856, p. 6–12. 15 Oct 1856, p. 1.
Iowa City, Iowa	15 Jul	James G. Willie (4th Handcart Co.)	abt. 500	120 (hc) 5 wagons	9 Nov 1856	J.H. 9 Nov 18–30; J.H. 15 Oct 1856, p. 2.
Iowa City, Iowa	28 Jul	Edward Martin (5th Handcart Co.)	575	146 (hc) handcarts; 7 wagons	30 Nov 1856	J.H. 30 Nov 1856, p. 7–8, 60–76, 15 Oct 1856, p. 2.

Pioneer Companies That Crossed the Plains 1847–1868 *(continued)*

Outfitting Post	Date of Departure	Captain of Company and Company No.	Number Leaving Outfitting Post People/Wagons		Date Arrived	Roster (J.H. = Journal History of the Church) *Partial Roster
Florence, Neb.	5 Jun	Philemon C. Merrill (1st Wagon Company)	200	50	13–18 Aug 1856	J.H. 5 Jun 1856, p. 1.
Florence, Neb (Now Omaha)	abt. 10 Jun	Canute Peterson (2)	abt. 320	abt. 60	20 Sep 1856	J.H. 20 Sep 1856, p. 1–8, 15 Oct 1856, p. 12–13.
Florence, Neb	Middle of June	John Banks (3) [St. Louis Company]	300	abt. 60	1–2 Oct 1856	J.H. 3 Oct 1856, p. 2–9. 15 Oct 1856, p. 3.
Iowa City, Iowa	30 Jul	William B. Hodgetts (4)	abt. 150	33	10 Dec 1856 (some later)	J.H. 15 Oct 1856, p. 3. 15 Dec 1856, p. 1–6.
Iowa City, Iowa	1 Aug	Dan Jones (then John A. Hunt) (5)	abt. 300	56	10–15 Dec 1856	J.H. 15 Dec 1856, p. 7–15, 15 Oct 1856, p. 2.
Mormon Grove, Kan	10 Aug	Abraham O. Smoot [mostly merchandise]	abt. 97	abt. 34	9 Nov 1856	some names end of 1856
	1857					
Iowa City, Iowa	abt. 22 May	Israel Evans (6th Handcart Co.)	149	28 h.c.	11–12 Sep 1857	
Iowa City, Iowa	abt. 15 Jun	Christian Christiansen (7th Handcart Co.) [first headed by James Park, David Dille and George Thurston]	abt. 330	68 h.c. 3 wagons	13 Sep 1857	J.H. 13 Sep 1856, p. 12–26.
Florence, Neb. (Omaha)	13 Jun	William Walker's Freight Train	86	28	4 Sep 1857 (others a few days later)	no roster.
Iowa City, Iowa	early Jun	Jesse B. Martin (1st Wagon Co.)	192	34	12 Sep 1857	no roster.
Iowa City, Iowa	abt. 15 June	Matthias Cowley (2) [Scandinavian Co.]	198	31	13 Sep 1857	no roster.
Iowa City, Iowa	early Jun	Jacob Hoffheins (3) [New York Co. later the St. Louis Co.]	abt. 204	41	21 Sep 1857	no roster.
From Texas	Jul	Homer Duncan (returning from a mission)			14 and 20 Sep 1857	no roster.
Iowa City, Iowa	Jun	William G. Young	abt. 55	19	26 Sep 1857	no roster.
	1858					
[Very few emigrants crossed the plains in 1858 due to the approaching U.S. Army which was sent to suppress a supposed rebellion in Utah]						
Iowa City, Iowa	left Loupe Fork 8 Jun	Horace S. Eldredge (1st Wagon Company) men	39	13	9 Jul 1858	Church Emigration Book 1858.*
Iowa City, Iowa	Middle of Jun	Iver N. Iversen (2)	abt. 50	8	20 Sep 1858	J.H. 13 Jul 1858, p. 1.
Iowa City, Iowa	19 Jun	Russell K. Homer (3) [from ship "John Bright"]	abt. 60		6 Oct 1858	no roster, see Ms. History of Scandinavian Mission 21 Feb 1858, p. 3–5.
	1859					
Florence, Neb. (Omaha)	9 Jun	George Rowley (8th Handcart Company)	235	60 h.c. 8 wagons	4 Sep 1859	J.H. 12 Jun 1859, p. 4. Hafen's *Handcarts to Zion*
Florence, Neb.	13 Jun	James Brown, III (1st Wagon Company)	353	59	29 Aug 1859	J.H. 12 Jun 1859, p. 4.
Florence, Neb.	June	Horton O. Haight (2) [Merchandise Train]	154	71	1 Sep 1859	J.H. 12 Jun 1859, p. 4.

Pioneer Companies That Crossed the Plains 1847–1868 *(continued)*

Outfitting Post	Date of Departure	Captain of Company and Company No.	Number Leaving Outfitting Post People/Wagons		Date Arrived	Roster (J.H. = Journal History of the Church) *Partial Roster
Florence, Neb	26 or 28 Jun	Robert F. Neslen (3)	380	58	15 Sep 1859	J.H. 12 Jun 1859, p. 4.
Florence, Neb.	26 Jun	Edward Stevenson (4)	285	54	16 Sep 1859	no roster.
Geona, Neb.		A. S. Beckwith	22		1 Aug 1859	J.H. 1 Aug 1859.

Deseret News for 14 Sep 1859 notes that several small companies arrived in Salt Lake City after 1 Aug 1859. These Saints may have traveled with P. H. Buzzard's, D. Davis', J. H. Lemon's, F. Little's, and Redfield and Smith's freight trains.

Outfitting Post	Date of Departure	Captain of Company and Company No.	Number Leaving Outfitting Post People/Wagons		Date Arrived	Roster
	1860					
Florence, Neb.	6 Jun	Daniel Robinson (9th Handcard Co.)	233	43 (hc) 6 wagons	27 Aug 1860	J.H. 31 Dec 1860 Supp., p. 13–18.
Florence, Neb.	6 Jul	Oscar O. Stoddard (10th and last Handcart Co.)	126	22 hc 6 wagons	24 Sep 1860	J.H. Supp. after 31 Dec 1860, p. 34–37.
Florence, Neb.	30 May	Warren Walling (1st Wagon Co.)	172	30	9 Aug 1860	J. H. Supp. after 31 Dec 1860, p. 7–12.
Florence, Neb.	17 Jun	James D. Ross (2)	249	36	3 Sep 1860	J.H. Supp. after 31 Dec 1860, p. 19–25.
Florence, Neb	19 Jun	Jesse Murphy (3)	279	38	30 Aug 1860	J.H. Supp. after 31 Dec 1860, p. 26–33.
Florence, Neb.	abt. 15 Jun	John Smith (Patriarch of of Church) (4)	359	39	1 Sep 1860	J.H. Supp. after 31 Dec 1860, p. 38–46.
Florence, Neb.	20 Jul	William Budge (5)	400	55	5 Oct 1860	J.H. Supp. after 31 Dec. 1860, p. 47–57.
Florence, Neb.	3 Jul	John Taylor ["Iowa" Company]	123		17 Sep 1860	J.H. Supp. after 31, 1860 p. 58–62.
Florence, Neb.	23 Jul	Joseph W. Young [merchandise]	abt. 100	50	3 Oct 1860	no roster.
Florence, Neb.	latter part June	Franklin Brown [independent company]	60	14	27 Aug 1860	no roster.
Florence, Neb		Brigham H. Young [freight train]			14 Sep 1860	no roster.
	1861					
Florence, Neb. (Omaha)	29 May	David H. Cannon (1st Church Train)	225	57	16 Aug 1861	no roster.
Florence, Neb	7 Jun	Job Pingree [ind. co.]		33	24 Aug 1861	J.H. 24 Aug 1861.
Florence, Neb	abt. 20 Jun	Peter Ranck [ind. co.]		abt. 20	8 Sep 1861	no roster.
Florence, Neb	25 Jun	Homer Duncan (4)	264	47	13 Sep 1861	J.H. 13 Sep 1861, p. 2–5; Duncan's CEB 1861.
Florence, Neb	30 Jun	Ira Eldredge [2nd Church Train]		70	15 Sep 1861	no roster.
Florence, Neb	July	Milo Andrus	620	38	12 Sep 1861	no roster.
Florence, Neb	July	Thomas-Woolley	abt. 150	30	Sep 1861	no roster.
Florence, Neb	9 Jul	Joseph Horne [3rd Church Train]		62	13 Sep 1861	no roster.
Florence, Neb	13 Jul	Samuel Woolley	338	61	22 Sep 1861	J.H. 22 Sep 1861, p. 2–11.
Florence, Neb.	13 Jul	Joseph Porter [originally part Samuel Woolley Co.]			22 Sep 1861	roster for Wooley Co.
Florence, Neb.	July	John R. Murdock [4th Church Train] [mostly Scandinavian Saints from ship "Monarch of the Sea"]			12 Sep 1861	no roster, see See Ms. History of British Mission, 16 May 1861.

Pioneer Companies That Crossed the Plains 1847–1868 *(continued)*

Outfitting Post	Date of Departure	Captain of Company and Company No.	Number Leaving Outfitting Post People/Wagons		Date Arrived	Roster (J.H. = Journal History of the Church) *Partial Roster
Florence, Neb.	11 Jul	Joseph W. Young and later Heber P. Kimball [5th Church Train] (Merchandise)	90		23 Sep 1861	no roster.
Florence, Neb.	11 Jul	Ansel P. Harmon [Began as Joseph W. Young Co. Harmon organized 27 Jul]	40		23 Sep 1861	no roster.
Florence, Neb.	16 Jul	Sixtus E. Johnson	abt. 200	52	27 Sep 1861	no roster.

[In addition to the companies mentioned, several freight trains left Florence, Neb. during the months of July and Aug.]

Florence, Neb.	**1862** 17 Jun	Lewis Brunson (ind. co.)	212	48	29 Aug 1862	See *Deseret News* for 1861, vol. 12, p. 78. Also J.H. 20 Aug 1862, p. 2–7.*
Florence, Neb.	14 Jul	Ola N. Liljenquist (an ind. Scandinavian Co.)	abt. 250	40	23 Sep 1862	no roster.

See Ms. History of Scandinavian Mission for Apr. 1862, for rosters of people that left Hamburg, Germany. Liljenquist was leader of company on ship "Athenia".

Florence, Neb.	abt. 1st week in July	James Wargham (ind. co.)	250	46	26 Sep 1862	*Deseret News* for 1862, vol. 12, p. 93. Also J.H. 16 Sep 1862, p. 1.
Florence, Neb.	22 Jul	Homer Duncan (1st Church Train)	abt. 500		24 Sep 1862	J.H. 16 Sep 1862, p. 1. *Deseret News* vol. 12, p. 93.
Florence, Neb.	14 Jul	Christian A. Madsen (independent Scandinavian Company)	abt. 264	40	23 Sep 1862	no roster. see Ms. History of Scandinavian Mission, Apr 1862, for roster of ship "Franklin".
Florence, Neb.	24 Jul	John R. Murdock (2nd Church Train)	700	65	27 Sep 1862	*Deseret News* 1862, vol. 12, p. 93; J.H. 16 Sep 1862, p. 2.
Florence, Neb	28 Jul	James S. Brown (ind. co.)	200	46	2 Oct 1862	Partial roster See *Deseret News* 1862, vol. 12, p. 113. Also J.H. 2 Oct 1862, p. 1
Florence, Neb.	29 Jul	Joseph Horne (3rd Church Train)	570	52	1 Oct 1862	*Deseret News* 1862, vol. 12, p. 98. Also J.H. 24 Sep 1862, p. 1.
Florence, Neb.	abt. 30 Jul	Isaac A. Canfield (ind. co.)	abt. 120		16 Oct 1862	*Deseret News* 1862, vol. 12, p. 93. Also J.H. 16 Sep 1862, p. 3, and 16 Oct 1862 p. 1–14.
Florence, Neb.	early Aug	Ansel P. Harmon (4th Church Train)	abt. 500		5 Oct 1862	J.H. 24 Sep 1862, p. 2. Also *Deseret News* 1862, vol. 12, p. 98.
Florence, Neb.	8 Aug	Henry W. Miller (5th Church Train)	665	60	17 Oct 1862	*Deseret News* 1862, vol. 12, p. 92.
Florence, Neb.	early Aug	Horton D. Haight (6th Church Train)	650		19 Oct 1862	J.H. 24 Sep 1862, p. 2. Also *Deseret News* 1862, vol. 12, p. 98.
Florence, Neb.	14 Aug	William H. Dame (7th Church Train)	150	50	29 Oct 1862	J.H. 24 Sep 1862, p. 3. *Deseret News* 1862, vol. 12, p. 98.

In addition to these companies, a large number of freight trains brought small companies of L.D.S. emigrants.

Florence, Neb.	**1863** 29 Jun	John R. Murdock (1st Church Train)	275 or 375	55	29 Aug 1863	no roster, but mentioned in J.H. 14 Jul, 21, 29 Aug 1883 and *Deseret News* 1863, vol. 13, p. 57.

Pioneer Companies That Crossed the Plains 1847–1868 (continued)

Outfitting Post	Date of Departure	Captain of Company and Company No.	Number Leaving Outfitting Post People/Wagons		Date Arrived	Roster (J.H. = Journal History of the Church) *Partial Roster
Florence, Neb.	6 Jul	John F. Sanders (2nd Church Train)			5 Sep 1863	no roster, but J.H. 5 Sep 1863 and *Deseret News* 1863 vol. 13, p. 57.
Florence, Neb.	30 Jun	Alvus H. Petterson (ind. co.)	abt. 200	50	4 Sep 1863	J.H. 4 Sep 1863, p. 1–3.
Florence, Neb.	6 Jul	John R. Young (ind. co.)			12 Sep 1863	no roster, J.H. 12 Sep 1863, p. 2–9, for camp history.
Florence, Neb.	9 Jul	William B. Preston (3rd Church Train)	abt. 300	55	10 Sep 1863	no roster, J.H. 5, 16, 24 Aug 1863, and *Deseret News*, vol. 13, p. 64.
Florence, Neb.	25 Jul	Peter Nebeker (4th Church Train)	abt. 500	70	25 Sep 1863	no roster.
Florence, Neb	6 Aug	Daniel D. McArthur (5th Church Train)	abt. 500	75	3 Oct 1863	no roster.
Florence, Neb.	8 Aug	Horton D. Haight (6th Church Train)	abt. 200 (freight)		4 Oct 1863	no roster.
Florence, Neb.	9 Aug	John W. Woolley (7th Church Train)	abt. 200		4 Oct 1863	no roster.
Florence, Neb.	10 Aug	Thomas E. Ricks (8th Church Train)	abt. 400		4 Oct 1863	no roster.
Florence, Neb.	11 Aug	Rosel Hyde (9th Church Train)	abt. 300		13 Oct 1863	no roster.
Florence, Neb.	14 Aug	Samuel D. White (10th Church Train)	abt. 300 (freight)		15 Oct 1863	no roster.

Freight Trains under the charge of Captains Canfield, Jakeman, Shurtliff, and others also left Florence, Nebraska, for Salt Lake City.

Outfitting Post	Date of Departure	Captain of Company and Company No.	Number Leaving Outfitting Post People/Wagons		Date Arrived	Roster
	1864					
Wyoming, Neb. (west bank of Missouri River about 40 miles south of Omaha)	25 Jun	John D. Chase (ind. co.)	85	28	abt. 20 Sep 1864	J.H. 20 Sep 1864, p. 2.
Wyoming, Neb.	29 Jun	John R. Murdock (1st Church Train) [large amount of freight]	78		26 Aug 1864	J.H. 26 Aug 1864.
Wyoming, Neb.	8 Jul	William G. Preston (2nd Church Train)	abt. 400	50	15 Sep 1864	*Deseret News* 17 Aug 1864, p. 369; J.H. 8 Jul, 14 Sep, 19 Oct 1864.
Wyoming, Neb.	15 Jul	Joseph S. Rawlins (3rd Church Train)	abt. 400	abt. 50	20 Sep 1864	*Deseret News* 17 Aug 1864, p. 369.
Wyoming, Neb.	19 or 22 Jul	William S. Warren (4th Church Train)	abt. 329	abt. 65	4 Oct 1864	*Deseret News* 17 Aug 1864, p. 369.
Wyoming, Neb.	27 Jul	Isaac A. Canfield (5th Church Train)	abt. 211	abt. 50	5 Oct 1864	*Deseret News* 17 Aug 1864, p. 369.*
Wyoming, Neb.	July	John Smith (Presiding Patriarch) [ind. co.]	abt. 150	20	1 Oct 1864	no roster.
Wyoming, Neb.	9 Aug	William Hyde (6th Church Train)	abt. 350	62	26 Oct 1864	*Deseret News* 19 Oct 1864, p. 18.*
Wyoming, Neb.	middle Aug	Warren S. Snow	abt. 400		2 Nov 1864	no roster.
	1865					
Wyoming, Neb.	31 Jul	Miner G. Atwood	abt. 400	45	8 Nov 1865	*Deseret News* 1865, vol. 14 p. 403; J.H. 8 Nov 1865.
Wyoming, Neb.	12 Aug	Henson Walker	abt. 200	abt. 50	9 Nov 1865	J.H. 9 Nov 1865; *Deseret News* 1865, vol. 14, p. 403.
Wyoming, Neb.	12, 15 Aug	William S. S. Willis	abt. 200	abt. 50	11 Nov 1865 others 29 Nov 1865	J.H. 29 Nov 1865, *Deseret News* 1865, vol. 14 p. 204.

Pioneer Companies That Crossed the Plains 1847–1868 *(continued)*

Outfitting Post	Date of Departure	Captain of Company and Company No.	Number Leaving Outfitting Post People/Wagons		Date Arrived	Roster (J.H. = Journal History of the Church) *Partial Roster
	1866					
Wyoming, Neb.	6 Jul	Thomas E. Ricks (1st Church Train)	251	46	4 Sep 1866	*Deseret News* 16 Aug 1866. Also J.H. 4 Sep 1866.
Wyoming, Neb.	7 Jul	Samuel D. White (2nd Church Train)	230	46	5 Sep 1866	*Deseret News* 16 Aug 1866.
Wyoming, Neb	13 Jul	William Henry Chipman (3rd Church Train)	375	abt. 60	15 Sep 1866	J.H. 15 Sep 1866, p. 3–4.
Wyoming Neb.	19 Jul	John D. Holladay (4th Church Train)	350	69	25 Sep 1866	J.H. 25 Sep 1866.*
Wyoming, Neb.	4 Aug	Peter Nebeker (5th Church Train)	400	62	29 Sep 1866	J.H. 25 Sep 1866.*
Wyoming, Neb.	25 Jul	Daniel Thompson (6th Church Train)	abt. 500	85	29 Sep 1866	Those born and died in J.H. 29 Sep 1866.*
Wyoming, Neb.	2 Aug	Joseph S. Rawlins (7th Church Train)	over 400	65	1 Oct 1866	J.H. 1 Oct 1866.
Wyoming, Neb.	8 Aug	Andrew H. Scott (8th Church Train)	abt. 300	49	8 Oct. 1866	no roster, Ms. Hist. of Wyoming, Nebraska.
Wyoming, Neb.	early Aug	Horton B. Haight (9th Church Train) [included 500 miles of wire for Deseret Telegraph Line]	4 families	65	15 Oct 1866	no roster.
Wyoming, Neb.	8 Aug	Abner Lowery (10th Church Train)	300		22 Oct 1866	J.H. 22 Oct 1866.
	1867					
North Platte, Neb. [Western Terminus of the Union Pacific Railroad]	middle Aug	Leonard G. Rice	abt. 500	abt. 50	5 Oct 1867	no roster.
	1868					
Laramie, Wyo.	25 Jul	Chester Loveland	abt. 400	40	20 Aug 1868	J.H. 25 Jul 1868, p. 2.
Laramie, Wyo.	25 Jul	Joseph S. Rawlins	nearly 300	31	20 Aug 1868	no roster.
Laramie, Wyo.	27 Jul	John R. Murdock	abt. 600	50	19 Aug 1868	no roster.
Laramie, Wyo.	27 Jul	Horton D. Haight	275	abt. 30	24 Aug 1868	no roster.
Laramie, Wyo.	1 Aug	William S. Seeley	272	39	29 Aug 1868	J.H. 1 Aug 1868, p. 1.
Benton, Wyo.	13 Aug	Simpson A. Molen	300	61	2 Sep 1868	no roster.
Benton, Wyo.	14 Aug	Daniel D. McArthur	411	51	2 Sep 1868	no roster.
Benton, Wyo.	24 Aug	John Gillespie	abt. 500	50	15 Sep 1868	no roster.
Benton, Wyo.	31 Aug	John G. Holman	abt. 650	62	25 Sep 1868	J.H. 25 Sep 1868.
Benton, Wyo.	1 Sep	Edward T. Mumford	250	28	24 Sep 1868	J.H. 24 Sep 1868, p. 1.

1869

With the arrival of Holman's and Mumford's trains, travel across the plains with ox or mule teams was terminated. The construction of the Transcontinental Railroad from the Missouri River to San Francisco, California was completed 10 May 1869 with the driving of the last spike at Promintory Point, Utah.

NOTES

Preface

[1] Stegner, *The Gathering of Zion: The Story of the Mormon Trail*, (Lincoln, Nebraska: University of Nebraska Press, 1964), 13.

[2] Rachel Maines, "Textiles as History," *American Quilts, A Handmade Legacy*, ed. by Thomas Frye (Oakland, Calif: Oakland Museum of Art, 1981) 41.

[3] Ann Leppich, conversation with the author, June 1996.

[4] Ruby Shepherd Karpowitz, "History of Elizabeth Jane Rogers Shepherd: Pioneer of 1866," Manuscript Collection, Pioneer Memorial Museum.

Introduction

[1] Margaret Gay Judd Clawson, "Reminiscences," as cited in Susan Arrington Madsen, *I Walked to Zion: True Stories of Young Pioneers on the Mormon Trail* (Salt Lake City: Deseret Book Company, 1994), 143.

[2] Allen, James and Glen Leonard, *The Story of Latter-day Saints* (Salt Lake City: Deseret Books, 1992), 390.

[3] Stegner, *The Gathering of Zion*, 177.

[4] Thomas A. Bailey and David M. Kennedy, *The American Pageant* (Lexington, MA: D.C. Heath, 1983), 231.

[5] Whitney Cross, *The Burned-over District: The Social and Intellectual History of Enthusiastic Religion in Western New York, 1800–1850*, (Ithaca, New York: Cornell University Press, 1950).

[6] Norma B. Ricketts, *Melissa's Journey with the Mormon Battalion* (Salt Lake City: International Society of Daughters of Utah Pioneers, 1994), 3.

[7] Sarah Dall Weech and Hyrum Weech, *Our Pioneer Parents: Autobiographies* (n.p.: Weech Genealogical Association, n.d.), p. 38. The hill at the Big Colorado River crossing at Lee Ferry's, known as Lee's Backbone, was one of the steepest and most dangerous climbs on the southern routes.

[8] Charles Dickens, quoted in William W. Slaughter, *Life in Zion* (Salt Lake City: Deseret Book Company, 1995), 45.

Part One: Seeking the Place

[1] "History of Margaret T. McMeans Smoot, Pioneer of 1847," Manuscript Collection, Daughters of Utah Pioneers, Salt Lake City, Utah.

[2] Allen and Leonard, *The Story of Latter-day Saints*, 124–125.

[3] Amanda Barnes Smith, *Amanda's Journal*, comp. Lura D. Dunn (self-published, 1977), 2.

[4] "History of the Church of Jesus Christ of Latter-day Saints, Period I, History of Joseph Smith, the Prophet, By Himself [DHC]," (Salt Lake City: Deseret News, 1949) IV:605-607, as cited in Relief Society of the Church of Jesus Christ of Latter-day Saints, *History of Relief Society 1842–1966* (Salt Lake City: General Board of Relief Society, 1966), 21.

[5] Allen and Leonard, *The Story of Latter-day Saints*, 216.

[6] Stegner, *The Gathering of Zion*, 40.

[7] John Taylor, "Address to the Saints in Great Britain," *Millennial Star* 8 (15 November 1846): 114, as cited in Gentry, "Mormon Way Stations," 445.

[8] B.H. Roberts, *A Comprehensive History of the Church of Jesus Christ of Latter-day Saints*, vol. 1, 539–540 as cited in Stanley B. Kimball, *Historic Resource Study: Mormon Pioneer National Historic Trail* (Washington, D.C.: United States Department of the Interior/National Park Service, 1991), 129.

[9] Eliza R. Snow, *Biography and Family Record of Lorenzo Snow*, (Salt Lake City: Deseret News, 1884), 91–92, as cited in Gentry, "Mormon Way Stations," 459.

[10] John Henry Evans, *Charles Coulson Rich: Pioneer Builder of the West* (New York: Macmillan, 1936) as cited in Leland H. Gentry, "The Mormon Way Stations: Garden Grove and Mt. Pisgah," *Brigham Young University Studies* 24, no. 4 (1981): 460.

[11] Annie Caroline Carlston Bills, "Mary Young Wilcox," Manuscript file, International Society of Daughters of Utah Pioneers, Pioneer Memorial Museum, Salt Lake City, p. 5–6.

[12] Stegner, *The Gathering of Zion*, 106.

[13] Matthias F. Cowley, *Wilford Woodruff: History of His Life and Labors* (Salt Lake City: Deseret News, 1909), 250, as cited in Gentry, "Mormon Way Stations," 454.

[14] Kenneth Barker, interview by author, Winter Quarters Historical Site, Omaha, Nebr., September 1994.

[15] Sarah DeArmon Pea Rich, Autobiographical sketch, 1885, relating experiences in Missouri during 1836–1838, as cited in Nina Palmer, *Rich Family and Church History Tour* (Salt Lake City, Utah: self-published, 1991), 7–8.

[16] Patsy and Myron Orlofsky, *Quilts in America* (New York: McGraw-Hill, 1974), 256.

[17] Allen and Leonard, *The Story of the Latter-day Saints*, 104.

[18] Ron Romig, Church Archivist, Reorganized Church of Jesus Christ of Latter Day Saints, Independence, Missouri, interview with author, January 20, 1995.

[19] Accession sheet #03739, Pioneer Memorial Museum, Salt Lake City. However, the information is incorrect: the quiltmaker died in 1893 at age 79.

[20] Ida Rich Strong, *Sketch of the Life and History of Sarah DeArmon Pea Rich: Pioneer of 1847*, Manuscript Collection, Pioneer Memorial Museum, Salt Lake City.

[21] Ibid., 9.

[22] Nedra Watkins Reese, *Charles Coulson Rich: The Man and His Family* (Orem, Utah: self-published, 1988), 84.

[23] Rita Adrosko, *Natural Dyes and Home Dyeing* (New York: Dover Publications, 1971), 31–39.

[24] Allen and Leonard, *The Story of Latter-day Saints*, 42.

[25] Timothy Wilson, *Flags at Sea* (London: Her Majesty's Stationery Office, 1986), 74.

[26] Sarah Harris Passey, "Autobiography of Margaret McMeans T. Smoot, First Wife of A. O. Smoot Came to Utah 1847," Manuscript Collection, Pioneer Pioneer Museum, Salt Lake City, 33–39.

[27] Relief Society, *History*, 102.

[28] "Life Sketch of Sophronia Carter: Early Dixie Pioneer," Family History Library, Salt Lake City, microfilm #485,341.

[29] "William Carter-Scout," in vol. 2 of *Our Pioneer Heritage*, ed. Kate B. Carter (Salt Lake City: Daughters of Utah Pioneers, 1959), 551.

[30] "History on Sophronia Turnbow Carter," Manuscript Collection, Daughters of Utah Pioneers, McQuarrie Memorial Museum, St. George, Utah.

[31] Ibid.

[32] Virginia Fleming, "Mary Wilcox Young," Manuscript Collection of Virginia Fleming, Arcadia, California.

[33] James Jakeman, "Pioneer Mothers and Daughters," *Daughters of Utah Pioneers and Their Mothers* (n.p.: Western Album Publishing Company, n.d.)

[34] Ibid.

[35] Florence H. Petit, *America's Printed and Painted Fabrics 1600–1900* (New York: Hastings House, 1970), 237.

[36] Kathryn Fairbanks Kirk, *The Fairbanks Family in the West: Four Generations* (Salt Lake City: Paragon Press, 1983) 669.

[37] Edna Ashby Thorley, "Nancy Garr Badger Stringham," Manuscript Collection, Pioneer Memorial Museum, Salt Lake City.

[38] Hal Morgan, *Symbols of America* (New York: Viking Penguin, 1986), 104.

[39] Annie B. Johnson, "Another Crazy Quilt," in *Pioneer Quilts*, ed. Kate B. Carter (Salt Lake City: Daughters of the Utah Pioneers, n.d.), 93–94.

[40] Florence Montgomery, *Printed Textiles: English and American Cottons and Linens 1700–1850* (New York: Viking Press, 1970), 212.

[41] Florence Montgomery, *Textiles in America 1650–1870* (New York: W. W. Norton, 1984), pl. D-93.

[42] Abigail Chase Gudmundson, "Biography of Samantha (Crismon) Chase," Manuscript Collection, Pioneer Memorial Museum, Salt Lake City.

[43] Montgomery, Ibid.

[44] Ruth Ashby Corley, interview with author, Kearns, Utah, July 26, 1995.

[45] Beatrice S. Winsor, "A Sketch of the Life of Erastus Snow: Immigrant Pioneer 1847," Manuscript File, Daughters of the Utah Pioneers, Salt Lake City.

[46] James Jakeman, Ibid.

[47] Kate B. Carter, "Brigham Young—His Wives and Family," *Our Pioneer Heritage* (Salt Lake City, Utah: Daughters of Utah Pioneers, 1958), 431.

[48] Allen and Leonard, *The Story of Latter-day Saints*, 389.

[49] Relief Society, *History*, 13.

[50] Melvin Bashore and Linda L. Haslam, *Mormon Pioneer Companies Crossing the Plains* (Salt Lake City: Church Historical Department, 1990).

[51] Amelia Peck, *American Quilts and Coverlets in The Metropolitan Museum of Art* (New York: Metropolitan Museum of Art, 1990), 122–123.

[52] Bill Ormon, conversation with Christine Briscoe and the author, March 1995.

[53] Montgomery, Ibid., 287.

[54] "History of Sarah Heward Stocks," Manuscript Collection, Daughters of Utah Pioneers, Salt Lake City.

[55] Ibid.

56 Ricky Clark, George Knepper, and Ellice Ronsheim, *Quilts in Community: Ohio Traditions* (Nashville, Tenn.: Rutledge Hill Press, 1991), 61.

57 Daniel Duncan McArthur, *Daniel Duncan McArthur: Mormon Pioneer* (Bountiful, Utah: R. McArthur, 1987) 35–36.

58 Ibid., 61.

59 Wilford W. McArthur as told to Lola H. McArthur, quoted in ibid., 174.

60 Matilda Ann Duncan Winters, Obituary, Manuscript file, Pioneer Memorial Museum, Salt Lake City.

61 Matilda Burningham, Statement, Accession File #6295, Pioneer Memorial Museum, Salt Lake City.

62 Ancestral File #AFN:FL81-91, Church of Jesus Christ of Latter-day Saints, Salt Lake City, Utah.

63 Martha Doane, "History of Nancy Crosby Bankhead," Manuscript Collection, Pioneer Memorial Museum.

64 Inez Rhead Allen, "Hannah Johnson Staley, Born in Albany, New York, July 31, 1806," Manuscript File, Pioneer Memorial Museum.

65 Susan La Nez Cragun, "Sarah Ann Huffman Pitkin," Manuscript Collection, Pioneer Memorial Museum, 13–14.

66 *Family Histories and Record of William Walton Burton: and Wives Rachel Fielding Burton, Ellen Fielding Burton, and Sarah Ann Fielding Burton* (Salt Lake City: William Walton Burton Family Organization, 1981).

67 Kate B. Carter, *An Enduring Legacy*, Daughters of the Utah Pioneers, 1985, Volume 8, 253–254.

68 Acquisition Sheet #12930, Pioneer Memorial Museum.

69 Relief Society, *History*, 22.

70 Church Family History Ancestral File, International Genealogical Index, Early Church Membership Files.

71 Maurine Carr Ward, "The Winter Quarters Journals of Mary Haskin Parker Richards," journal 3, Manuscript collection of Janet Burton Seegmiller, Cedar City, Utah, 79.

Part Two: Gathering in Zion
1 Eliza Roxcy Snow, Diaries, 1846–49, holograph, Huntington Libraries, San Marino, California. Transcribed by Maureen Ursenbach Beecher, Joseph Smith Institute for Church History, Brigham Young University, Provo, Utah.

2 Stanley B. Kimball, *Historic Resource Study: Mormon Pioneer National Historic Trail* (Washington, D.C.: United States Department of the Interior/National Park Service, 1991), 9.

3 Susan Arrington Madsen, *I Walked to Zion: True Stories of Young Pioneers on the Mormon Trail* (Salt Lake City: Deseret Book Company, 1994), 144.

4 Kimball, Ibid., 10.

5 Madsen, Ibid., 144.

6 Kathryn Fairbanks Kirk, *The Fairbanks Family in the West: Four Generations* (Salt Lake City: Paragon Press, 1983), 670.

7 Glenn Leonard, interview with author, May 10, 1995.

8 Kate B. Carter, *Our Pioneer Heritage*, (Salt Lake City, Utah: Daughters of Utah Pioneers, 1965), vol. 8, 289.

9 Ibid., 1960, Volume 3, 242.

10 S. Kent Brown, Donald Q. Cannon, and Richard H. Jackson, *Historical Atlas of Mormonism* (New York: Simon and Schuster, 1994), 116–117.

11 Leona George Smith and Hilda Mann Condie, "Life Sketch of Ann Mariah Bowen Call," Manuscript Collection, Pioneer Memorial Museum.

12 James McClintock, *Mormon Settlement in Arizona* (reprint, Tucson: University of Arizona Press, 1985), 112.

13 Smith and Condie, Ibid.

14 Elly Sienkiewicz, *Spoken Without a Word* (Washington, D.C.: Turtle Hill Press, 1983), 49.

15 Suellen Meyer, "Pine Tree Quilts," *The Quilt Digest* (San Francisco: Quilt Digest Press, 1986), 14.

16 Norma B. Ricketts, ed., *An Enduring Legacy* (Salt Lake City: Daughters of Utah Pioneers, 1981), vol.4, 125.

17 Norma B. Ricketts, *Melissa's Journey with the Mormon Battalion* (Salt Lake City: International Society of Daughters of Utah Pioneers, 1994).

18 Madsen, *I Walked to Zion*, 143.

19 Stanley B. Kimball, *Historic Resource Study*, 146.

20 Anne Woolin, Descendant, interview with author, May 1995.

21 Cornelia Crane Butterfield, "History of Mary Jane Parker Butterfield", Manuscript File, Daughters of Utah Pioneers, Salt Lake City.

22 Ibid.

23 This would indicate the family traveled on their own or made their own arrangements.

24 Donald Kloster, Curator of Military History, National Museum of American History, Smithsonian Institution, Washington, D.C., interview with author, January 1995.

25 Ron Romig, Church Archivist, Reorganized Church of Jesus Christ of Latter Day Saints, Independence, Missouri, Conversation with the author, January 20, 1995.

26 Relief Society of the Church of Jesus Christ of Latter-day Saints, *History of Relief Society 1842–1966* (Salt Lake City: General Board of Relief Society, 1966), 102.

27 Amanda Barnes Smith, *Amanda's Journal*, comp. Lura S. Dunn (self-published, 1977), 1–6.

28 Rozilla M. Dalton Tolman, Accession File #6126, Pioneer Memorial Museum.

29 Ibid.

30 "Biography of Lee and Nancy Bybee," Manuscript Collection, Pioneer Memorial Museum.

31 Ibid.

32 *An Enduring Legacy*, (Salt Lake City: Daughters of the Utah Pioneers, 1982), Volume 5, 46–47.

33 Cuma Bond Goodwin, "Lucy Jane Clark Barkdull," Manuscript Collection, Pioneer Memorial Museum, 2.

34 Florence N. Riddle et al., "History of Matilda Robison King," Manuscript Collection, Pioneer Memorial Museum.

35 Gayle B. Frandsen, "Matilda Robison King," Unpublished manuscript.

36 Quilt #01839 documentation, Pioneer Memorial Museum.

37 Vernon Lunt, *The Life of Henry Lunt* (n.p., 1944), 77–79.

38 Ibid., 83.

39 Ibid., 83–86.

40 Averil Colby, *Patchwork* (Newton Centre, Mass.: Charles T. Branford, 1958), 56.

41 Carter, vol. 8, Ibid., 290–294.

42 Accession Record #208320-MUSM-90, Church Museum of History and Art, Salt Lake City.

43 Ibid., 293.

44 Laura Allen, "A Sketch of the Life of Sarah M. Chaffin," Manuscript File, Pioneer Memorial Museum.

45 "Biography of Louis R. Chaffin," Manuscript Collection, Daughters of Utah Pioneers, McQuarrie Memorial Museum, St. George, Utah.

46 *World Book Encyclopedia*, ed., S.V. "."

47 Pearl J. Cordon, "Eliza Melissa Hall," Manuscript File, Daughters of Utah Pioneers, Salt Lake City.

48 "Sketch of the Life of Eliza Melissa Hall Hall," Manuscript Collection, Daughters of Utah Pioneers, Ogden, Utah.

49 Frank Esshom, *Pioneers and Prominent Men of Utah* (Salt Lake City: Western Epics, 1966).

50 Sadie Leffler Russon, "Life Sketch of Eliza Dorsey Ashworth," Manuscript File, Pioneer Memorial Museum, 1.

51 Pearl Lence, "History of Sage Treharne Jones," Manuscript Collection, McQuarrie Memorial Museum, St. George, Utah.

52 Dorothy Osler, *Traditional British Quilts* (London, B. T. Batsford, 1987), 26–28.

53 Asa Wettre, *Old Swedish Quilts* (Loveland, Colo.: Interweave Press), 1995, 46–47, 96–98.

54 *Box Elder Lore of the Nineteenth Century*, (Brigham City, Utah: Box Elder Chapter of Sons of Utah Pioneers, 1951), 41–48, 56–61.

55 Brown, Cannon, and Jackson, *Historical Atlas*, 90.

56 James Allen and Glen Leonard, *The Story of Latter-day Saints* (Salt Lake City: Deseret Books,), 279.

57 Ruth Gunnell Victor, "History of Ann Sewell Hawkins," Ogden, Utah, 1980.

58 Hazel Murphy McRae, "Sketch of the Life of Isabella C. MacKay, A Utah Pioneer of 1852," Manuscript File, Pioneer Memorial Museum, 2.

59 Ibid., 3.

60 Quilt documentation #6A, Daughters of Utah Pioneers, Salt Lake City.

61 Accession donation #6517.

62 Florence Montgomery, *Textiles in America 1650–1870* (New York: W. W. Norton, 1984), 291–292.

63 Ibid., 214.

64 Ibid., 320.

65 Florence Montgomery, *Printed Textiles: English and American Cottons and Linens 1700–1850* (New York: Viking Press, 1970), 306.

66 Helen Orr Smith, *History of Sarah Henry Wickle*, Manuscript Collection, Daughters of Utah Pioneers, Salt Lake City.

67 June Kasteler, "Story of Elizabeth Jones Fox," *Treasures of Pioneer History*, vol. 1 (Salt Lake City: Daughters of Utah Pioneers, 1952), 129–130.

68 Norma B. Winn, ed., "Desdamona Fox Brown, Pioneer of 1855," *An Enduring Legacy* vol. 3 (Salt Lake City: Daughters of Utah Pioneers, 1980), 369.

Part Three: Welcoming the Faithful

1 William Hepworth Dixon, *New America*, Vol. 1 (London: Hurst and Blackett, 1867), 252–53, as cited in James Allen and Glen Leonard, *The Story of Latter-day Saints* (Salt Lake City: Deseret Books,), 294.

2 Kate B. Carter, comp., "Mormon Emigration 1840–1869," (Salt Lake City: Daughters of Utah Pioneers, 1963), 261.

3 Mary Gobel Pay, "Reminiscence," *Our Pioneer Heritage* (Salt Lake City, Utah: Daughters of Utah Pioneers, 1970), vol. 13, p. 430.

4 Lyndia McDowell Carter, "The Mormon Handcart Companies," *Overland Journal* 13, no. 1, (spring 1995): 9.

5 Ibid., 4–15.

6 Leonard J. Arrington, *Great Basin Kingdom* (Cambridge: Harvard University Press, 1958), 194, as cited in Allen and Leonard, *The Story of Latter-day Saints*, 317.

7 William G. Hartley, "Down-and-Back Wagon Trains: Travelers on the Mormon Trail in 1861," *Overland Journal* 11, no. 4 (winter 1993): 25.

8 Kate B. Carter, "Mormon Emigration 1840–1869," 266.

9 Journal History, July 17, 1861, LDS Archives, Church History Department, Salt Lake City, as cited in Hartley, "Down-and-Back Wagon Trains," 25.

10 Washington County Chapter DUP, *Under Dixie Sun: A History of Washington County by Those Who Loved Their Forebears* (Panguitch, Utah: Garfield County News, 1950), 183–84.

11 "Family History 1987: Brighton, Thornley, Timmons," Manuscript Collection, Family History Library, Salt Lake City, 45.

12 Paul E. Dahl, " 'All Is Well . . .': The Story of 'the Hymn That Went around the World,' " *Brigham Young University Studies,* Volume 21, Number 4, Fall 1981, 515–527.

13 Quilt documentation, Collection of Floyd D. Ahlstrom, Kanash, Utah.

14 Carolyn O'Bagy Davis, *Pioneer Quiltmaker: The Story of Dorinda Moody Slade 1808–1895* (Tucson, Ariz.: Sanpete Publications, 1990).

15 Ibid., 38.

16 Ibid.

17 Henry W. Miller, "Journal of Henry W. Miller: April 1855–Spring 1862," Manuscript Collection, Utah State Historical Society, Salt Lake City.

18 Jack E. and Patricia K. A. Fletcher, "The Cherokee Trail," *Overland Journal* 13, no. 2: 24–25.

19 E. Grant Moody, ed., *The John Wyatt Moody Family: Past and Present* (Tempe, Ariz.: Dr. Thomas Moody Family Organization Inc., 1985), as cited in Davis, *Pioneer Quiltmaker*, 28.

20 Carolyn Davis, Letter to author, June 17, 1995.

21 Warren A. Beck and Ynez D. Haase, *Historical Atlas of the American West* (Norman, Okla.: University of Oklahoma Press, 1989), 28–29.

22 Fletcher, Ibid., 21–33.

23 The 1860 census listed only forty-three permanent citizens: ten men, eight women, and twenty-five children under the age of fourteen.

24 Moody, *John Wyatt Moody Family*, 46, as cited in Davis, *Pioneer Quiltmaker*, 51.

25 Barbara Brackman, *Encyclopedia of Pieced Quilt Patterns* (Lawrence, Kans.: Prairie Flower Publishing, 1984), #1081.

26 Carolyn Davis, interview with author, Santa Fe, New Mexico, April 1, 1995.

27 Davis, *Pioneer Quiltmaker*, 54–55.

28 Arzella Knight Gylling, "Life Story of My Grand Mother Betsy Williamson Smith," Manuscript Collection, Pioneer Memorial Museum.

29 The damaged area's not having been repaired or altered was an appropriate action by the donor. The most approved method of treatment would be to stabilize the area by putting fabric on the back and carefully attaching the quilt using a couching stitch. A transparent fabric could also be placed over the top and stitched in the same fashion. This would allow the original work to be preserved and enjoyed.

30 Theo Dedrickson Sr., "A Brief Story of Theo Dedrickson, Sr.," *Pioneer Histories*, vol. 2, cited in Carter, Ibid., p. 6.

31 Gylling, Ibid., 2.

32 Daniel Robinson, "Autobiography," *Treasures of Pioneer History* compiled by Kate B. Carter, (Salt Lake City, Utah: Daughters of the Utah Pioneers, 1956), Volume 5, p. 288 as found in Carter, Ibid., p. 5.

33 Muriel Colton Johnson, "History of Eleanor Jones Young, Pioneer of 1856," Manuscript File, Pioneer Memorial Museum.

34 Johnson, "Eleanor Jones Young," 2.

35 Deon S. Seedall, Documentation on Quilt #06926, Pioneer Memorial Museum.

36 Dorothy Osler, *Traditional British Quilts* (London: B. T. Batsford, 1987), 34.

37 Florence Montgomery, *Printed Textiles: English and American Cottons and Linens 1700–1850* (New York: Viking Press, 1970), 137.

38 Seedall, Quilt #06926.

39 Washington County Chapter DUP, *Under Dixie Sun*, 309.

40 Le Landgren, *A Whitmore Family History 1793–1990* (West Linn, Ore.: Family Gathering, 1990), 4, 10–11.

41 Averil Colby, *Patchwork* (Newton Centre, Mass.: Charles T. Branford, 1958), 42.

42 Montgomery, *Printed Textiles*, 287–305.

43 Jane Rawlinson Geertson, *Life Story of Charles Rawlinson: Heirs to the Kingdom* (self-published, n.d.).

44 Ibid.

45 Elly Sienkiewicz, *Spoken Without A Word* (Washington, D.C.: Turtle Hill Press, 1983), 43.

46 Sarah Dall Weech and Hyrum Weech, *Our Pioneer Parents: Autobiographies* (n.p.: Weech Genealogical Association, md.), 24.

⁴⁷ Allen and Leonard, *The Story of Latter-day Saints*, 345.

⁴⁸ Davis, *Pioneer Quiltmaker*, 39.

⁴⁹ David Moses, Telephone conversation with the author, May 4, 1995.

⁵⁰ Brackman, *Pieced Quilt Patterns*, #2020.

⁵¹ Margaret Noall, "History of Mary Ellen Salisbury Parsons," Unpublished manuscript, 1995.

⁵² Margaret Noall, letter to author, April 1995.

⁵³ Noall, "History of Mary Ellen Salisbury Parsons," Ibid.

⁵⁴ Osler, *Traditional British Quilts*, 36.

⁵⁵ Barbara Brackman, *Clues in the Calico: A Guide to Identifying and Dating Antique Quilts* (McLean, Va.: EPM Publications, 1989), 62.

⁵⁶ Osler, *Traditional British Quilts*, 57–58.

⁵⁷ Jean Christensen, Letter to author, April 18, 1995.

⁵⁸ Jean Christensen, Conversation with author, December 1994.

⁵⁹ Ibid.

⁶⁰ Colby, *Patchwork*, figs. 112, 123, 126.

⁶¹ Montgomery, *Printed Textiles*, 137–140, 300–304.

⁶² Barton Howell, "Elizabeth Bell Barton," Manuscript File, Pioneer Memorial Museum.

⁶³ Kate B. Carter, *Our Pioneer Heritage*, (Salt Lake City: Daughters of the Utah Pioneers, 1961), Volume 4, 32–33.

⁶⁴ Florence Smith Bowns, "History of Eliza Jane Eynon Ricks," Manuscript Collection, Pioneer Memorial Museum, 3.

⁶⁵ Ibid., 5.

⁶⁶ Ibid., 2.

⁶⁷ Colby, *Patchwork*, 48.

⁶⁸ Ibid., 70–71.

⁶⁹ Accession Sheet #10685, ISDUP Pioneers Museum Collection, Salt Lake City.

⁷⁰ Ruby Shepherd Karpowitz, "History of Elizabeth Jane Rogers Shepherd, Pioneer of 1866," Manuscript File, Pioneer Memorial Museum, 1–2.

⁷¹ Ibid.

⁷² Accession Sheet #12503, Pioneer Memorial Museum.

⁷³ M. David Potter and Bernard P. Corbman, *Fiber to Fabric* (New York: McGraw-Hill, 1959), 154.

Part Four: Settling the Inter-mountain West

¹ Beatrice Winsor, "A Sketch of the Life of Erastus Snow Immigrant Pioneer 1847," Manuscript File, Daughters of Utah Pioneers, Salt Lake City, p. 18.

² James Allen and Glen Leonard, *The Story of Latter-day Saints* (Salt Lake City: Deseret Books), 398.

³ Jennie N. Weeks and Katherine Taylor, *Coray and Lusk Family History* (Salt Lake City: self-published, 1960), 1.

⁴ Ibid., 420.

⁵ Ibid., 454.

⁶ Accession Sheet #32-17, Museum of Church History and Art, Salt Lake City.

⁷ Weeks and Taylor, Ibid.

⁸ Louise B. Pearce, *Early Mormon Settlements* (Salt Lake City, Utah: Daughters of Utah Pioneers, 1988), 210–14.

⁹ Joyce Peaden, letter to author, April 5, 1995, p. 6.

¹⁰ Penny McMorris, *Crazy Quilts*, (New York: E. P. Dutton, 1984), 21.

¹¹ Averil Colby, *Patchwork* (Newton Centre, Mass.: Charles T. Branford, 1958), 187.

¹² Raye Price, "Utah's Leading Ladies of the Arts," *Utah Historical Quarterly* 38 (winter 1970): 79, as cited in Vicky Burgess-Olson, *Sister Saints* (Salt Lake City: self-published, 1978), 265.

¹³ "Deseret News," April 30, 1847, as cited in Burgess-Olson, *Ibid.*, 266.

¹⁴ Raye Price, "Utah's Leading Ladies," 81, as cited in Burgess-Olson, Ibid., 265.

¹⁵ "Biography of Ann West Neville", January 1929, Manuscript Collection of Edwin and Geri Neville, Byron, Wyoming.

¹⁶ Ibid., 16.

¹⁷ Mark M. Partridge, *With Book and Plow: History of Mormon Settlement* (Lovell, Wyoming: Mountain States Printing, 1967), 48.

¹⁸ "Julia Ann England Denney," Manuscript Collection of Edwin and Geri Neville, Byron, Wyoming.

¹⁹ Johnson Family genealogy papers, Collection of Zelda Moore, Cody, Wyoming.

²⁰ Wilford Woodruff, *Wilford Woodruff's Journal*, vol. 7, ed. Scott G. Kenny (Midvale, Utah: Signature Books, 1985), 473, as cited in W. L. Rusho, *Lee's Ferry: Desert River Crossing*, (Salt Lake City: Cricket Productions, 1992), 46.

²¹ Johnson Family genealogy papers.

²² Partridge, Ibid., 47–48.

²³ Stella Jones, *Hawaiian Quilts* (Honolulu: Daughters of Hawaii, Honolulu Academy of Arts, and Mission Houses Museum, 1973), 15, 24, 25.

²⁴ Matthew Noall, *To My Children: An Autobiographic Sketch* (Salt Lake City: self-published, 1946), 27–28.

[25] Ibid., 12.

[26] Ibid., 78–79.

[27] Ibid., 77.

Conclusion

[1] Kathryn Fairbanks Kirk, *The Fairbanks Family in the West: Four Generations* (Salt Lake City: Paragon Press, 1983).

[2] Christopher Carlson, "The Rural Family in the 19th Century: A Case Study in Oregon's Willamette Valley," (Ph.D. diss., University of Oregon, 1980), 180–93.

[3] Sarah Harris Passey, "Autobioglraphy of Margaret McMeans T. Smoot, first wife of A.O. Smoot came to Utah 1847," Manuscript Collection, Pioneer Memorial Museum, Salt Lake City, 33–39.

[4] Kenneth W. Godfrey, Audrey M. Godfrey, and Jill Mulvay Derr, *Women's Voices: An Untold History of the Latter-day Saints 1830–1900* (Salt Lake City: Deseret Book Company, 1982), 9.

[5] Leonard J. Arrington and David Bitton, *The Mormon Experience: A History of the Latter-day Saints* (New York: Alfred A. Knopf, 1979), 185.

[6] Florence A. Merriam, *My Summer in a Mormon Village* (Boston: Houghton Mifflin, 1894), 102, 107.

[7] Cherrel B. Weech, Pima, Arizona, conversation with the author, June 9, 1995.

[8] Nedra Watkins Reese, *Charles C. Rich: The Man and His Family*, (Orem, Utah: H.W. Reese, 1988), 99.

[9] Winifred S. Cannon, "History of Amanda Barnes Smith," Manuscript Collection, Daughters of Utah Pioneers Museum, 7.

[10] Leona George Smith and Hilda Mann Condie, "Life Sketch of Ann Mariah Bowen Call," Manuscript Collection, Pioneer Memorial Museum, 3.

Appendix A

[1] See Asa Wettre, *Old Swedish Quilts* (Loveland, Colo.: Interweave Press, 1995) and *Quilted Treasures of Great Britain: The Heritage Search of the Quilter's Guild* (Nashville, Tenn.: Rutledge Hill Press, 1996).

[2] Nellie McArthur Gubler, Coordinator of Swiss Days in Santa Clara, Utah, conversation with the author, May 1995.

[3] Ricky Clark, *Quilted Gardens: Floral Quilts of the Nineteenth Century* (Nashville, Tenn.: Rutledge Hill Press, 1994), 3.

[4] Dorothy Osler, *Traditional British Quilts* (London: B. T. Batsford, 1987), 35–36.

[5] Jacqueline M. Atkins and Phyllis A. Tepper, *New York Beauties: Quilts from the Empire State* (New York: Dutton Studio Books, 1992), illustrations 28 and 29; Ricky Clark, George Knepper, and Ellice Ronsheim, *Quilts in Community: Ohio Traditions* (Nashville, Tenn.: Rutledge Hill Press, 1991), illustration 173.

[6] Averil Colby, *Patchwork* (Newton Center, Mass.: Charles T. Branford, 1958), illustrations 127 and 128; Dorothy Osler, *Traditional British Quilts*, illustrations 49 and 70.

[7] Jean Christensen, conversation with the author, December 1994.

[8] Susan H. Armitage, "The Challenge of Women's History," in *Women in Pacific Northwest History: An Anthology,* ed. Karen Blair (Seattle: University of Washington Press, 1988), 233–241.

[9] Glenn Leonard, Director, Museum of Church History and Art, Salt Lake City, conversation with the author, May 10, 1995.

[10] Cora Bell Stewart Littlefield, "History of Mary Priscilla S. Burreston," Manuscript collection, ISDUP Pioneer Memorial Museum.

[11] Mary Bywater Cross, *Treasures in the Trunk: Quilts of the Oregon Trail* (Nashville, Tenn.: Rutledge Hill Press, 1993).

Appendix B

[1] David and Ruth Moses, conversation with the author, May 1995.

[2] Terri Schindel, Buffalo Bill Historical Center, Cody, Wyoming, *Examination and Treatment Proposal for #A-952* , Fremont County Pioneer Museum, Lander, Wyoming, December 4, 1994.

[3] Sandra L. Troon, Oregon Textile Workshop, Portland, Oregon, conversation with the author, May 9, 1996.

[4] Jane C. Nylander, *Fabrics for Historic Buildings: A Guide to Selecting Reproduction Fabrics* (Washington, D.C.: National Trust for Historic Preservation, 1983), 35.

[5] Barbara Norin, E. E. Schenck Company, Portland, Oregon, conversation with the author, May 9, 1996.

[6] Camillia Carter Sullivan Higgins, correspondence with the author, Spring 1995.

[7] Joyce Toland Weeks, personal statement, Salt Lake City, March 16, 1995.

BIBLIOGRAPHY

Quilts and Quilt History

Adrosko, Rita. *Natural Dyes and Home Dyeing.* New York: Dover Publications, 1971.

Arizona Quilt Project. *Grand Endeavors: Vintage Arizona Quilts and Their Makers.* Flagstaff, Ariz.: Northland Publishing, 1992.

Armitage, Susan H. Introduction in *Patterns and Passages: Quilts as An Expression of Human Experience.* An exhibition catalog. Bothell, Wash.: That Patchwork Place, 1994.

Atkins, Jacqueline, and Phyllis Tepper. *New York Beauties: Quilts from the Empire State.* New York: Dutton Studios, 1992.

Bacon, Lenice Ingram. *American Patchwork Quilts.* New York: Bonanza Books, 1973.

Bowman, Doris. *The Smithsonian Treasury American Quilts.* Washington, D.C.: Smithsonian Institution, 1991.

Brackman, Barbara. *An Encyclopedia of Pieced Quilt Patterns.* Lawrence, Kans.: Prairie Flower Publishing, 1984.

_____. *Clues in the Calico: A Guide to Identifying and Dating Antique Quilts.* McLean, Va.: EPM Publications, 1989.

_____. *Encyclopedia of Appliqué.* McLean, Va.: EPM Publications, 1993.

Bresenhan, Karoline Patterson, and Nancy O'Bryant Puentes. *Lone Stars: A Legacy of Texas Quilts, 1836–1936.* Austin, Tex.: University of Texas Press, 1986.

Bullard, Lacy Folmar, and Betty Jo Shiell. *Chintz Quilts: Unfading Glory.* Tallahassee, Fla.: Serendipity Publishers, 1983.

Burnham, Dorothy. *Pieced Quilts of Ontario.* Toronto: Royal Ontario Museum, 1975.

Carlisle, Lilian Baker. *Pieced Work and Appliqué Quilts at Shelburne Museum.* Shelburne, Vt.: Shelburne Museum, 1957.

Carter, Kate B. *Pioneer Quilts.* Salt Lake City: ISDUP, n.d.

Clabburn, Pamela. *Patchwork.* Shire Album 101. Aylesbury, England: Shire Publications, 1983.

Clark, Ricky. *Quilted Gardens: Floral Quilts of the Nineteenth Century.* Nashville, Tenn.: Rutledge Hill Press, 1994.

Clark, Ricky, George Knepper, and Ellice Ronsheim. *Quilts in Community: Ohio Traditions.* Nashville, Tenn.: Rutledge Hill Press, 1991.

Colby, Averil. *Patchwork.* Newton Center, Mass.: Charles T. Branford, 1958.

_____. *Patchwork Quilts.* New York: Charles Scribner, 1965.

Conroy, Mary. *Three Hundred Years of Canada's Quilts.* Toronto: Griffin House, 1976.

Curtis, Phillip H. *American Quilts in the Newark Museum Collection.* Newark, N.J. Newark Museum, 1973.

Davis, Carolyn O'Bagy. *Pioneer Quiltmaker: The Story of Dorinda Moody Slade 1808–1895.* Tucson, Ariz.: Sanpete Publications, 1990.

Finley, Ruth. *Old Patchwork Quilts and the Women Who Made Them.* Newton Center, Mass.: Charles T. Branford, 1929.

Fisher, Laura. *Quilts of Illusion.* London: Blandford, 1988.

Foundation of the American Insitute for Conservation of Historic and Artistic Works (FAIC). 1717 K St. NW, Washington, D.C. 20006. (202) 452-9545.

Fox, Sandi. *Quilts in Utah: A Reflection of the Western Experience.* Salt Lake City: Salt Lake Art Center, 1981.

Frye, Thomas, ed. *American Quilts: A Handmade Legacy.* Oakland, Calif.: Oakland Museum of Art, 1981.

Hall, Carrie, and Rose Kretzinger. *The Romance of the Patchwork Quilt in America.* Caldwell, Idaho: Caxton Printers, 1935.

Heritage Quilt Project of New Jersey. *New Jersey Quilts, 1777 to 1950.* Padacuh, Ky.: American Quilter's Society, 1992.

Horton, Laurel, and Lynn Robertson Myers. *Social Fabric South Carolina's Traditional Quilts.* Columbia, S.C.: McKissick Museum, n.d.

Jones, Stella. *Hawaiian Quilts.* Honolulu: Daughters of Hawaii, Honolulu Academy of Arts, and Mission Houses Museum, 1973.

Kiracofe, Roderick, and Mary Elizabeth Johnson. *The American Quilt: A History of Cloth and Comfort, 1750–1950.* New York: Clarkson Potter Publishers, 1993.

Leman, Bonnie, and Judy Martin. *Log Cabin Quilts.* Denver: Moon Over Mountain Publishing, 1980.

McKendry, Ruth. *Quilts and Other Bed Coverings in the Canadian Tradition.* Toronto: Van Nostrand /Reinhold, 1979.

McMorris, Penny. *Crazy Quilts.* New York: E. P. Dutton, 1984.

Meyer, Suellen. "Pine Tree Quilts." In *The Quilt Digest 4.* Michael Kile, editor. San Francisco: The Quilt Digest Press, 1986.

Montgomery, Florence. *Printed Textiles: English and American Cottons and Linens, 1700–1850.* New York: Viking Press, 1970.

_____. *Textiles in America, 1650–1870.* New York: W. W. Norton, 1984.

Morgan, Hal. *Symbols of America.* New York: Viking Penguin, 1986.

Nylander, Jane C. *Fabrics for Historic Buildings: A Guide to Selecting Reproduction Fabrics.* Washington, D.C.: National Trust for Historic Preservation, 1983.

_____. *Our Own Snug Fireside: Images of the New England Home, 1760–1860.* New York: Alfred A. Knopf, 1993.

Orlofsky, Patsy, and Myron Orlofsky. *Quilts in America.* New York: McGraw-Hill, 1974.

Osler, Dorothy. *Traditional British Quilts.* London: B. T. Batsford, 1987.

Peck, Amelia. *American Quilts and Coverlets in the Metropolitan Museum of Art.* New York: Metropolitan Museum of Art, 1990.

Penny, Prudence. *Old-time Quilts.* Seattle: Seattle Post-Intelligencer, 1927.

Petit, Florence H. *America's Printed and Painted Fabrics, 1600–1900.* New York: Hastings House, 1970.

Potter, M. David, and Bernard P. Corbman. *Fiber to Fabric.* New York: McGraw-Hill, 1959.

Schoeser, Mary, and Celia Rufey. *English and American Textiles from 1790 to the Present.* London: Thames and Hudson, 1989.

Sienkiewicz, Elly. *Spoken Without a Word.* Washington, D.C.: Turtle Hill Press, 1983.

Stitches in Time: A Legacy of Ozark Quilts. Rogers, Ark.: Rogers Historical Museum, 1986.

Webster, Marie. *Quilts: Their Story and How to Make Them.* New York: Tudor, 1915.

Wettre, Asa. *Old Swedish Quilts.* Loveland, Colo.: Interweave Press, 1995.

Western History

Armitage, Susan, and Elizabeth Jameson, eds. *The Women's West.* Norman: University of Oklahoma Press, 1987.

Bailey, Thomas A., and David M. Kennedy. *The American Pageant.* Lexington, Mass.: D. C. Heath, 1983.

Beck, Warren A., and Ynez D. Haase. *Historical Atlas of the American West.* Norman: University of Oklahoma Press, 1989.

Blair, Roger. "That Bourn From Which No Traveler Returns." Oregon-California Trails Association Summer Conference, 1995.

Jeffrey, Julie Roy. *Frontier Women: The Trans-Mississippi West, 1840–1880.* New York: Hill and Wang, 1979.

Mattes, Merrill. *The Great Platte River Road.* Lincoln: University of Nebraska Press, 1969.

Myres, Sandra. *Westering Women and the Frontier Experience, 1800–1915.* Albuquerque: University of New Mexico Press, 1982.

Niederman, Sharon. *A Quilt of Words: Women's Diaries, Letters, and Original Accounts of Life in the Southwest, 1860–1960.* Boulder, Colo.: Johnson Publishing, 1988.

Petersen, William J. *Steamboating on the Upper Mississippi: The Water Way to Iowa.* Iowa City: State Historical Society of Iowa, 1937.

Riley, Glenda. *Women and Indians on the Frontier, 1825–1915.* Albuquerque: University of New Mexico Press, 1984.

_____. *A Place to Grow: Women in the American West.* Arlington Heights, Ill.: Harlan Davidson, 1992.

Schlissel, Lillian. *Women's Diaries of the Westward Journey.* New York: Schocken, 1982.

Twain, Mark. *Roughing It.* New York: Harper and Brothers, 1871.

Unruh, John D. Jr. *The Plains Across: The Overland Emigrants and the Trans-Mississippi West, 1840–1860.* Chicago: University of Illinois Press, 1979.

Wilson, Timothy. *Flags at Sea.* London, England: Her Majesty's Stationery Office, 1986.

World Book Encyclopedia. Chicago, Field Enterprises, 1977. Volume 20.

Mormon History

Allen, James, and Glen Leonard. *The Story of the Latter-day Saints.* Salt Lake City: Deseret Book Company, 1992.

Arrington, Leonard J., and David Bitton. *The Mormon Experience: A History of the Latter-day Saints.* New York: Alfred Knopf, 1979.

Arrington, Leonard J., and Susan Arrington Madsen. *Sunbonnet Sisters: True Stories of Mormon Women and Frontier Life.* Salt Lake City: Bookcraft, 1984.

Bashore, Melvin, and Linda L. Haslam. *Mormon Pioneer Companies Crossing the Plains.* Salt Lake City: Church Historical Department, 1990.

Bennett, Richard. *Mormons at the Missouri, 1846–1852: "And Should We Die."* Norman: University of Oklahoma Press, 1987.

Britsch, R. Lanier. *Moramona: The Mormons in Hawaii.* Laie, Hawaii: Institute for Polynesian Studies, 1989.

Brown, S. Kent, Donald Q. Cannon, and Richard H. Jackson. *Historical Atlas of Mormonism.* New York: Simon and Schuster, 1994.

Burgess-Olson, Vicky, ed. *Sister Saints.* Salt Lake City: Self-published, 1978.

Cannon, Donald Q., and Lyndon W. Cook, eds. *Far West Record: Minutes of the Church of Jesus Christ of Latter-day Saints, 1830–1844.* Salt Lake City: Deseret Book Company, 1983.

Carter, Kate B., ed. *Mormon Emigration, 1840–1869.* Salt Lake City: International Society of Daughters of Utah Pioneers (ISDUP), 1963.

_____. *The Story of the Negro Pioneer*. Salt Lake City: ISDUP, 1965.

_____. *Our Pioneer Heritage*. Vol. 8. Salt Lake City: ISDUP, 1965.

_____. *Our Pioneer Heritage*. Vol. 3 Salt Lake City: ISDUP, 1960.

_____. *Our Pioneer Heritage*. Vol. 4. Salt Lake City: ISDUP, 1961.

Clayton, William. *The Latter-day Saints' Emigrants' Guide*. Edited by Stanley B. Kimball. St. Louis: Patrice Press, 1983.

Cross, Whitney. *The Burned-over District: The Social and Intellectual History of Enthusiastic Religion in Western New York, 1800–1850*. Ithaca, N.Y.: Cornell University Press, 1950.

Derr, Jill Mulvay, Janath Russell Cannon, and Maureen Ursenbach Beecher. *Women of Covenant: The Story of the Relief Society*. Salt Lake City: Deseret Book Company, 1992.

Esshom, Frank. *Pioneers and Prominent Men of Utah*. Salt Lake City: Western Epics, 1966.

Fillerup, Melvin M. *Sidon: The Canal That Faith Built*. Cody, Wyo.: Ptarmigan Company, 1988.

Givens, George W. *In Old Nauvoo: Everyday Life in the City of Joseph*. Salt Lake City: Deseret Book Company, 1990.

Godfrey, Kenneth W., Audrey M. Godfrey, and Jill Mulvay Derr. *Women's Voices: An Untold History of the Latter-day Saints, 1830–1900*. Salt Lake City: Deseret Book Company, 1982.

Hafen, May Ann. *Recollections of a Handcart Pioneer of 1860: A Woman's Life on the Mormon Frontier*. Lincoln: University of Nebraska Press, 1983.

Holzapfel, Richard, and T. Jeffery Cottle. *Old Mormon Kirtland and Missouri*. Santa Ana, Calif.: Fieldbrook Productions, 1991.

_____. *Old Mormon Palmyra and New England*. Santa Ana, Calif.: Fieldbrook Productions, 1991.

International Society of Daughters of Utah Pioneers. *Pioneer Museum*. Salt Lake City: ISDUP, 1983.

Kane, Elizabeth Wood. *Twelve Mormon Homes*. Tanner Trust Fund. Salt Lake City: University of Utah Library, 1974.

Kimball, Stanley B. *Historic Resource Study: Mormon Pioneer National Historic Trail*. Washington, D.C.: United States Department of the Interior, National Park Service, 1991.

Landgren, Le. *A Whitmore Family History, 1793–1990*. West Linn, Oreg.: Family Gathering, 1990.

Launius, Roger Dale. "Zion's Camp and the Redemption of Jackson County, Missouri." Master's thesis. Graceland College, Lamoni, Iowa, 1978.

Madsen, Carol Cornwall. *In Their Own Words: Women and the Story of Nauvoo*. Salt Lake City: Deseret Book Company, 1994.

Madsen, Susan Arrington. *I Walked to Zion: True Stories of Young Pioneers on the Mormon Trail*. Salt Lake City: Deseret Book Company, 1994.

Malouf, Beatrice. *An Enduring Legacy*. Vol. 11. Salt Lake City: ISDUP, 1988.

McArthur, Daniel Duncan. *Daniel Duncan McArthur: Mormon Pioneer*. Bountiful, Utah: R. McArthur, 1987.

McClintock, James. *Mormon Settlement in Arizona*. Reprint, Tucson: University of Arizona Press, 1985.

McConkie, Bruce R. *Mormon Doctrine*. Salt Lake City: Bookcraft, 1979.

Merriam, Florence A. *My Summer in a Mormon Village*. Boston: Houghton Mifflin, 1894.

Miller, David E. *Hole in the Rock*. Salt Lake City: University of Utah Press, 1959. Reprint, Publishers Press, 1995.

Noall, Matthew. *To My Children: An Autobiographic Sketch*. Salt Lake City: Self-published, 1946.

Partridge, Mark N. *With Book and Plow: History of Mormon Settlement*. Lovell, Wyoming: Mountain States Printing Co., 1967.

Reay, Lee. *Incredible Passage through the Hole-in-the-Rock*. Provo, Utah: Meadow Lane Publications, 1980.

Relief Society of the Church of Jesus Christ of Latter-day Saints. *History of Relief Society, 1842–1966*. Salt Lake City: General Board of Relief Society, 1966.

Ricketts, Norma B. *Melissa's Journey with the Mormon Battalion*. Salt Lake City: ISDUP, 1994.

Rusho, W. L. *Lee's Ferry: Desert River Crossing*. Salt Lake City: Cricket Productions, 1992.

Slaughter, William W. *Life in Zion*. Salt Lake City: Deseret Book Company, 1995.

Smith, Joseph Jr. *History of the Church of Jesus Christ of Latter-day Saints*. Vol. 3. Edited by B. H. Roberts. Salt Lake City: Deseret Book Company, 1964.

Sonne, Conway B. *Saints on the Seas: A Martime History of Mormon Migration, 1830–1890*. Salt Lake City: University of Utah Press, 1983.

Stegner, Wallace. *The Gathering of Zion: The Story of the Mormon Trail*. Lincoln: University of Nebraska Press, 1964.

Washington County Chapter, Daughters of Utah Pioneers. *Under Dixie Sun: A History of Washington County by Those Who Loved Their Forebears*. Panguitch, Utah: Garfield County News, 1950.

Welch, Charles A. *History of the Big Horn Basin*. Salt Lake City: Desert News Press, 1940.

Winn, Norma B. *An Enduring Legacy*. Vol. 4. Salt Lake City: ISDUP, 1981.

_____. *An Enduring Legacy*. Vol. 5. Salt Lake City: ISDUP, 1982.

Articles, Family Histories, Letters, Magazines, Pamphlets, Papers

Adamson, Ida Sheets. "History of Ann Leaver Musser." Manuscript Collection. International Society of Daughters of Utah Pioneers (ISDUP) Pioneer Memorial Museum, Salt Lake City.

Allen, Inez Rhead. "Hannah Johnson Staley, Born in Albany, New York, July 31, 1806." Manuscript Collection, ISDUP Pioneer Memorial Museum, Salt Lake City.

Allen, Laura, "A Sketch of the Life of Sarah M. Chaffin." Manuscript Collection, ISDUP Pioneer Memorial Museum, Salt Lake City.

Arrington, Leonard J. "In Honorable Remembrance: Thomas L. Kane's Services to the Mormons." In *Brigham Young University Studies* 21, no.4 (1981): 389–403.

Bills, Annie Caroline Carlston. "Mary Young Wilcox." Manuscript Collection, ISDUP Pioneer Memorial Museum, Salt Lake City.

"Biography of Louis R. Chaffin." Manuscript Collection, International Society of Daughters of Utah Pioneers McQuarrie Memorial Museum, St. George, Utah.

"Biography of Ann West Neville." January 1929. Manuscript Collection of Edwin and Geri Neville. Byron, Wyoming.

"Biolgraphy of Lee and Nancy Bybee." Manuscript Collection, ISDUP Pioneer Memorial Museum, Salt Lake City.

Bowns, Florence Smith. "History of Eliza Jane Eynon Ricks." Manuscript Collection, ISDUP Pioneer Memorial Museum, Salt Lake City.

Box Elder Lore of the Nineteenth Century. Brigham City, Utah: Box Elder Chapter of Sons of Utah Pioneers. September 1951.

Butterfield, Cornelia C. "History of Mary Jane Parker Butterfield." Manuscript Collection, ISDUP Pioneer Memorial Museum, Salt Lake City.

Carter, Kate B., comp. "Pioneer Quilts." In *Heart Throbs of the West.* Vol. 2. Salt Lake City: ISDUP, 1940.

_____. "Brigham Young: His Wives and Family." In *Our Pioneer Heritage.* Vol. 1. Salt Lake City: ISDUP, 1958.

_____. "William Carter-Scout." In *Our Pioneer Heritage.* Vol. 2. Salt Lake City: ISDUP, 1959.

_____. "The Mormons in San Bernadino." In *Our Pioneer Heritage.* Vol. 4 Salt Lake City: ISDUP, April 1961.

_____. "The Mormons from Scotland and Wales." In *Our Pioneer Heritage.* Vol. 9. Salt Lake City: ISDUP, March 1970.

Carter, Lyndia McDowell. "The Mormon Handcart Companies." In *Overland Journal:Quarterly Journal of the Oregon-California Trails Association* 13, no. 1 (Spring 1995).

Christensen, Jean. Letter to author, April 18, 1995.

Cordon, Pearl J. "Eliza Melisa Hall." Manuscript Collection, ISDUP Pioneer Memorial Museum, Salt Lake City, Utah.

Cottam, Naomi. "The Mormon Corridor." In *Chronicles of Courage.* Salt Lake City: ISDUP, 1991.

Cragun, Susan La Nez. "Sarah Ann Huffman Pitkin". Manuscript Collection, ISDUP Pioneer Memorial Mueum, Salt Lake City.

Dahl, Paul E. " 'All Is Well...': The Story of 'the Hymn That Went around the World.' " In *Brigham Young University Studies* 21, no. 4 (1981).

Davis, Carolyn. Letter to author, June 17, 1995.

Family Histories and Record of William Walton Burton: and Wives Rachel Fielding Burton, Ellen Fielding Burton, and Sarah Ann Fielding Burton. Salt Lake City: William Walton Burton Family Organization, 1981.

"Family History 1987: Brighton, Thornley, Timmons." Manuscript Collection, Family History Library, Salt Lake City, Utah.

Fleming, Virginia. "Mary Wilcox Young." Manuscript Collection of Virginia Fleming, Arcadia, California.

Fletcher, Jack E., and Patricia K. A. "The Cherokee Trail." In *Overland Journal* 13, no.2 (1995).

Frandsen, Gayle B. "Matilda Robison King." Unpublished manuscript, Sandy, Utah.

Geertson, Jane Rawlinson. *Life Story of Charles Rawlinson: Heirs to the Kingdom.* Self-published, n.d.

Gentry, Leland H. "The Mormon Way Stations: Garden Grove and Mt. Pisgah." In *Brigham Young University Studies* 21, no. 4 (1981).

Goodwin, Cuma Bond. "Lucy Jane Clark Barkdull." Manuscript Collection, ISDUP Pioneer Memorial Museum, Salt Lake City.

Green, Louise C. "The First Latter-day Saint Apostles." In *An Enduring Legacy.* Salt Lake City: ISDUP, December 1984.

Gudmundson, Abigial Chase. "Biography of Samantha (Crismon) Chase." Manuscript Collection, ISDUP Pioneer Memorial Museum, Salt Lake City.

Gylling, Arzella Knight. "Life Story of My Grand Mother Besy Williamson Smith" Manuscript Collection, ISDUP Pioneer Memorial Museum, Salt Lake City.

Hartley, William G. "Down-and-Back Wagon Trains: Travelers on the Mormon Trail in 1861." *Overland Journal* 11, no. 4 (Winter 1993).

"History of Margaret T. McMeans Smoot, Pioneer of 1847." Manuscript Collection, ISDUP Pioneer Memorial Museum, Salt Lake City.

"History on Sophronia Turnbow Carter." Manuscript Collection, ISDUP McQuarrie Memorial Museum, St. George, Utah.

"History of Sarah Heward Stocks." Manuscript Collection, ISDUP Pioneer Memorial Museum, Salt Lake City, Utah.

Howell, Barton. "Elizabeth Bell Barton." Manuscript Collection, ISDUP Pioneer Memorial Museum, Salt Lake City.

International Society of Daughters of Utah Pioneeres (ISDUP). Manuscript Collection. McQuarrie Memorial Museum, St. George, Utah.

ISDUP. Manuscript Collection. Pioneer Memorial Museum, Salt Lake City, Utah.

Jakeman, James. "Pioneer Mothers and Daughters". *Daughters of Utah Pioneers and Their Mothers.* N.p.: Western Album Publishing Company, n.d.

Johnson Family genealogy papers. Collection of Zelda Moore, Cody, Wyoming.

Johnson, Muriel Colton. "History of Eleanor Jones Young, Pioneer of 1856." Manuscript Collection, ISDUP Pioneer Memorial Museum, Salt Lake City, Utah.

"Julia Ann England Denney." Manuscript Collection of Edwin and Geri Neville. Byron, Wyoming.

Karpowitz, Ruby Shepherd. "History of Elizabeth Jane Rogers Shepherd, Pioneer of 1866." Manuscript Collection, ISDUP Pioneer Memorial Museum, Salt Lake City.

Kasteler, June. "Story of Elizabeth Jones Fox." In *Treasures of Pioneer History*. Vol. 1. Salt Lake City: Daughters of Utah Pioneers, 1952.

Kimball, Stanley B. "The Mormon Trail Network in Iowa." In *Brigham Young University Studies* 21, no. 4 (1981).

Kirk, Kathryn Fairbanks. *The Fairbanks Family in the West: Four Generations*. Salt Lake City: Paragon Press, 1983.

Lence, Pearl. "History of Sage Treharne Jones." Manuscript Collection. ISDUP McQuarrie Memorial Museum, St. George, Utah.

"Life Sketch of Sophronia Carter: Early Dixie Pioneer." Microfilm #485,341. Family History Library, Salt Lake City, Utah.

Lunt, Vernon. The Life of Henry Lunt. Manuscript Collection. Family History Library, Salt Lake City.

Lyon, T. Edgar. "Mormon Colonization in the Far West." In *The Improvement Era* 73, nos. 7, 14 (1970).

McRae, Hazel Murphy. "Sketch of the Life of Iabella C. MacKay, A Utah Pioneer of 1852." Manuscript Collection. ISDUP Pioneer Memorial Museum, Salt Lake City.

Miller, Henry W. "Journal of Henry W. Miller: April 1855–Spring 1862." Manuscript Collection. Utah State Historical Society, Salt Lake City, Utah.

Noall, Margaret. History of Mary Ellen Salisbury Parsons. Unpublished manuscript, 1995.

Noall, Margaret. Letter to author, April 1995.

Passey, Sarah Harris. "Autobiography of Margaret McMeans T. Smoot, First Wife of A.O. Smoot Came to Utah 1847." Manuscript Collection, ISDUP Pioneer Memorial Museum, Salt Lake City, Utah.

Pay, Mary Gobel. "Reminiscence." In *Our Pioneer Heritage*. Salt Lake City, Utah: Daughters of Utah Pioneers, 1970.

Peaden, Joyce. Letter to author, April 5, 1995.

Pearce, Louise B. "Historic Western Trails." In *An Enduring Legacy*. Salt Lake City, Utah: ISDUP, March and April 1983.

_____. "New Settlements." In *An Enduring Legacy*. Salt Lake City: ISDUP, 1983, Volume 6.

_____. "Pioneer Vacations." In *An Enduring Legacy*. Salt Lake City: ISDUP, February 1985.

_____. "Pioneer Fashions." In *An Enduring Legacy*. Salt Lake City: ISDUP, March 1985.

_____. "Early Foreign Missions." In *An Enduring Legacy*. Salt Lake City: ISDUP, 1986. Volume 9.

_____. "Pioneer Stories." In *An Enduring Legacy*. Salt Lake City: ISDUP, 1986. Volume 9

_____. "British Immigrants." In *An Enduring Legacy*. Salt Lake City: ISDUP, November 1986.

_____. *Early Mormon Settlements*. Salt Lake City, Utah: ISDUP, January 1988.

_____. "DUP Camps in States Other Than Utah." In *An Enduring Legacy*. Salt Lake City: ISDUP, March and April 1988.

Palmer, Nina. *Rich Family and Church History Tour*. Salt Lake City: Self-published, 1991.

Reese, Nedra Watkins. *Charles Coulson Rich: The Man and His Family*. Orem, Utah: Self-published, 1988.

Riddle, Florence N., et al. "History of Matilda Robison King." Manuscript Collection, ISDUP Pioneer Memorial Museum, Salt Lake City.

Russon, Sadie Leffler. "Life Sketch of Eliza Dorsey Ashworth." Manuscript Collection, ISDUP Pioneer Memorial Museum. Salt Lake City, Utah.

Schindel, Terri. *Examination and Treatment Proposal for #A-952*. Fremont County Pioneer Museum, Lander, Wyoming, December 4, 1994.

"Sketch of the Life of Eliza Melissa Hall Hall." Manuscript Collection. International Society of Daughters of Utah Pioneers, Ogden, Utah.

Smith, Amanda Barnes. *Amanda's Journal*. Compiled by Lura S. Dunn. Self-published, 1977

Smith, Cordelia Thurston. "To My Children and Grandchildren." Manuscript Collection. ISDUP Pioneer Memorial Museum, Salt Lake City.

Smith, Helen Orr. "History of Sarah Henry Wickle." Manuscript Collection, ISDUP Pioneer Memorial Museum, Salt Lake City, Utah.

Smith, Leona George and Hilda Mann Condie. "Life Sketch of Ann Mariah Bowen Call." Manuscript Collection, ISDUP Pioneer Memorial Museum, Salt Lake City.

Snow, Eliza Roxcy. Diaries, 1846–49. Holograph. Huntington Libraries, San Marino, California. Transcribed by Maureen Ursenbach Beecher, Joseph Smith Institute for Church History, Brigham Young University, Provo, Utah.

Strong, Ida Rich. "Sketch of the Life and History of Sarah DeArmon Pea Rich: Pioneer of 1847." Manuscript Collection, ISDUP Pioneer Memorial Museum, Salt Lake City.

Thorley, Edna Ashby. "Nancy Garr Badger Stringham." Manuscript Collection, ISDUP Pioneer Memorial Museum, Salt Lake City.

Victor, Ruth Gunnell. "History of Ann Sewell Hawkins." Ogden, Utah: n.p., 1980.

Ward, Maurine Carr. "The Winter Quarters Journals of Mary Haskin Parker Richards." Journal Number Three. Unpublished draft. Manuscript Collection of Janet Burton Seegmiller, Cedar City, Utah.

Weech, Sarah Dall, and Hyrum Weech. *Our Pioneer Parents: Autobiographies.* Weech Genealogical Association, n.d.

Weeks, Jennie N., and Katherine Taylor. *Coray and Lusk Family History.* Salt Lake City: self-published, 1960.

Winn, Norma B. ed. "The Pioneer Home." In *An Enduring Legacy.* Salt Lake City: ISDUP, 1978. Volume 1.

_____. "Freighters and Freighting," *An Enduring Legacy.* Salt Lake City, Utah: ISDUP, 1979. Volume 2.

_____. "Desdamona Fox Brown, Pioneer of 1855." In *An Enduring Legacy.* Salt Lake City, Utah: ISDUP, 1980. Volume 3.

_____. "Emigrant Pioneers." In *An Enduring Legacy.* Salt Lake City: ISDUP, March 1980.

_____. "The Texas Expedition." In *An Enduring Legacy.* Salt Lake City: ISDUP, April 1985. Volume 8.

Winsor, Beatrice. "A Sketch of the Life of Erastus Snow Immigrant Pioneer 1847." Manuscript Collection, ISDUP Pioneer Memorial Museum, Salt Lake City.

Winters, Matilda Ann Duncan. Obituary. Manuscript Collection, ISDUP Pioneer Memorial Museum, Salt Lake City, Utah.

ACKNOWLEDGMENTS

THIS MIGRATION QUILT PROJECT HAS ENRICHED MY life immeasurably. It began with a grant for an exploratory survey with Utahan Jude Daurelle, investigating the availability of historic quilts connected to their migrations. This grant was under the sponsorship of the International Society of Daughters of Utah Pioneers (ISDUP) with funding from the Utah Humanities Council (UHC) and guidance from Associate UHC Director Cynthia Buckingham.

Individuals and institutions alike welcomed me, a non-Mormon quilt historian from Oregon, to review their collections for quilts that would qualify for the study. These, in turn, led to my discovery of the rich histories and traditions of the women and their faith.

The Daughters' generosity in sharing their invaluable resources of stitched and penned artifacts and records brought this project to reality. Not only have they worked in the past to preserve their heirlooms, record their experiences, and maintain their traditions, they continue to seek new information, expand their programs, and reach out in new directions to educate future generations. It is an honor to dedicate this book to their organization.

Beginning with the ISDUP Board led by President Louise C. Green, they made the decison to participate in and contribute to the project. Directly involved were members Elma Odegard, Isabelle Meadows, Orella Carver, and Ann Brest Van Kampen. Another, Edith Menna, the volunteer director of their Pioneer Memorial Museum, became a valued resource and a respected friend. The support of time and effort provided by receptionist Evelyn Belnap and volunteers Elva Smith, Bonnie Brunner, Dayle White, and Morgan Abbott is much appreciated. Wanda Kerr of Portland is especially thanked for lending her entire library of lessons Daughters of Utah Pioneers for my research.

Responding to the call for quilts and facilitating my on-site studies were the ISDUP Museums of Ogden and St. George, where I was assisted by Ruth White, Diane Parker, and Delores Riggs. Recognizing the special relationship involved in housing the collections of the

ISDUP, the Territorial Statehouse State Park Museum and the Brigham City Museum both responded. At both locations, Mark Trotter and Larry Douglas assisted my searches and later provided transportation for the quilts so that they could be photographed. Special thanks to Karen Kreiger, Site Coordinator of the Utah Heritage Parks, and Bill Ormond, Curator of Collections of This Is the Place State Park, for their special assistance and guidance.

The other major institution providing enthusiastic support and interest for the project has been the Museum of Church History and Art in Salt Lake City. The staff support, led by Director Glenn Leonard, was fostered by Richard Oman, Robert Davis, Jennifer Lund, and Marjorie Conder. Special thanks to Art Registrar Gloria Scovill, Media Coordinator Ron Read, and volunteer Jan Fletcher for their assistance and research with the quilt collection.

Within the Church organization, other key individuals who answered my questions and guided my research were Mary Gifford, Melvin Bashore, and Bill Slaughter of the Church Historical Department Library and Archives; Ken Nelson of the Family History Library; and Diane Harris of the Portland Institute of Religion. In addition, at the Family History Centers in Salt Lake and in Beaverton and Oregon City, Oregon, volunteers like Beverly Westerfield were always eager to serve with a smile and ready answer.

The Church has had a significant history in parts of North America other than the West. Key people who provided information about the various historic sites include the following: Ronald Romig, Church Archivist of the Reorganized Church of Jesus Christ of Latter Day Saints, Independence, Missouri; Michael Riggs, Garnett, Kansas; Joyce Harrop, Director of Public Affairs, and Kenneth and Jackie Barker, Directors, Winter Quarters Historic Site, Nebraska; and Carol E. Hill, Nauvoo Restoration Incorporated, Nauvoo, Illinois.

Other institutions across the West responded with generous support from the following staff members: Dean Knudsen of Scotts Bluff National Monument, Scottsbluff, Nebraska; Martha Brace of Fremont County Pioneer Museum, Lander, Wyoming; Terri Schindel of Buffalo Bill Historical Center, Cody, Wyoming; Judith Durant of Interweave Press, Loveland, Colorado; Todd Guenther, Curator of South Pass City State Historical Site, Wyoming; Patti Owens of Gentler Times Quilt Shop, Salt Lake City, Utah; Sandra Troon of the Oregon Textile Workshop, Portland, Oregon; Linda Thatcher and Susan Whetstone of the Utah State Historical Society; and the staff of the Eastern Arizona Museum, Pima, Arizona.

As I worked in Salt Lake City for extended periods of time, a number of people and places became special friends and welcoming sites. Such Utah women include, among others, Cynthia Overturf, Cody Mazuran, Joyce Robison, Cammy Higgins, and Beverly Ellis. An important acknowledgment goes to the staff of the Downtown Residence Inn by Marriott under the leadership of Katherine M. Halter. It became a place where I always felt welcome and experienced a sense of returning home.

As the research progressed and the paths of discovery turned to the eastern seaboard and beyond to Europe, several individuals responded to my inquiries, including Jeanne H. Watson of the Morris County Historical Society, Morristown, New Jersey; Doris Bowman of the Textile Division of the Smithsonian's Museum of American History, Washington, D.C.; Deborah E. Kraak of Winterthur Museum, Winterthur, Delaware; Dorothy Osler, Newcastle upon Tyne, England; and Gill Turley of the European Quilt Association, Surrey, England. Working within the network of quilt historians of the American Quilt Study Group has again provided a sharing of information and assistance across the country from a number of people, including Judy Elsley, Barbara Brackman, Ricky Clark, Stacie Seeger, Laurene Sinema, Sandi Fox, and Carolyn O'Bagy Davis. Also providing assistance were members of the Columbia-Willamette Quilt Study Group who participated in a focus group studying quilts, photographs, and artwork.

Acknowledgment for information and guidance also goes to the following members of the Oregon-California Trails Association: Will Bagley, Michael Bateman, Lamar Berrett, David Bigler, Roger Blair, Lyndia Carter, Susan Badger Doyle, George Ivory, Stanley Kimball, Shann Rupp, and Jeanne Watson.

Natasha Mink of Rutledge Hill Press deserves a special credit for providing contacts in the print media to facilitate the regional survey for historic quilts. Rutledge Hill Press owners Larry Stone and Ron Pitkin receive great appreciation for accepting the project's book proposal.

As public awareness grew about the Mormon Migration Quilt Project, I came in contact with others who generously shared their ideas, answered my questions, and suggested resources. Some were descendants of Utah Pioneers who have carefully preserved and stored a treasured heirloom from an ancestor's past. Others were current quilters who are continuing the tradition of quiltmaking throughout the Mormon intermountain area by recreating the special quilts of their heritage. Still others were contemporary scholars working in the fields of western history and women's history to educate others about the important role these and other women had in settling the West.

Descendants and family members who generously provided their heirloom quilts and stories included Barbara Pack, Evelyn Lucas, Renee Jones, Chris Reynolds, Trice Cunningham, Louis and Zela Moore, Cal and Geraldean Jones, Joyce Weeks, Sharon Ahlstrom, Pat Evans, Mary Louise Stromness, Margaret Noall, Jean Christensen, Janet Calvert, Virginia Fleming, Cody Mazuran, Cherrel B. Weech, Joyce Bennion Peaden, and Dorothy Bennion Potter.

I made many personal contacts for confirming information or providing new leads. Many people responded by sharing personal stories, information, and photographs. I also made many calls to donors and their descendants in attempts to confirm the traceable link in a quilt's history from a maker to a current family member or donor. Many people responded, but special acknowledgment must go to those who provided key leads, including Beverly Robertson, Janet Seegmiller, Wanda Rowley, Rudger McArthur, Ethel Jarman, Helen Gardner, Dottie Zimmerman, Susan Timothy Burton, Anne Wollen, Le Landgren, Nellie McArthur, Beth Ransom, Afton Lindsey, Carol Madsen, Norma B. Ricketts, Joyce Weeks, Gayle Franszen, Ruth Ashby Corley, Diane Forsgren, Afton Alder, Edwin and Jeri Neville, Ron Dennis, Eleanor Bogart, and David and Ruth Moses.

One of the project's biggest challenges was the logistics of studying and photographing the quilts. The ISDUP Pioneer Memorial Museum was gracious to allow on-site photographing of both their quilts and many that belonged to other individuals and institutions. This work could not have been concluded in a timely and efficient manner without the assistance of the volunteers from the Utah Quilt Guild: Joyce Robison, Irene Parker, Saundra Tripp, Sandra Robison, and Ruth Moon. Other quilters who helped under the able direction of Beverly Ellis were Marie Scoffield, Shelba Steadman, Barbara Strong, Evelyn Erkelens, Eunice Davis, and Norma Hallmark. Overseeing and facilitating the photography process was Donald E. Green, with help from Frieda and Mel Jacobsen.

Photographic services were provided by Lucille Warters of Cody, Wyoming; Dale Holloday of Safford, Arizona; Lynne Clark of St. George, Utah; Ron Read of the Church Museum of History and Art; Dave Labrum of Busath Photography in Salt Lake City; and Bill Bachhuber of Portland, Oregon.

Special guidance in researching was provided by recognized scholars and friends in the fields of western and Mormon history, including Loren Horton, Senior Historian at the State Historical Society of Iowa, Iowa City, on the Mormon migration experience in Iowa; Dr. Glenda Riley, Alexander M. Bracken Professor of History at Ball State University, Muncie, Indiana, in the area of westering women; Dr. Stanley B. Kimball, Professor of History at Southern Illinois University, Edwardsville, Illinois, in the field of Mormon migration; and Dr. Maureen Ursenbach Beecher, Professor of English and Research Historian, Joseph Smith Institute for Church History, Brigham Young University, Provo, Utah, in the field of Mormon women's history.

A very special honor is the opportunity to publish the previously unseen work "Mormon Washday" by artist William Henry Jackson. This offer was generously made by Jackson scholar John Osterberg.

Unique assistance was provided by Robert Burco. He placed my research discoveries into the broader historical context of the infrastructure of nineteenth-century transportation systems in America. His ability to relate the economic and political movements of the migration eras across America to the individual quilts and their owners' and makers' stories is unique; it represents an extension of his recent research on historical transportation routes, their regular users, and the pioneers.

Special acknowledgment goes to those many people who provide encouragement and assistance in my life—from my Mien work crew led by Yuen Chien to my Methodist ministers, the late H. Laron Hall and Ross Miller. For their continuing friendship and interest, I acknowledge the friends of the Seamsters and the Needlework Group. I appreciate the valuable editorial comments and interest of historian Harry Stein. I especially recognize Marjolaine Renfro, my friend and tenant who showed support and interest throughout all phases of the project, from providing transportation to giving editorial assistance.

Above all, the assistance and support provided by my sister Nancy Bywater Dornfeld, my son Steven Mercer Cross, and my daughter Carol Hutchins Cross has been especially rewarding. From doing research by reading files and indexes to carrying my equipment, their interest has been reaffirming and fulfilling as we shared the experiences of doing the work and enjoyed the opportunities to be together as family and friends. May they always proudly wear their "Treasures in the Trunk Quilt Projects Staff" T-shirts.

PHOTO PERMISSIONS

Brigham City Museum, 90, 143

Brigham Young University Department of Geography, Jeffry S. Bird, cartographer, Provo, 2, 8, 54, 104, 150

Brigham Young University Museum of Art, Provo, © Copyright and all rights reserved, 10, 42 (top), 52–53, 66 (top), 70

International Society of Daughters of Utah Pioneers (ISDUP)
McQuarrie Memorial Museum, St. George, 20 (top), 40 (top)
Odgen Museum, 65, 72, 73, 85
Pioneer Memorial Museum, Salt Lake City, 14, 16, 18, 19, 21, 22, 25, 31, 33, 35, 37, 38, 41, 43, 45, 47, 48, 49, 51, 61, 63, 66, 67, 68, 69, 71, 75, 80, 83, 86 (top), 87, 89, 91, 92, 93, 97, 99, 100, 101, 102–103, 118, 121, 123, 124 (bottom), 125, 127, 132, 141, 145, 147, 169, 176

LDS Church Historical Department, vi, 14, 20, 34 (bottom, left), 36 (bottom, right), 79 (bottom), 107, 156, 157

Museum of Church History and Art, © The Church of Jesus Christ of Latter-day Saints and used by permission, xvi (both), 7, 12 (bottom), 13, 24, 55, 58 (bottom), 81, 86 (bottom), 92 (top), 95, 98 (top), 105, 108, 109, 111, 113 (top), 129, 140, 142 (bottom), 148–149, 152, 159, 161

Territorial Statehouse Museum, Fillmore, 28, 29, 61, 74, 76, 77, 119

This Is the Place State Park, Salt Lake City, 17, 27

Utah State Historical Society, xvii, 34, 46 (top), 58 (top), 113 (bottom), 122, 124 (top), 146 (bottom), 153, 168

Library Archives, Reorganized Church of Jesus Christ of Latter Day Saints, The Auditorium, Independence, Missouri, 12

Byron Museum, Byron, Wyoming, 171

Fremont County Pioneer Museum, Lander, Wyoming, 167

Eastern Arizona Museum, Pima, Arizona, 131

Fredonia, Arizona, Public Library, 174, 175

Scotts Bluff National Monument, Gering, Nebraska, 207

Mrs. Edith Cannon, xx–1

Norma B. Ricketts, 11

Virginia Fleming, 23

Glenn Snow, 34 (bottom, right)

Norma Taggart Estate, 36

Barbara Pack, 39

Trice Cunningham, artist, 39

Rutger McArthur, 40 (bottom)

Zella Matheson, 79 (top)

Ronald Dennis, 88 (bottom, right)

Archie Wallis, 110

Floyd Ahlstrom, 115

Carolyn O'Bagy Davis, 116

Wanda Rowley, 126

Cherrel B. Weech, 130 (top)

J. William Christensen, 134 (top)

Margaret Noall, 134, 135

Jean Christensen, 136, 137, 138, 139

Edwin Neville, 155, 170, 172, 173

Dorothy Bennion Potter, 163

Joyce Bennion Peaden, 165

Mary Louise Stromness, 177

John Osterberg, 188

PHOTO CREDITS

Bill Bachhuber, 23, 135, 163, 165

Dale Holladay, 131

Dave Labrum, Busath Photography, 15, 19, 21, 25, 27, 29, 31, 33, 35, 37, 38, 39, 41, 43, 45, 47, 49, 51, 61, 63, 65, 67, 69, 71, 72, 73, 75, 77, 78, 83, 85, 87, 89, 90, 91, 93, 97, 99, 101, 115, 118, 119, 125, 127, 132, 137, 139, 141, 145, 147, 167, 169, 170, 177, 206

Ron Read, 81, 95, 129, 159, 161

Lucille Warters, 171

FACSIMILE PHOTO CREDITS

Photographs of earlier photos are credited to the following:

Bill Bachhuber, 11, 39, 88 (bottom right), 130 (top), 134 (bottom), 162, 164

Nelson Wadsworth, 14, 16, 18, 22, 48, 62, 66, 68, 80, 82, 86, 92, 100, 124, 175, 183

Dave Labrum, Busath Photography, 28, 60, 72, 74, 76, 126, 136, 138, 155, 172, 173

Lynn Clark, 20, 34 (top and bottom, right), 40, 79, 88 (top), 110, 153, 174, 175

INDEX

NOTE: *Specific quilts are indexed on page 202 in the Quilt List; if they are indexed here, it is only by maker/owner's name. Names of quiltmakers and owners are in bold print. Places in the United States are indexed according to current state location.*